The Folk-Lore

FOR COLLECTING AND PRINTING

RELICS OF POPULAR ANTIQUITIES, &c.

ESTABLISHED IN

THE YEAR MDCCCLXXVIII

PUBLICATIONS

OF

THE FOLK-LORE SOCIETY

CIV

BRITISH
CALENDAR CUSTOMS

SCOTLAND

VOL. II:
THE SEASONS
THE QUARTERS
HOGMANAY
JANUARY TO MAY

BY

Mrs. M. MACLEOD BANKS

PAST PRESIDENT OF THE FOLK-LORE SOCIETY

1939
PUBLISHED FOR THE FOLK-LORE SOCIETY
LONDON: WILLIAM GLAISHER LTD., 265 HIGH HOLBORN, W.C. 1
GLASGOW: JOHN WYLIE & CO., 27 GORDON STREET, C. 1

PRINTED IN GREAT BRITAIN BY ROBERT MACLEHOSE AND CO. LTD.
THE UNIVERSITY PRESS, GLASGOW

H. 26. 11.

INTRODUCTION

VOLUME II of *Scottish Calendar Customs* sets out upon the broad stream of customs at fixed seasonal dates which the editor hopes to see continue its course through its successor, Volume III. The material here dealt with is more characteristic of the land and folk of Scotland than that of the Movable Festivals, most of these having been tied to the ecclesiastical calendar. It is perhaps on that account more connected with theories of origin and more noticeably marked by variation, more disputable therefore at many points. Discussion of these points, however, has not been undertaken and very few references to comparative instances in other lands have been made. The method adopted throughout this series is one of simple presentation, with such local variants as seemed essential to its faithfulness.

Fishermen's customs have been better collected and more thoroughly noted along Scottish shores than elsewhere in the British Isles, but as they are rarely connected with the calendar they find only occasional reference among Calendar Customs.

The saints have come in for ample notice. They had absorbed many local traditions often foreign to themselves and introduce details from lives of saints in other lands, a transplantation sometimes interesting to observe. They are intimately connected with the calendar and a record of its features would be incomplete without their pagan associations.

Readers observant of regional traits will find many gaps, for in Scotland as in England a thorough geographical survey is still to be looked for. One is surprised to find that among the estimable company of competent collectors none has been found to define and compare one geographical area with another. We do not know, for instance, with any certainty, where St John's fires prevail over those of Beltane, in which district stones were believed to move, or whether phantom funerals were seen passing only on Highland roads. Yet the regional delimitation of such beliefs and rites goes far in helping us to trace the various tribes or races which have blended on Scottish soil.

Acknowledgments made in the Introduction to Volume I are gladly repeated here and for Volume III. Very specially is that true for the generous help and support given by the late Hon. Secretary. He was an unfailing friend in need to all who took up work for the Folk-Lore Society ; deep is the sense of their loss. Sincere thanks are also due to the Hon. Treasurer, Dr. Heather, for proof-reading of the later pages of this volume.

The index will be found at the end of Volume III, which should carry the record to Yuletide, the close of the calendar year.

M. MACLEOD BANKS

16 Houston Court, London, W. 8
May 1939

CONTENTS

LIST OF PLATES

AUTHORITIES QUOTED WITH ABBREVIATED TITLES

An^t Ch. Ded. : J. M. Mackinlay, *Ancient Church Dedications in Scotland*, 1910.

An^t Ch. Ded. N.S. : J. M. Mackinlay, *Ancient Church Dedications in Scotland, Non-Scriptural*, 1914.

Book of Saints : *The Book of Saints*, compiled from the Roman and other Martyrologies by the Benedictine monks, St. Augustine's Abbey, Ramsgate, 1921.

Brand : John Brand, M.A., *Observations on the Popular Antiquities of Gt. Britain*, ed. T. F. Thistleton Dyer, 1876.

Car. Gad. : Alexander Carmichael, LL.D., *Carmina Gadelica*, 1900.

Celt. Pl.-Names : J. W. Watson, LL.D., *The History of the Celtic Place-Names of Scotland*, 1926.

Dalyell : J. G. Dalyell, *The Darker Superstitions of Scotland*, 1835.

Descrip. of Orkney : John Brand, *Description of Orkney, Zetland and Caithness*, 1703 (J. Pinkerton).

Dwelly : Ed. Dwelly, *The Illustrated Gaelic Dictionary*, 1930.

E.D.D. : Joseph Wright, D.C.L., *The English Dialect Dictionary*, 1878-1905.

Emblems : F. C. Husenbeth, D.D., *Emblems of Saints*, 1882.

F.-L. : *Folk-Lore*, the Quarterly Trans. of the Folk-Lore Society, 1890 to date.

F.-L. Journal : *The Folk-Lore Journal*, Folk-Lore Society, 1883-1889.

F.-L. Record : *The Folk-Lore Record*, Folk-Lore Society, 1878-1882.

F.-L. of Scot. Lochs : J. M. Mackinlay, *The Folk-Lore of Scottish Lochs and Springs*, 1893.

Forbes, Kal. : Alex. P. Forbes, *Kalendar of Scottish Saints*, 1872.

Geogr. Coll. ; Ed. Sir Arthur Mitchell, *Geographical Collections Relating to Scotland*, from Macfarlane's MS. in the Advocates' Library, Edinburgh, 1906.

Greg. : Rev. W. Gregor, *Notes on the Folk-Lore of the North-East of Scotland*. Published for the Folk-Lore Society, 1881.

H. Miller : Hugh Miller, *Scenes and Legends of the North of Scotland*, 1889.

Hghlds. & W. Isles : J. McCulloch, M.D., *The Highlands and Western Isles of Scotland*, 1824.

Hone : William Hone, *The Every-Day Book*, 1826-1827.

J. E. Cr. : J. E. Crombie, MS. notes.

Jamieson : John Jamieson, D.D., *An Etymological Dictionary of the Scottish Language*, and *Supplement*, 2nd edition, 1840-1841.

Martin : Martin Martin, *A Description of the Western Isles of Scotland*, ed. 1716.

Marwick, and Mwk. : Sir James D. Marwick, LL.D., Town Clerk of Glasgow, *List of Markets and Fairs Now and Formerly Held in Scotland*, with Notes as to Charters, Acts of Parliament, and other Documents by which the Right to hold them has been Conferred. Prepared for the Royal Commissioners of Market Rights and Tolls, 1890.

Mlan MS. : Dr. Maclagan, Collection of Folk-Lore in MS. bequeathed to the Folk-Lore Society, parts of which had already appeared in print.

Napier : James Napier, *Folk-Lore Beliefs in the West of Scotland within this Century*, etc., 1879.

N. & Q. : *Notes and Queries*, 1849 to date, in several series.

New Sp. Club : New Spalding Club, *Publications*.

N.S.A. : *New Statistical Account of Scotland*, by the Ministers of the Respective Parishes, 1834-1845.

O.S.A. : *Statistical Account of Scotland*, Drawn up from the Communications of the Ministers of the Respective Parishes. Ed. by Sir John Sinclair, 1791-1799.

Old Times : A. D. Cumming, *Old Times in Scotland*, 1910.

Pennant : Thomas Pennant, *A Tour in Scotland*, etc., ed. 1772.

Pop. Rhymes : Robert Chambers, *The Popular Rhymes of Scotland*, from 1822, several editions.

Pop. Superst[ns] : W. Grant Stewart, *The Popular Superstitions and Festive Amusements of the Highlanders of Scotland*, 1822.

P.S.A. Scot. : *Proceedings of the Society of Antiquaries of Scotland*, 1852 to date.

Rev. W. Gregor : MS. Notes by the Rev. W. Gregor, sent to J. E. Crombie and presented to the Folk-Lore Society by Mrs. Crombie.

Sp. Club : Spalding Club, *Publications*, from 1841.

Sc. N. & Q. : *Scottish Notes and Queries*, from 1887.

Sup[s] of Hghlds. : J. Gregorson Campbell, *Superstitions of the Highlands and Western Islands of Scotland*, 1900.

Wcrft. & Sec. Sight : J. Gregorson Campbell, *Witchcraft and Second Sight in the Highlands and Isles of Scotland*, 1900-1903.

ABBREVIATIONS OF SCOTTISH COUNTIES

Ab. : Aberdeen.
Ar. : Argyll.
Bf. : Banff.[1]
Bwk. : Berwick.
Bte. : Bute.
Cths. : Caithness.
Cln. : Clackmannan.
Dbn. : Dumbarton.
Dfs. : Dumfries.
Edin. : Edinburgh.
E. Ln. : East Lothian.

El. : Elgin.[1]
Ffe. : Fife.
Hdn. : Haddington.
Iness. : Inverness.
Hdes. : Hebrides.
Kin. : Kincardine.
Krs. : Kinross.
Kcbt. : Kirkcudbright.
Lnk. : Lanark.
Llgw. : Linlithgow.
Nn. : Nairn.

Ps. : Peebles.
Pth. : Perth.
Rfw. : Renfrew.
Rs. : Ross & Cromarty.
Rxb. : Roxburgh.
Slk. : Selkirk.
Stg. : Stirling.
Sld. : Sutherland.
Wtn. : Wigtown.

[1] In Morayshire.

CLASSIFICATION

The Month.

  I. Names.

  II. Sayings, proverbs, rhymes.

  III. Omens.

  IV. Observances :

    (*a*) Festivals, general festivals ; local marked †.

    (*b*) Visiting of wells, stones, etc.

Days.

  I. Names.

  II. Sayings, proverbs, rhymes.

  III. Saints.

  IV. Omens :

    (*a*) Weather and heavenly bodies.

    (*b*) Fire, ashes.

    (*c*) Water.

    (*d*) Persons.

    (*e*) Animals, birds, insects.

    (*f*) Plants.

    (*g*) Food.

  V. Observances : local observances and customs are marked †.

    (*a*) Unlucky or forbidden.

    (*b*) Lucky or enjoined.

    (*c*) Fire, ashes, torches, candles.

    (*d*) Rites of divination or augury.

    (*e*) The farm, barn, byre.

    (*f*) Household ; churning, spinning, sweeping, etc.

    (*g*) Fishing and sea-faring.

Days.—*Continued.*

V. Observances.—*continued.*

(*h*) Water.

(*i*) Visiting wells, stones, altars.

(*j*) Sacrifice, blood shedding, scapegoat.

(*k*) Doles and gifts.

(*l*) Begging.

(*m*) Food and drink.

(*n*) Pranks and tricks ; indoor games.

(*o*) Habits of animals, birds, insects.

VI. Witchcraft and superstitious beliefs ; fairies.

VII. Natural phenomena.

VIII. Folk medicines.

IX. Mumming, guizing, dramatic performances, dancing.

X. Processions.

XI. Outdoor games, races, mock combats, holiday making.

XII. Festivals, fasts, religious observances.

XIII. Business transactions :

(*a*) Municipal and civic.

(*b*) Private.

XIV. Prohibitions.

THE SEASONS

I. Names.
II. Sayings, Rhymes.

Folk sayings and riddles referring to a year of four seasons date from the time when the changes of the year had been fitted into a calendar marked by the victory of the sun in the long struggle to reconcile the differences of lunar and solar time-reckoning. The calendar was established by the ruling powers in Scotland as elsewhere, and used for business and public affairs. But the people in country districts, among the Isles, in the north, and over the Highlands, only slowly and by necessity consented to this official notation. Long after it had been adopted popular notions of the seasons lived on, and when adjustment was attempted, the change of style in 1752 brought fresh difficulties and some resistance ; for matters had been puzzling enough while many church festivals continued to move along lines decreed by the moon. The observance of New Year on January 1st held good in Scotland from 1600. The four seasons, harmonising with the four quarters, were held in the official framework with some security and could be dated with more or less assurance, but the shorter seasons fell out of the reckoning. We find the dating of these, known under their Gaelic names as the *Gobag*, the *Gearran*, the *Faoilleach*, etc., variable and uncertain. These names, peculiar to Scotland, reflect a consideration of seasonal change and weather based on out-of-door occupations, on cares of the livestock or crops of the farm, and on the anxieties of fishermen. The time of their origin is unknown. Older Gaels used them and they are quoted by every collector of popular sayings in the Highlands and Western Isles as a common heritage. They are not attached to ecclesiastical notation or to any fixed calendar, but have the character of earliest time-reckoning and note the seasons as they specially affect man in his endeavour to win sustenance from the world about him. They cover the active period between the end of winter and harvest.

A rhyme of the four seasons is given as a riddle :

> Four came over,
> Without boat or ship ;
> One yellow and white,

One brown, abounding in twigs, (*slatagach*)
One to handle the flail,
One to strip the trees.

This translation by J. Gregorson Campbell treats of the four
seasons as we know them ; even here the point of view is that
of the countryman. The shorter seasons in the following list
are given with dates assigned to them by different authorities.

Gobag, a'Ghobag, is a dogfish, also the beaked one or the
voracious. It is reckoned as a short week, as three days, or as
one day only. In the *Celt. Review*, V, p. 67, *a'Ghobag* is called
mother of the *Faoilleach*, therefore immediately preceding it,
and should belong to the middle of January. In *Carmina
Gadelica* it is a day preceding St Bride's day, which in other
reckonings cuts the *Faoilleach* in two.

The *Gearran, an Gearran*, is a gelding or horse, and may be
the period between March 15th and April 11th, the month of
February, or the nine days after *Faoilleach*. Some men called
it the *Gearan*, meaning sighing or moaning, and there is a
Seachduin a'Ghearain, the week of complaining. [Mlan MS.]

In a Perthshire rann it plays a vicious trick :

I will put the big cow in the mire
Till the flood comes over her head.

[*Wcrft. & Sec. Sight*, p. 253.]

The *Gearran* is also counted as the month before St Patrick's
day, O.S., March 29th, or as fourteen days before it and fifteen
after. [*Ibid.*]

The *Feadag* is a whistle, also the plover. Dwelly's *Dictionary*
says ' the third week in February ' ; the ' week of whistles '
thus following the *Faoilleach*. But a Highland rann puts it
earlier :

Feadag! Feadag! Mother of the cold Faoilleach,
It kills sheep and lambs,
It kills the big kine one by one,
And the horse at the same time.

To the *Sguabag*, the broom or sweeper, three days are
usually assigned ; it is not so frequently mentioned as other
seasons.

Faoilleach, or *Faoilteach*, the season of the wolf-ravage, is
' proverbial for variableness '. The first half was called the
Faoilleach of winter, the second the *Faoilleach* of spring.

Notes on the Scottish short seasons that follow are by noted
Gaelic scholars.

Those by Mrs E. C. Watson are :

Faoilleach, Faoilteach, Foiltheachd, is the last month of winter, from *faol,* wolf. During this month the wolf approached . . . the dwellings.

Mi Faoillich, month of *Faoilleach,* sharp, ravenous . . . wind.

Naoi la Gearrain, nine days of *Gearran,* galloping wind, like a garron.

Seachdain Feadaig, a week of *Feadag,* sharp, piping wind.

Seachdain Caillich, a week of *Cailleach,* a few semi-calm days.

Tri la Sguabaig, three days of *Sguabag,* the soughing blast which ushers in the spring.

Suas an t-earrach! Up with the spring!

Her *Gobag* rann is :

> Gobag, Gobag, mother of the wolf-month cold,
> That didst kill the sheep and the lean lamb,
> That didst kill the grey goat in two watches
> And the speckled stirk in one.

[*Celt. Rev.* V, pp. 66 f.] Hghlds.

The notes by the Rev. J. Macrury of Snizort were contributed to the Gael. Soc. of Inverness, and printed in the *Transactions,* XVII (1890, 1). A shortened translation follows :

Faoilleach is the name given by the old people to the last fortnight of winter, and the first of spring. As they say, ' Fifteen days before the Feast of Bride and fifteen days after it.' I believe that it began and ended on a Friday ; on a Friday Christ was crucified, and many believe that this is the worst day of the week.[1] The *Faoilleach* lasted for a month and the *Gearran* and the *Sguabag* followed. I have heard the rann of the *Faoilleach* in two versions :

> A month of Faoilleach,
> Nine days of the Gearran,
> Three days of the Sguabag,
> Then up with the spring!

The other version has ' a week of the *Cailleach* ' between the *Gearran* and the *Sguabag.*

The old folk had no grudge against the *Faoilleach.* From my own experience I know that they taught that nothing was better than that hard weather should come in its proper time, Once the *Faoilleach* was there they liked it to show its full force, they looked for no calm weather meanwhile.

[1] In the Island of Lewis it comes on Friday and departs on Tuesday [Macdonald's *Dict.*]

Faoilleach! Faoilleach! The hand on the girdle ;
A good welcome is due to it.
Cattle and sheep run to and fro,
Weeping and wailing are greeting due.

But they looked for a respite of three days of calm, borrowed from *Iuchar*, the time of the dog days.

Three days of Iuchar in the Faoilleach
And three days of the Faoilleach at Iuchar.

Faoilleach should have ' the three fillings of the furrow ', the filling with water, the filling with snow, and the filling with thatch from the house-roofs, for a fair *Faoilleach* is as ' unnatural as a calf lowing in its mother's womb '. A spell of fine weather that lasts only a short time is called ' fair weather of *Faoilleach* '. Frost at this time is known as ' the frost of the full puddle ', which holds only to the third hour. Another saying has it that the weather of *Faoilleach* should be ' as changeable as if the seven elements were each in turn striving for dominance '.

The nine days of *Gearran* which follow are cutting and cold ; they bring death to weak creatures left alive after the *Faoilleach* :

Says Faoilleach to Gearran,
' Where hast thou left the wretched stirk? '
Gearran answers,
' I put its hide on the litter,
And its head on the rubbish heap.'

Later again comes *Sguabag*, the Sweeper, the raging storm that sweeps along everything on the face of the earth. And then the spring.
The old folk say :

Autumn till Nollaig,
Winter till St Patrick's day,
Spring till St Peter's day,
Summer till Michaelmas.

St Patrick's day, March 29th, O.S., was hailed with joy ;

Day of Feill Padraig,
Day of my heart and of my creel,
Day of service to man,
And on which man serves him.

The first part of March is bitterly cold, but the month ends mildly ; it has ' a serpent's head and a peacock's tail '. If it does not come in like a lion it will depart in that character.

About the time of Beltane, O.S., there came three or four days of wintry weather, with showers and wind from the north, known as ' the sad old man of Beltane '. But in the time of *Iuchar* the three cold days of *Faoilleach* were greeted as a short break in the sultry heat of this month, ' two weeks before Lammas and three after it.'

Tempests about Michaelmas were called the Harvest storms, and frost in summer ' the sting of summer '. *Nollaig* should have snow : ' it is a lean Christmas without snow.'

All through the year, even in the depth of winter, it was believed that the sun would show his face on Wednesday, for that was the day of his creation.

(Weather portents at New Year quoted by the same authority on Gaelic lore and customs will be found under December 31st and January 1st.)

In Mr Macrury's rann the *Cailleach* follows the *Gearran*. This is the *Cailleach* of spring, an envious old woman who tries to fight against the return of life. It is possible to look upon her as the *Cailleach* of the cornfield recognised in the reapers' rites, who resents the fresh growth of the spring. (See *Harvest* and *New Year*.) She sees the growing grass and attempts to beat it down, but the vigour of the young year is too strong for her, and rises in fresh shoots under her feet. The versions of her rann closely resemble one another. That quoted below is given by Dr Maclagan in *F.-L.* VI (1895), pp. 148 f., translated from a Gaelic original :

> It escapes me up and down,
> 'Twixt my very ears has flown ;
> It escapes me here and there,
> 'Twixt my feet and everywhere.
> This 'neath holly tree I'll throw
> Where no grass nor leaf shall grow.

And the rod or wand is cast angrily under the holly, where growing grass is never found. [Ed.]

The period of *Gearran* was the best time for sowing seed ; the winds had dried the ground, and ' a dry bed for the seed ' was an agricultural adage. These were the winds said to send ' seven bolls of driving snow through one auger hole '. [*Wcrft. & Sec. Sight*, pp. 252 f.]

Such ranns were not inspired by indoor occupations and the less active winter season, but the west wind might blow at any time and brought treasure in the form of seaweed, ware, valuable as manure for the fields. ' Wind from the west brings

fish and bread ', or ' fish and milk '. Fertile fields gave good
crops with grain for bread and fodder for the milch cow.

J. Gregorson Campbell's *Faoilleach* rann is from Tiree, and
reverses the parts played by it and the *Gearran* :

> Then said Gearran to Faoilleach,
> ' Where left you the poor stirk? '
> ' I left it with him who made the elements,
> Staring at a stack of fodder.'
> ' If I catch it,' said the May month,
> ' With the breath in the points of his ears,
> I will send it racing to the hill,
> With its tail upon its shoulders.'

The beast will pull through if it can ' lift its ear higher than its
horn ', which at that age (one year) it ought to do.

Gearran extends over a month, and in Skye is made to succeed to the *Faoilleach*.   There was a rule known to old men that
' the first Tuesday of March (O.S.) is the last day of *Gearran* '.
It is quite possible that the original name may have been
Gearan, complaint, as there is always associated with it a
period called *Caoile*, leanness [usually *a'Chaoile*].   [*Wcrft. &
Sec. Sight*, pp. 251 f.]   Skye and Tiree, Iness and Ar.

Mrs Watson's version of the *Faoilleach* rann differs considerably :

> The Gearran said to the Faoilleach,
> ' Where, love, is the lean stirk? '
> ' Thou who didst send me into the world,
> I placed his paunch upon the stake.'
> ' O! my grief! ' said the Ceitein [May month],
> ' Great the ransom upon thee,
> Had I at all got hold of his ears,
> I would have sent him up the hill.'

[*Celt. Rev.* V, p. 67.]

It is worth noting that rivalry in severity of cold between
two months is mentioned in a Finnish tale.   In this February
says to January, ' If I were in thy place I would freeze the foal
in its mother's womb, the hands of the housewife to the dough,
and the feet of the swine to the ground. . . .'   Also a proverb of
the Teutons runs, February to January ' hätt ich die Macht
wie du, liess ich erfrieren das Kalb in der Kuh '.   [See Uno
Holmberg, *Finno-Ugric Mythology* (1927), p. 226.]

Another note on *Iuchar, Futhar*, the Dog Days.

In West Ross-shire the last two weeks of July and the first

two of August (i.e. *Futhar*) are known as *Futhar*, *Uthar*, or
Iuthar. [*Trans. Gaelic Soc. of Inverness*, xxiv, 1899-1901.]   Rs.
  Futhar = Dog-days.   Pth.
  Futhar an fhoghair = the height of autumn, latter half of
August.   N. Ar.
  Futhar an earraich = the height of spring.   N. Ar.
  Futhar an t-samhraidh = the latter half of July.   N. Ar.
[Dwelly.]
Some of these sayings, with others, are given again under the
Months. [Ed.]

SPRING

I. Names. *Earrach.* Among the old Gaels it was divided
into two parts, *e. geamhraidh* and *e. samhraidh*, winter spring and
summer spring. [Dwelly.]
The Galloway name, Ware, is from Lat. *ver.*

II. Sayings, Rhymes. Winter never comes till ware comes.
The cuckoo rhyme belongs to this season :

> The cuckoo comes in the middle of March,
> And sings in the middle of April,
> And passes away at the Lammas-tide,
> When the corn begins to fill.

[*Round the Grange Farm*, p. 108.]   Ps.
In May begins the golk to gail. [Alex. Scott, *Gratulation to
the Moneth of May*, p. 50.]
About April 24th ; 'the gowk has come hame.' [*Ibid.*,
p. 52.]
The Lanarkshire ploughman believes that 'the cuckoo
comes wi' a haw leaf and gangs away wi' a bear (four-rowed
barley) head '.   Lnk.
It is also said in the west of Scotland that the cuckoo flies
away at the first sight she obtains of barley in the ear. [*Ibid.*
p. 50.]   W. Scot.
Cf. other sayings about spring in the section dealing with
the short Scottish Seasons.

III. Omens.
Foals and lambs to be seen from the front.
Referring to the common notion that it is unlucky for one
to see the first lamb or foal of the season with its tail to him, a
native of Ross-shire says that in his part of the country that is
held to be quite true, but only with regard to those engaged
in farming. The idea is that if, when a farmer sees his first

lamb, or first foal of the season, its tail should be towards him, it indicates that either he will have no more, or at any rate a shortage of that kind during that season. It is said in such a case, if it be a lamb, ' The lambs are going from him.' And if a foal, ' The foals are going from him.' [Mlan Ms.]   Rs.

Harrows.

When harrows are seen at work for the first time in spring it is lucky to see them going uphill not downhill. [J. E. Cr.]   Bf.

Cuckoo, swallow and foal.

It is accounted fortunate to be seated when we see the first swallow in spring, to be walking when we hear the first cuckoo, and to see for the first time in the year a foal going before the eyes of its dam.

> Gang an' hear the gowk yell,
> Sit an' see the swallow flee,
> See the foal before its mither's e'e,
> 'Twill be a thriving year wi' thee.
>
> [*Pop. Rhymes*,[1] p. 284.]

V. Observances, a. *Things unlucky or forbidden. To leave the partly emptied grain-bags in the fields.* The bags of grain when once put out in the fields for the sowing are not taken in till the sowing is over, whatever the weather may be, or ill luck would result. [J. E. Cr.]   Bf.

V b. *Things lucky. To put a Bumble Bee in the purse.* We catch the first Bum bee we see in spring and put it in our purse and we are sure not to be out of money till next spring. [Mlan Ms.]   Skye, Iness.

V d. *Rite of divination. By a hair.* The first time the cuckoo's note was heard the hearer turned round three times on the left heel against the sun, searched in the hollow made by the heel, and in it a hair of the colour of the future husband or wife was found. [Greg. p. 83.]   N.E. Scot.

V e. *Farm Customs. Ploughing rhyme.* It was till lately believed by the ploughmen of Clydesdale, that if they repeated the rhyme,

> Fairy, fairy, bake me a bannock, and roast me a collop,
> And I'll gie ye a spurtle aff my gad end,

three several times on turning their cattle at the termination of ridges, they would find the said fare prepared for them on reaching the end of the fourth furrow. [*Pop. Rhymes*,[3] p. 106.]
    Lnk.

For magical virtue attached to soil from the plough or other implement see Hallowe'en.

Butter put in the horses' ears. To bring luck, she says, her father used to put butter in the horses' ears the first day they went to plough. [Mlan Ms.] Islay, Ar.

Butter given with the Cailleach. Many a time I have seen people putting butter in the horses' ears, and rubbing it on their shoulders and breasts when they were going out for the first time in spring to plough. And they would also give them the cailleach of the preceding harvest to eat. [*Ibid.*] Ibid.

The ploughman also gets butter. Mr Mac. says that he remembers quite well when it was the custom, before going out the first day of the season to plough, the ears of the horses would be stuffed with butter, and a large piece of bread, thickly laid over with butter would be given to the man who was to plough. This was, of course, outside of the regular meals for the day, and the reciter believes it took its rise from some superstitious belief. [*Ibid.*] Ibid.

Earth from the plough lucky. It used to be a common custom in parts of the Highlands, to take a little earth from the plough and rub it on the horse's neck and shoulders on the first day they would go to plough for the season. This was supposed to secure the safety of the horses for that whole season against all danger of being injured either by an evil eye or by witch-craft. [*Ibid.*] W. Hghlds.

Cf. fairy-rhyme above.

Salt and water. Immediately before beginning the spring labour, just when the horses were yoked to the plough and on the very spot of the farm where they were to begin the work of the season, the horses' harness and plough were three times carefully besprinkled with water in which some salt had been dissolved, and a little of the same solution was then poured into the horses' ears. After this last part of the ceremony had been gone through, the spring labour was considered to have been duly inaugurated. This ceremony was performed in the island of Arran within the last ninety years. [*F.-L.* XI, p. 439.]
Hdes.

A common custom among the natives of Eriskay for a man when going to sow seed is to sprinkle both himself and the seed with salt and water before sowing it. [Mlan Ms.]
Eriskay, Hdes.

Fishermen also sprinkle themselves in Islay before setting out to fish. [*Ibid.*]

Dry salt used. An old man, who is a native of Islay, says that it was common enough in his young days to throw dry salt on cattle when being let out for the first time in spring on the grass. [*Ibid.*]   Islay, Ar.

A young man serving with a farmer in Renfrewshire told that his master was in the habit of sprinkling a little dry salt on the backs of all his calving cows every spring at calving time. . . . The first cow calving was the first to receive the sprinkling, after her he went over them all.   Rfw.

In Islay each cow was sprinkled as she calved. The same in Campbeltown, and in addition a small handful of the salt was sprinkled over the calf and left there for a few minutes, when the cow was encouraged to lick it thoroughly all over. [*Ibid.*]   Islay and Kintyre, Ar.

Sprinkling with urine. It used to be customary when the cattle were being put out on the grass in spring or the early part of summer for the first time that season to take the bedroom slops (urine) and a broom and to sprinkle the slops on the cattle as they were passing out of the byre. This was to prevent *cronachadh* (hurt from the evil eye). [*Ibid.*]   Islay, Ar.

When the plough is first yoked horses and coulter are sprinkled with urine. [J. Ramsay, *Scotland and Scotsmen in the Eighteenth Century*, p. 454.]   Breadalbane, Pth.

Sprinkling wisp thrown on plough. The wisp of straw used for the sprinkling is thrown between the mould-board and the beam. [*Ibid.*]   *Ibid.*

See also under *Quarters*.

Sprinkling with water, walking sunwise. Three days before sowing the seed is sprinkled with clear cold water, in the name of Father, Son, and Spirit, the person sprinkling walking sunwise the while. [*F.-L.*, March, 1913 ; quoting *Car. Gad.*]
                                                           Hghlds. and W. Isles.

Holy Water used. In South Uist (a Roman Catholic district), when the ploughing season is being begun, the owner, just when ready to put the ploughshare into the soil, besprinkles the horses and all the ploughing implements with ' holy water '. This is regarded much more than an ordinary ceremony, as it is a matter of great interest to the whole family. [*F.-L.* XI, p. 439.]   Hdes.

On the day the plough was first put into the soil—' streekit ', or ' strykit ' after harvest—a few cakes of oaten bread were baked. To make them a little more dainty, they were commonly rubbed with cream before they were placed on ' the girdle ' over the fire to be baked. Cream, which, if scarce, was saved up with much care, was churned, and made into butter.

When the bread and the butter were ready, the guidwife took some of them, along with a ' kebback ' and whisky, and went to the field to the ploughman—commonly the guidman himself or a son, for in those old days in many districts each family tilled its own holding. He cut the cheese, and partook of the dainties carried to the field. A piece of the cakes was given to each horse, if the animal was accustomed to eat them. The whole household partook at supper of the bread, the butter, and the cheese.—Told by one whose mother carried out the custom in Pitsligo, Aberdeenshire. [*F.-L. J.*, Vol. II (1884), p. 329.] Ab.

When the plough was first yoked for the season . . . bread and cheese were carried to the field and given to the ploughman. Corgarff, Ab.

Such an entertainment was called the ' Pleuch-Fehst '. [*Trans. Buchan Field Club*, IV, p. 148.] Strathdon, Ab.

There were some who would begin to plough for the first time during the season on Saturday. . . . By the time the ploughman was at the end of . . . the first furrow, his master was beside him carrying bread and cheese, and then received a glass of whisky. The old man drank a glass of the whisky, then filled the glass again and poured (the contents) over the bridle of the plough, and repeated the words, ' Weel fah the lawbour! ' Pieces of the bread and cheese were carefully wrapped up in paper and tied firmly to the beam of the plough by the farmer, who at the same time laid strict orders on the servant not to take them off ; ' It may fa' aff o't sell, or the dogs may eht it. Nae maitter, but dinna ye touch't,' were his words. When all this was done and said, the old man added, ' Noo, just tak.ye anither fur (furrow) and syne lowse (and then loosen) ; ye'll be ready for yir wark on Muninday's mornin'.' [*Ibid.*] Strachan, Ab.

Streeking the plough—an event marked in many parts of the district by a species of semi-religious custom, and this as recently as the beginning of the present century (19th). About an hour after the plough was at work, the gudewife, or the principal female servant, proceeded to the field with bread, cheese, and a jar of home-brewed ale. The salutation to the ploughman was . . . ' Guid speed the wark! ' to which he replied, ' May Guid speed it! ' He then seated himself on the beam of the plough, and after sundry forms of good wishes for the health and prosperity of the family . . . partook of the refreshment. [Rev. J. B. Pratt, *Buchan*[3] (1870), p. 21.]
Quoted also from Bf. and Ab.

My grand-uncle . . . was, I believe, the last in the district if not the last in Scotland who observed that custom of break-fasting at the plough-tail on the first day that the plough was yoked in spring. [*F.-L. J.*, VII, p. 175.]   Lewis, Hdes.

The unused seed corn. *Lite-cuire* (Sowing porridge), otherwise *Lite-Mhannta[i]n* (Manntan's porridge), was porridge made of *Ulag*-meal, and made *once a year only*, of what remained over, after the sowing, of the grain that had been prepared and set apart for seed-corn. Thick porridge was made of this *Ulag*-meal. The thicker and richer the porridge the heavier and richer would be the crops in harvest. This custom came down almost to our own times embodied in the following rhyme :

> *Là lite Mhanntain,*
> *Là 'us fearr air bith ;*
> *An coire 'us an crocan,*
> *'S a' maide crom air chrith.*

> The day of Manntan's porridge,
> The best day of all ;
> Kettle, crook, and crooket-stick,
> Shaking like to fall.

Ulag was grain expeditiously dried for the quern, either in a pot over the fire or by a red-hot stone that was being kept perpetually rolling among the grain in a tub. The operator preserved his hands from being injured by the hot stone by keeping both his hands full of grain as he rapidly rolled the stone round. *Ulag* so made is the origin of the Gaelic proverb, which not many understand now : *Clach fo shiol* (stone under grain) ; or in full : *Tionndadh na cloiche fo'n t-siol* (turning the stone under the grain) ; in other words, ' A rolling stone gathers no moss.' [Rev. Malcolm Macphail in *F.-L.* (1900), XI, pp. 440-1.]   Lewis, Hdes.

Sowing with the rising tide. I remember distinctly that in some of the districts of the island of Lewis the time of day selected for starting the sowing for the season was during the rising of the tide, and to avoid doing so during its fall, and, if at all convenient, to begin during spring-tide. It was con-sidered more in harmony with the course of nature and more conducive to a rich harvest to begin the sowing during those seasons than at the falling of the tide or during neap-tide. [*F.-L.* XI (1900), p. 440.]   Lewis, Hdes.

Symbols in the sowing-basket. A nail and an egg were placed in the *Sgeap a' chuire* (sowing basket) beneath the corn-seed. The bottom of the *sgeap* was not to be seen till the sowing season was over. The nail was emblematical of long, strong, straight stalks of corn ; the egg was symbolical of corn as full of substance as the egg is of meat ; and the not seeing the bottom of the sowing-*sgeap* during the sowing season was an augury of abundance for the ensuing year. [*Ibid.*] *Ibid.*

Burning heather to draw down rain. In the Highlands of Scotland, where at this season (spring) the heather is burned by the shepherds, the belief (that burning fern brings rain) is general among the people. . . . It is believed in the neighbourhood of Melrose that burning the heather brings rain. . . . In Scotland . . . it is the practice of shepherds in spring, when the heather is dry enough, to set fire to it . . . in order to get rid of the old woody plants. . . . It is the general belief throughout the south of Scotland, and in the Cheviot range, that this burning ' doth draw downe rain '. [*Choice Notes from N. & Q.* (1859), pp. 149 f.] Mid Lothian and Hghlds.

Peas not sown till the swallows appear. It was a custom among the farmers in the southern counties of Scotland never to sow their peas till the swallows made their appearance. [Alex. Scott, *Gratulation to the Moneth of May*, p. 50 ; quoted from Thomas Wilkie's MSS.] S. Scot.

St Brianan invoked. The people [of Barvas, Lewis] used in the spring to proceed to the end of a reef, and invoke St Brianan to send a strong north wind to drive plenty of sea-weed ashore.[1] [W. C. Mackenzie, *History of the Outer Hebrides* (1903), p. 526.] Lewis, Hdes.

Collection of ware. There is a curious custom in Bernera ; . . . when the second moon of the spring is full, they go to a part of the shore and cut some sea-ware, saying when cutting it, *Tha mi a'gearradh so air son ' luck '* (I am cutting this for luck), or repeating a rhyme which they use for the purpose. They take the ware home and spread it on a little bit of ground, marking the place where it has been spread. This is a kind of test, and should that bit of ground yield a good crop that season, it is taken as a good augury for the season following, and when the time comes round for manuring the land they go to that part of the shore for their seaweed from which they had previously taken the test sample. [Mlan MS.] Ar.

V f. *House and household. Whitewashing in Autumn and Spring.* One of the time-honoured customs . . . is that of whitewashing on a certain night in autumn when the weavers began to light their lamps, and in the spring when the days have . . .

---

[1] Seaweed was used as manure.

lengthened and it is unnecessary to work by artificial light in the evenings.

The windows, and in some cases the doors, of all the leading 'loomshops' in Paisley were bespattered with whitening, which was allowed to remain until dry. The rising generation will . . . view the white 'splarges' with wonder, and ponder as to what can be their meaning ; and possibly the ancient-looking mortal who sits at the loom may be as much at a loss to tell its origin, and can only say that his father did the same thing before him on ' Whitewashing Nicht '. [I. H., *Northern N. & Q.*, vols. I and II (1888), pp. 173-4.]

V g. *Fishermen's beliefs. Gentle Annie.* The Cromarty fisher-people refer to the spring equinox as ' Gentle Annie weather ' . . . which lasts sometimes for six weeks. ' Gentle Annie ' is without doubt the Hag of the south-west wind. After she has spent her fury good weather ensues. ' We'll have to be keeping a shilling or twa beside us for the time o' Gentle Annie,' say the fisherwomen. Waves flecked with white foam are ' the feather in Gentle Annie's hat '. [*Celt. Rev.* VII, pp. 341 ff.]   Cromarty, Rs.

VII. Natural phenomena. With the advance of spring ' as horses grow lean, crabs grow fat '. Others have it, ' when the horse is lean the whelk is fat '. [*Wcrft. & Sec. Sight*, p. 260.] Hghlds. and W. Isles.

VIII. Popular medicine. *Letting blood.* In the spring time let blood at the right side, and in the fall of the leaf at the left side. [Ed. Raban, *Prognostication* for 1626.]

XII. Festivals, Fasts. *Public fasts before seed-time and harvest.* It is appointed by the Lord Bishop and Synod—that, upon the two Lord's dayes immediately preceeding the publick fasts befor seed time and harvest, intimation be made by the severall ministers to their respective congregations . . . and that no minister shall homolgate the non-observance of the forsaid fasts in their people. [*Records of Meeting of the Exercise of Alford*, Oct. 1687, pp. 384 f. N. Sp. Club.]   Ab.

SUMMER

I. Names. *Samhradh*, also *Sail-ùrlair*, ' the central beam of a floor that receives the joists '. [Dwelly.] The first week of summer is called ' the whistling week ', alluding to the winds of that time.

II. Sayings, Rhymes. A speckled, chequered summer makes a white, sunny harvest. [*Wcrft. & Sec. Sight*, p. 303.]

Hghlds. and W. Is.

III. Weather omen. See **II**, above.

V. Observances, a. *Things unlucky. To do field work during the first week.* It is unlucky during the 'whistling week' to proceed with field operations. [*Ibid.*, p. 273.]

Hghlds. and W. Is.

V e. *Farm customs. Going to the sheilings.* The people here (Kyle of Durness) live very hardy, principally on milk, curds, whey and a little oatmeal, specially when they are at the sheales in the mountain, that is, the cabins or hutts in which they live when they go to the mountains with their cattle during the months of June, July and August. [Rd. Pococke, *Tours in Scotland*, 1747, 1750, 1760, p. 127 (Scot. Hist. Soc.).] Sld.

Life at the Sheilings is described in quotations for the months of summer. [Ed.]

AUTUMN

I. Names. *Foghar*, which means also Harvest.

II. Sayings. Forecast from earlier weather, see *Summer*, **II** ; for cuckoo at Lammas see *Spring*, **II**.

The ware (spring) evening is long and tough,
The harvest evening runs soon over the heugh (dell).

[Js. Kelly, *Scottish Proverbs* (1721), p. 334.]

III. Omen. *From the rose.* At this season the blooming of a white rose meant an early death, of a red rose, an early marriage. [Napier, p. 129.]

V. Observances, c. *Rites of fire*, etc. *Fire carried round sunwise, Teine deiseil.* The first night the cattle were brought home and housed for the winter, fire was carried round them three times sunways. [*F.-L.* VI (1895), p. 170. From MS. notes made about thirty years before by the Rev. Malcolm Macphail.]

Is. of Lewis, Hdes.

V e. *Farm and byre. Customs at 'stryking the plough' at spring and autumn*, see *Spring*, **V e.**

V f. *Whitewashing*, see *Spring*, **V f.**

V g. *Fishing custom. Burning the water.* Burning the water took place in the late autumn, and at night. One man carried a lighted torch to attract the salmon, and another speared them with a trident when they came near it. This was later forbidden by law. [Quoted from Sir Eneas Mackintosh by I. F. Grant, *Every-day Life in a Highland Farm, 1769-1783* (1924), p. 130.]

VI. Beliefs in spirits, fairies, etc. *A goblin a friend of the red autumn cock.* A goblin came to a door one night and failed to get admittance. He said, ' If it were the red cock of autumn that were in the house he would open the door for me. It isn't that that is in it, but the black cock of the spring March. [A. Goodrich Freer, *Outer Isles* (1902), p. 240.]   Outer Is.

IX. Dancing. *The Rinche Fada.* The Ring dance was formerly . . . the common dance at the *kirn* or feast of cutting down the grain, and was always danced with peculiar glee by the reapers at that farm where the harvest was first finished in any district. . . . They danced on an eminence in view of the reapers . . . to the music of the Lowland bagpipe ; commencing the dance with three loud shouts of triumph, and thrice tossing up their hooks in the air. The intervals of labour during harvest were often occupied by dancing the Ring, to the music of the piper who formerly attended the reapers. . . . The dance is still retained among the Highlanders, who frequently dance the Ring in the open fields when they visit the south of Scotland as reapers during the autumnal months. Similar seems to be the Rinceadhf(h)ada, Rinkey, or field dance of the Irish. [J. A. H. Murray, ed. *Complaynt of Scotlande*, E. Eng. Text Soc., Extra series, XVII, p. xciii, quoting J. Leyden, 1801.]

Description from the *Complaynt* : After singing, the shepherds ' began to dance in ane ryng, euyrie ald scheiphyrd led his vyfe be the hand, and euyrie yong scheiphird led hyr quhome he luffit best '.

Cf. *Journal of the English Folk Dance and Song Society*, III, 1, p. 31.

WINTER

I. Names. *Geamhradh.* The depth of winter was known as *an Dùdlachd*, gloom.

II. Sayings, Rhymes. Winter thunder summer hunger. [Js. Kelly, *Scottish Proverbs* (1721), p. 353.]

The rhyme about the Seven Sleepers, the seven winged

PLATE I

Sheelins in JURA and a distant View of the Paps.

From Pennant, 1772

creatures which disappeared in winter and were believed to
have gone underground, belongs to this period :

> Seven sleepers there be ;
> The bat, the bee, the butterflee,
> The cuckoo and the swallow,
> The kittiwake and the corn-craik,
> Sleep a' in a little hollie.

[Js. Hardy, in *F.-L. Record*, II (1879), p. 106.]

IX. **Dancing.** *Winter death revel. Geigean, Righ Geigean ;* King
Geigean. This was the term applied to the man who presided
over the death revels. These were held in winter. Lots were
cast and the man upon whom the lot fell was elected king of the
revels, over which he reigned from midnight till the old cock
crew. A tub of cold water was poured over his head and down
his throat, after which his face and neck were smeared with soot.
When the man had been made as formidable and hideous as
possible, a sword, scythe or sickle was placed in his hand as an
emblem of office.   Creich, Sld.

The ceremony was described by the Rev. Donald Mackay
of Cross, Lewis. He had seen it in the first decade of the (19th)
century in his native parish of Creich. Dr. Carmichael had
failed to find any trace of the ceremony further south.

A reference to *Geigean* is found in a rhyme common among
boys at play :

> I came from small peril,
> I came from great peril,
> I came from Geigean,
> I came from Guaigean,
> And I will come from thee if I can.

[*Car. Gad.* II, p. 285.]   W. Isles.

In Dwelly's *Gaelic Dictionary Geigean* is quoted as a Uist form
of *Ceigean*, a diminutive and unhandsome person . . . a bundle
of straw or hay. *Gigean* is also quoted as a term of contempt.
The king of the death revels therefore, by degradation of
meaning, may have passed into a mock king or king of straw.
[Ed.]

Mr C. I. Paton sends a note on a boys' game in the Isle of
Man which may be allied to the ceremony Dr. Carmichael
was unable to trace south of the Hebrides. The rhyme used
was, as translated from the Manx version :

> This to thee—the doagan. What said the doagan?
> Upon the cross—upon the lot—

Upon the little stick, straight and crooked,
In the little wood over yonder,
If thou wilt bring the head of the doagan
I will give the head of thee for it.

This refers to the head of Doagan being broken off.

Mr Paton adds : I do not pretend to understand this, but I believe the game was one which Mr N. M. C. Kermode told me that he had played when a child, the rule of which was that a lighted twig was passed from hand to hand by a circle of children, one being selected out of the number by the spark expiring whilst he or she held the twig. I have seen somewhere . . . that this selection was made in ancient times in order that a victim might be made for sacrifice. As to the change from D to G, or the reverse, I do not see that there is any insuperable difficulty ; . . . there are words which Scot. Gaelic has in g which Manks has in d. For instance, Scot. Gael. *gus*, to or until, is *dys* or *gys* in Manks . . . *gach*, each, is usually *dagh* in Manks, though *gagh* is also used. The adverbial *gu* is *dy* in Manks, *dy bragh* for *gu brath*. . . . Scot. Gael. *gun*, without, is commonly *dyn* in Manks, though *gyn* is also used. . . .

The points in common are the formidable Geigean or Doagan himself and the casting of lots ; the Gaelic emblems of office also carry out the suggestion of sacrifice. But the Manx instance is to be judged merely as an interesting possibility. [Ed.]

THE QUARTERS

The Celtic year, on which most Scottish calendar customs are based, is believed by many authorities to have been divided into quarters ; others explain the divisions as three ; some allow two divisions only, those of winter and summer. The division may have been different among the different tribes and have changed with the changes in the occupations of the people, at one time pastoral, at another agricultural. In Scotland religious and magical observances are known to have taken place at the beginning of a ' raith ' or quarter and point to a quarterly division of the year.

Term days in Scotland followed the old manner, though they hold their local authority from Christian times, and were called Quarter-days ; these are of different date from English Quarter-days and are February 2nd, Candlemas ; May 15th, Whitsun ; August 1st, Lammas ; and November 11th, Martinmas. Whitsun and Martinmas are the regular rent days. May 28th and November 28th are removal days ; servants are engaged on these days. The election to councils and municipal bodies is at Michaelmas. In Shetland Christmas, St John's day in December, and Easter are also known as term days. (See *P.S.A. Scot.*, X, p. 716.) [Ed.]

I. Names. The Celtic name for quarter is *raith* or *raidhe*, which meant also season. *Ceitein*, now the name for the spring season or May, had earlier the meaning of season in general.

Winter began the year, as night began the day ; the seasons corresponding to the quarters were called ; *geamhradh*, winter ; *earrach*, spring ; *samhradh*, summer ; and *foghar*, autumn. A folk name for autumn was *Ceitein Oinnsich*, the foolish woman's *ceitein*. Dr. Alex. Carmichael [*Car. Gad.*, II, p. 243] reads this as a mistake for *Ceitein Oinich*, generous or liberal *Ceitein*. *Foghar* also means harvest-time. [Ed.]

III. Weather omen. The wind was said to blow during the quarter . . . in that direction in which it blew during the first day of the quarter. [Greg., p. 151.]   N.E. Scot.

V. Observances, a. *Forbidden or unlucky. To ' straddle ' the beginning of the quarter.* No person will be proclaimed for

19

marriage in the end of . . . even a quarter of the year, and be married in the beginning of the next. [*O.S.A.*, XV, p. 253.]

Pth.

Kindling not to be given out. Many people in the island of Mull hold superstitious notions regarding quarter-days. For one thing they would never allow a kindling to be taken out of their house by a neighbour on a quarter-day, for the reason, as is believed, that a kindling going out of a house on a quarter-day, takes along with it all the good luck that otherwise might belong to that house for that whole quarter. [Mlan MS.]

Mull, Ar.

To counteract the danger. On the first day of every quarter of the year . . . no fire should be given out of the house. On the two last days (Beltane and Lammas), especially, it should not be given, even to a neighbour whose fire had gone out. It would give him the means of taking the substance or benefit (*toradh*) from the cows. If given, after the person who had come for it left, a piece of burning peat . . . should be thrown into a tub of water to keep him from doing harm. It will also prevent his coming again. [*Sup*ˢ. *of Hghlds.*, pp. 234 f.]

Hghlds.

To give a loan. It appears that the first Monday of each quarter of the year is looked upon in some parts of the Highlands as a day which favours evil disposed persons to take to themselves such good luck as any neighbour may be supposed to possess. A common method by which good luck is believed to be obtainable, is by the one who seeks it getting the loan of something from the one who is supposed to have it ; and in view of this, there are many people who would not lend anything on the first Monday of a quarter. [Mlan MS.]

Islay and Harris, Ar. and Iness.

V b. *Things lucky or likely to be successful. A new undertaking.* The first day of every quarter, Midsummer and New Year's Day, are the most fortunate times for accomplishing any design. [John Ramsay, ed. *Scotland and Scotsmen in the 18th Cent.* (1888), II, p. 448.]

Hghlds.

Charms and spells. Those dealing with charms and incantations were careful to rise for that purpose before the sun (on the first day of the quarter). [*Ibid.*]

Elf child buried. It was usual with those who believed that their children were thus (in exchange for an elf child) taken away, to dig a grave in the fields upon quarter-day, and there to lay the fairy skeleton till next morning ; at which time the parents went to the place, where they doubted not to find their own child instead of this skeleton. [Martin,[2], p. 118.]

W. Isles.

See also **VI**, below.

See also **V g**.

First footing. First footing was practised at these dates in a few places. See *January 1st*.

V c. *Fire rite. The neid-fire*. The neid-fire was resorted to in imminent or actual calamity upon the first day of the quarter, and to ensure success in great or important events. [*Car. Gad*. II, p. 340.]   Hghlds. and W. Isles.

V d. *Rites of divination or augury. For marriage*. A native of the island of Lewis says that the first Monday of every quarter is an important day among the unmarried girls of his native place. They pay particular attention to the first male person they may happen to meet on that day, for it is believed that his surname will be the surname of the future husband of her whom he was the first male to meet on that day. [Mlan Ms.]

Is. of Lewis, Rs.

It was believed that the name of the first woman a young man would meet on the morning of the first Monday of the quarter was to be the name of his future wife, and the same belief was held by young women with regard to young men. [Norman Morrison, in *Stornoway Gazette*, Oct. 1931.]   *Ibid.*

A Frith. A Frith [an incantation used for divination] may be made at any time, but the first Monday of the quarter— *a'chiad Diluain de'n raithe*—is considered the most auspicious. [*Trans. Gael. Soc*[tv]. *of Inverness*, XVIII, 1891, 2.]

V e. *Farm customs. Cattle sprinkled with urine. Maister* [or *maistir*], stale urine, kept for the scouring of blankets and other cloth, when sprinkled on the cattle and on the door-posts and walls of the house, kept the Fairies, and indeed every mischief at a distance. This sprinkling was done in the last evening of every quarter of the year. [*Sups. of Hghlds.*, p. 49.]   Hghlds.

Upon the evening of every day at the end of a quarter of the year and sometimes oftener, it is customary to take a wisp of straw and dip it in human urine and sprinkle all the cattle in the byre with it. [John Ramsay, *Scotland and Scotsmen in the 18th Century*, II, p. 454.]

This custom mentioned also by T. Pennant [*Tour* [2], p. 205.]

Dew gathered with which to rinse milk utensils. To increase the quantity of milk at the expense of a neighbour, on the morning of the first day of each ' raith ' the dew was gathered off the pasture of his cows, and the milk utensils were rinsed with it. [Greg. p. 193.] N.E. Scot.

Water from the well to keep evil influence from a cow. To prevent a cow from being ' forespoken ' it was the custom to draw water from the well on the morning of the first day of each ' raith ', between the sun and the sky, pour it into a cog or pail over a new shilling, and give it to the animal as a draught. [*Ibid.* p. 192.] *Ibid.*

Lustration of cattle. The people were wont to lustrate their cattle with fire, ammonia, water, and salt, and with prayers and incantations to safeguard them from evil influences. These lustrations were performed on the first day of the quarter, but especially on the first day of summer and the first day of winter. [*Car. Gad.* II, p. 285.]

Hghlds. and W. Is.

V e. and f. *Farm and household custom. Quarter-day cakes baked.* The names of the individual cakes were rendered into diminutives to distinguish them from the family cake, while the sex of the person for whom they were intended was indicated by the termination, as *Bridean,* masculine diminutive, *Brideag,* feminine diminutive, after Bride ; *Bealltan, Bealltag,* after Beltane ; *Luinean, Luineag,* after Lammas ; and *Samhnan, Samhnag,* after Hallowmas. The people repaired to the fields, glens, and corries to eat their quarter cakes. When eating them, they threw a piece over each shoulder, alternately, saying ' Here to thee, wolf, spare my sheep ; there to thee, fox, spare my lambs ; here to thee eagle, spare my goats ; there to thee, raven, spare my kids ; here to thee, marten, spare my fowls ; there to thee, harrier, spare my chickens.' [*Car. Gad.* I, p. 211.] Hghlds. and W. Is.

V g. *Fishermen's observances.* The first Monday of the quarter is a critical time for fishermen to observe superstitious practices. [Alex. Polson, *Our Hghld. F.-lore Heritage* (1926), p. 124.]

N.E. Scot.

Fishing custom. First Monday of quarter a critical time. A fisherman had been unsuccessful for a long time, and therefore went to consult a lady who practised the diabolical art. She frankly told him that he had sold his luck to an acquaintance, and that this was done beyond recall for that season. She, however, expressed her willingness to arrange with him for next season if he promised secrecy, as without that nothing could be done. This he promised, and she then gave him a sixpence which resembled all other sixpences except that it had the letters ' G.L.' printed on it. When asked if these letters stood for ' Good Luck ', she said it was not his business to ask any questions. He was told that he was, at the beginning of the next season, to get this coin spliced in the rope which ties the fleet of nets to the boat. This he did, and began to make splendid fishing. Although he knew that the first Monday of the quarter was a critical time, he neglected to watch his boat, and when he looked he found that the sixpence was gone. . . . And, as sure as death, a fortnight passed before another scale was seen in the boat. [*Trans. Gaelic Soc. of Inverness*, Vol. XVIII, 1891-2.] Cths.

V i. *Visiting wells*, see *Section Wells ;* Vol. I.

V j. *Scapegoat.* On the first Monday of the quarter a living creature was thrust outside by the first person who rose in the morning and the door was shut again. This was a propitiatory sacrifice to evil spirits, usually a cock, hen, drake, duck, or cat ; rarely a dog. [*Car. Gad.* II, p. 243.]
W. Hghlds. and Hdes.

V k. *Doles and gifts. Handsel on first Monday of quarter.* The reciter says that she remembers, when she was young, of a woman who was living beside them who used to make a point of coming to her mother on the first Monday of every quarter for a handsel. The woman was noted for her superstitious nature, and her object in asking the handsel from the reciter's mother was because she believed that it would secure a prosperous season for her during that quarter. [Mlan Ms.]
Rothiemurchus, Iness.

VI. Beliefs in Supernatural occurrences, witches, etc. *Quarter Days called Witches' Days.* The first Monday and the first Friday of each quarter were days on which witches and fairies held revel. Dyke, El.

Rowan tree crosses used to be put into the houses every quarter-day (to ward off evil influences)—Braemar (told by one who has seen this done). [Rev. W. Gregor.] Ab.

The last night of the quarter is the time of fairy festivities and raids on helpless human beings. [*Sups. of Hghlds.*, p. 18.]
Hghlds.

How to detect Witches on the first Monday. Early in the morning on the first Monday of each of the four quarters of the year the smoke from a witch's house *goes against the wind.* This may be seen by any one . . . going (early) to an eminence whence the witch's house may be seen. [*Wcrft. and Sec. Sight*, p. 53.]   Hghlds.

Fairies, Sith-Folk, move at beginning of a quarter. These *Siths*, or Fairies, they call *Sleagh Maith* (*Sluagh math*), or the Good People . . . remove to other lodgings at the beginning of each quarter of the year, so travelling till Domesday . . . finding some ease by so journing [journeying] and changing habitations. Their chamaelion-lyke bodies swim in the air near the earth with bag and bagadge ; and at such revolution of time, Seers, or men of the Second Sight (females being seldom so qualified) have very terrifying encounters with them, even on high ways ; who therefoir usually shune to travell abroad at these four seasons of the year, and thereby have made it a custom to this day among the Scottish-Irish to keep church duely every first Sunday of the quarter to sene (sain) or hallow themselves, their corns and cattell, from the shots and stealth of these wandering tribes ; and many of these superstitious people will not be seen in church againe till the next quarter begin, as if . . . all the use of worship and sermons were to save them from these arrows that fly in the dark. [*The Secret Commonwealth of Elves, Fauns and Fairies*, pp. 7, 8. Text from MS. by Robert Kirk, M.A., Minister of Aberfoyle, 1691. Published with Comments by Andrew Lang (1893).]

HOGMANAY

DECEMBER 31ST, EVE OF JANUARY 1ST

Both Teutonic and Celtic peoples began the day with its eve, or the preceding night ; in the same way the years were reckoned from winters. Some of the names and rites quoted illustrate this clearly, and, in keeping with old custom, the year of the Scottish Calendar Customs is set out as beginning with Hogmanay, New Year's Eve, though at times the passing of the old year may seem to be the uppermost thought in the minds of the commemorators.

I. Names. Hogmanay ; New Year's Eve ; *Oidhche Chaluinne*, night [for eve] of *caluinn*, Lat. *calendae*. The form *Oidhche Choinnle* has an alternative genitive written in the same way as the genitive of *coinneal*, candle ; hence the name ' Night of the Candle ', perverted also occasionally to Candlemas. Singen'-e'en, a name given in Fife and Angus. [Ed.]

The singing of Yule-tide carols was formerly quite common in Scotland ; the favourite occasion being the last night of the year, which in consequence became known as Singin' E'en . . ., the name used in Fife and Forfar [1] in preference to the more common term of Hogmanay. . . . Singin' E'en became the one notable date that to the peasant mind checked off the passing years. [D. MacRitchie, *Scot. Review*, 1905, Dec. 21st.]

Hogmanay is, 1st, the last day of the year ; and 2nd, the entertainment given to a visitor on this day ; or a gift conferred on those who apply for it. [Jamieson.]

IV. Omens, a. *Weather and heavenly bodies.* Some claimed the power of divining what kind the coming harvest was to be from the appearance of the stars on the last night of the year. [Greg. p. 160.]   Keith, Bf.

Omens drawn from the direction of the wind are the same as those quoted for New Year's Day. The omen was from ' the wind the old year left '.

The *Tarbh Choinnle*, translated ' the Candlemas Bull ' by the confusion of names explained under **I. Names.** [Ed.]

This ' Bull ' was nothing more or less than a small passing cloud which Highland imagination shaped into the form of a

---

[1] Now called Angus.

bull. Much was to be gathered, so it was believed, from watching the place of its rise, the direction it took, and the place of its disappearance. [A. Polson, *Our Highland Folklore Heritage* (1926), pp. 153 f.]   Hghlds.

In the Highlands of Scotland ... if a black cloud is seen on New Year's Eve, it portends some dreadful calamity, either to the country or to the person on whose estate or house it appears. [R. T. Hampson, *Med. Aevi Kalendarium* (1841), p. 387.]

In Perthshire this cloud was watched all night. [Alex. Allardyce, *Scotland and Scotsmen in the 18th Cent.* II, p. 457.] Pth.

Much importance was attached to the last night of the year in forecasting the nature of the coming year both as to weather and fertility. Between eight and nine o'clock at night the sky was carefully scanned. If it was cloudless the year would be bad. If there were clouds, the largest was selected. It went by the name of ' Tarrow choil ' [*tarbh choinnle*]. If it lay toward the north, was densely black, and had a soft and not a hard frosty appearance, it would be a year of plenty for man and beast. If it lay to the east, the year would be fairly good. If it lay toward the south there would be plenty of straw but not very much grain. If it hang in the west, the year would be of the same kind as if the sky was cloudless,—unproductivity. [Rev. W. Gregor.]   Corgarff, Ab.

IV. d. *Personal clothing or house.* Empty pockets or an empty cupboard on New Year's Eve portend a year of poverty. The poet Burns makes mention of this in an epistle to Colonel de Payster, from whom he borrowed a small sum at this season :

> ' To make the old year go out groaning
> And keep the new year from coming in moaning.'

[Henderson, *F.-L. of the Northern Counties* (1879), p. 72.]

IV. g. *Food or drink.* Omens were drawn from the way in which the wort was boiled ; if the wort boiled up in the middle of the pot there was a ' fey ' [doomed] person's drink in the pot. [This was in the brewing of the New Year ale. ' Wort ' is the infusion of malt before it ferments into beer. Ed.] [A. C. R., *Sc. N. & Q.*, 3rd Series, III, p. 291 (1925).] See also **V m.** *Bannocks.*

V. Observances. Hogmanay . . . was much more popular than Christmas in Scotland. [*Old Times*, p. 148.]

These rites should be compared with those of New Year's Day.

V a. *Things forbidden. Sweeping.* A lady who was brought up in the neighbourhood of Edinburgh says that she remembers how her mother would not allow the floor to be swept, or ashes or anything to be put out from the middle of the day before New Year day till after the New Year. The reason she gave ;—' for the luck would be swept out along with the sweepings.' [Mlan MS.] Edin.

To leave work unfinished.

On *Auld Year's* morn the countra folk
Wi' gleesome speed rise soon,
Ere night, ilk lass maun end her rock,
An' get her reelin' doon.
The lads the byres an' stables muck,
An' clean the corn is dightit,—
A single life sall be their luck,
Wha's task's undone or slightit
By them this day.

Note. It is believed by the Scottish peasantry that if any part of the work in which they are engaged remains unfinished upon the last day of the old year, their matrimonial wishes, however sanguine, shall never be crowned with success. [Rev. Jˢ. Nicol, *Poems* (1805), I, pp. 25 f.] S. Scot.

(About 1800.) In my grandfather's house . . . on the 31st Dec. all household work was stopped, rock emptied, yarn reeled and hanked, and wheel and reel put into an outhouse. The house itself was whitewashed and cleaned. [Napier, Appendix, p. 150.] W. Scot.

Superstitious women are anxious to spin off all the flax that is on their rocks on the last night of the year, being persuaded that if they left any unspun the ' gyre-carlin ', or as they also pronounce the word, ' gy-carlin ', would carry it off before morning. [Jamieson.] Ffe.

There was no spinning at Christmas, and the rock had to be emptied of lint on Christmas Eve. To do so sometimes it was necessary to spin till very late. If any was left, the chimney was swept with it. [This reference is probably to ' Little Christmas ', New Year, and its Eve. Ed.] [Rev. W. Gregor.]
New Deer, Aberdour, Ab.

Cessation of work quoted also from the Hebrides. [Mlan MS.]

Unlucky. Marriage proclaimed. It is held to be unlucky to have the proclamation of marriage made at the end of the year, and the marriage not celebrated till the year following.

A native of Lochgilphead says that, in his native place, they called such marriages *posadh gobhlach* (straddling marriages). [Mlan MS.]　　　　　　　　　　　　　　　　　　　　Ar.

V b.　*Things enjoined. Rubbish carried out.*　All dirty water and ashes—in short, all that is usually carried out of a house each morning—are carried out on the last evening of the year. This is done that nothing may have to be taken out on New Year's Day.　[*Ethnog. Survey of the U. Kingdom*, 4th Report, p. 15.]　　　　　　　　　　　　　　　　Minnigaff, Galloway.

Keeping out ill luck.　When the house was cleaned out at Hogmanay, the ill luck of the past year was supposed to be driven out . . . and to prevent the powers of evil entering again the Bible was sometimes placed above the door during the last hours of the year, and the cat kept inside, so that if by any mishap an unlucky first foot should dare to enter in spite of this precaution, the evil could be got rid of by throwing out the cat—for pussy was believed to be able to carry out with it all the mischief which such a person was supposed to bring in.　[Contributed to *John o' Groats' Journal* (1911) by Rev. D. Beaton.]　　　　　　　　　　　　　　　Cths.

To pay debts.　Amongst the old residenters and their descendants any outstanding debts were always paid before the New Year came in.　Houses were cleaned up and papered in preparation for the New Year.　[Communicated by D. Rorie, M.D., *County F.-L.*, VII, p. 146.]　　　　　　　Ffe.

On Hogmanay Day tradesmen called personally with their yearly accounts, of which they received payment, along with some appropriate refreshment.　[R. and W. Chambers, *Memoirs* [13] (1884), p. 19.]　　　　　　　　　　　　Edin.

Holly on the house.　The house was hung with holly to keep out the fairies.　[*Wcrft & Sec. Sight*, p. 232.]　　　　Hghlds.

To wash children.　In my father's house in Partick [about the year 1825] on . . . Hogmanay evening children were all washed before going to bed. . . . All retired to bed before twelve o'clock, as it was unlucky not to be in bed as the New Year came in.　[Napier, p. 159.]　　　　　　　　W. Scot.

V c.　*Fire, ashes, etc.*　On Hogmanay the fire was ' happit ' with more than ordinary care to keep it from ' going out ', as such a thing would be most unlucky.　On the same evening everything was made ready for the fire of the morning of the New Year.　[*Ethnog. Survey of the U. Kingdom*, 5th Report (1897), pp. 456 f.]　　　　　　　　Kirkmaiden, Wgtn.

Keep (your fire) burning even on till the New Year is in. Letting the fire burn out may predict a death in the home before the end of the New Year and it certainly shall be all bad luck for those people who are foolish enough to give away any fire that day. [Mlan MS.]   Skye, Iness.

On Hogmanay the fire was ' ristit ' by the ' gueedeman '. The Sign of the Cross was made on the peat that was put among the burning ashes. The peat was then covered up with the ashes, and after the whole was smoothed, the Sign of the Cross was made over the whole. No woman was allowed to take a hand in this piece of work, though it was her province to do this work at all other times. (For footprints next morning see *New Year*, **V**.) [Rev. W. Gregor.]   Muir of Ord, Rs.

There was a rhyme (which the writer has not been able to recover) to be said when feeding the fire. By this means evil was kept away from the house for the subsequent year. [*Wcrft & Sec. Sight*, p. 237.]   Hghlds and W. Isles.

No one was to come near the fire but a friend, and, as an additional security against its going out, candles were kept burning. . . .   The women made use of the occasion to bake bread for next day. [*Ibid.*]   *Ibid.*

People bring a peat or small bits of wood on visiting their friends at Hogmanay or New Year's morning singing the *Rann na Coluinn*. These were put on the friend's fire to ' burn some evil away '. [Mlan MS.]   S. Knapdale, Ar.

The ashes carried out of the house. See **V b**.   Reported for W. Scot. [Napier, p. 159.]

Juniper dried for saining. Juniper bushes are as much in request this night as kail is on Hallowe'en. Brought home in Herculean loads, the juniper is arranged about the fire to dry till morning. (For household and byre fumigation, see *New Year*.) [*Pop. Superstitions*, p. 252.]   Hghlds.

Burning of ' The Clavie '

A singular custom takes place on New Year's Eve (old style) at the village of Burghead, on the southern shore of the Moray Firth, about nine miles from the town of Elgin. It has been observed there from time immemorial, and both its origin, and that of the peculiar appellation by which it is distinguished, form still matter of conjecture and dispute for antiquaries. The following extract from the *Banffshire Journal* presents . . . all that can be stated regarding this remarkable ceremonial :

' Any Hogmanay afternoon, a small group of seamen and coopers, dressed in blue overfrocks, and followed by numbers of noisy youngsters, may be seen rapidly wending their way to the south-western extremity of the village, where it is customary to build the Clavie. One of the men bears on his shoulders a stout Archangel tar-barrel, kindly presented for the occasion by one of the merchants, who has very considerately left a quantity of the resinous fluid in the bottom. Another carries a common herring-cask, while the remainder are laden with other raw materials, and the tools necessary for the construction of the Clavie. Arrived at the spot, three cheers being given for the success of the undertaking, operations are commenced forthwith. In the first place, the tar-barrel is sawn into two unequal parts ; the smaller forms the groundwork of the Clavie, the other is broken up for fuel. A common fir prop, some four feet in length, called the " spoke ", being then procured, a hole is bored through the tub-like machine, that, as we have already said, is to form the basis of the unique structure, and a long nail, made for the purpose, and furnished gratuitously by the village blacksmith, unites the two. Curiously enough, no hammer is allowed to drive this nail, which is " sent home " by a smooth stone. The herring-cask is next demolished, and the staves are soon undergoing a diminution at both extremities, in order to fit them for their proper position. They are nailed, at intervals of about two inches all round, to the lower edge of the Clavie-barrel, while the other ends are firmly fastened to the spoke, an aperture being left sufficiently large to admit the head of a man. Amid tremendous cheering, the finished Clavie is now set up against the wall, which is mounted by two stout young men, who proceed to the business of filling and lighting. A few pieces of the split-up tar-barrel are placed in a pyramidal form in the inside of the Clavie, enclosing a small space for the reception of a burning peat, when everything is ready. The tar, which had been previously removed to another vessel, is now poured over the wood ; and the same inflammable substance is freely used, while the barrel is being closely packed with timber and other combustible materials, that rise twelve or thirteen inches above the rim.

' By this time the shades of evening have begun to descend, and soon the subdued murmur of the crowd breaks forth into one loud, prolonged cheer, as the youth who was despatched for the fiery peat (for custom says no sulphurous lucifer, no patent congreve dare approach within the sacred precincts of the Clavie) arrives with his glowing charge. The master-builder relieving him of his precious trust, places it within the opening already noticed, where, revived by a hot blast from his powerful lungs, it ignites the surrounding wood and tar, which quickly bursts into flame. During the short time the fire is allowed to gather strength, cheers are given in rapid succession for " The Queen ", " The Laird ", " The Provost ", " The Town ", " The Harbour ", and " The Railway ", and then Clavie-bearer number one, popping his head between the staves, is away with his flaming burden. Formerly, the Clavie was carried in triumph round every vessel in the harbour, and a handful of grain thrown into each, in order to insure success for the coming year ; but as this part of the ceremony came to be tedious, it was dropped, and the procession confined to the boundaries of the town. As fast as his heavy load will permit him, the bearer hurries along the well-known route, followed by the shouting Burgheadians, the boiling tar meanwhile trickling down in dark sluggish streams all over his back. Nor is the danger of scalding the only one he who essays to carry the Clavie has to confront, since the least stumble is sufficient to destroy his equilibrium. Indeed, this untoward event, at one time looked on as a dire calamity, foretelling disaster to the place, and certain death to the bearer in the course of next year, not unfrequently occurs. Having reached the junction of two streets, the carrier of the Clavie is relieved ; and while the change is being effected, firebrands plucked from the barrel are thrown among the crowd, who eagerly scramble for the tarry treasure, the possession of which was of old deemed a sure safeguard against all unlucky contingencies. Again the multitude bound along ; again they halt for a moment as another individual takes his place as bearer—a post for the honour of which there is sometimes no little striving. The circuit of the town being at length completed, the Clavie is borne along the principal street to a small hill near the northern extremity of the promontory called the " Doorie ", on the summit of which a freestone pillar, very much resembling an ancient altar, has been built for its reception, the spoke fitting into a socket in the centre. Being now firmly seated on its throne, fresh fuel is heaped on the Clavie, while, to make the fire burn the brighter, a barrel with the ends knocked out is placed on the top. Cheer after cheer rises from the crowd below, as the efforts made to increase the blaze are crowned with success.

' Though formerly allowed to remain on the Doorie the

whole night, the Clavie is now removed when it has burned
about half an hour.   Then comes the most exciting scene of
all.   The barrel is lifted from the socket, and thrown down on
the western slope of the hill, which appears to be all in one
mass of flame—a state of matters that does not, however,
prevent a rush to the spot in search of embers.   Two stout men,
instantly seizing the fallen Clavie, attempt to demolish it by
dashing it to the ground : which is no sooner accomplished
than a final charge is made among the blazing fragments,
that are snatched up in total, in spite of all the powers of combustion, in an incredibly short space of time.'   [Chambers'
Book of Days, vol. II, pp. 789-91.]   El.

No stranger may join the band of workers but as an on-
looker.   The sons of the original inhabitants only handle the
primitive tools that make the ' Clavie '.   Unwritten but unvarying laws regulate all their actions.   Every article required
is borrowed, nothing bought.   As darkness comes on a band
of coopers and sailors makes its way to a particular spot over-
looking the bay to the west of the village.   The band, till a
few years ago, was headed by an old man who superintended
the building of the Clavie.   Now he has resigned his post, and
a young man of another family is the recognised chief.   A tar
barrel is sawn in two, and the bottom half is retained.   A long
nail is specially made by the village smith and with it the
bottom half of the barrel is firmly nailed to a pole.   The staves
of another are nailed to the lower rim of the half barrel, and
their lower edges to the pole some distance down.   Sufficient
space is left between two of the staves for a man's head to be
thrust in, for the Clavie is carried round the village on the
head and shoulders.   The pole or ' spoke ' as it is called, to
which the half barrel has thus been nailed, is set up, and there
stands the empty Clavie.   As each additional performance is
completed, the workers stop and give three cheers, the crowd
of children and onlookers usually joining.   ' Three cheers for
that ' rings out again and again, and as the sounds rise a
strange feeling of excitement gets abroad.   When the last
stave is nailed on, the greater part of the work is over.   The
round stone used for a hammer is thrown aside, and the work
of filling the Clavie with sticks and tar begins.

When all is ready, one of the band is sent for a burning peat,
which is always supplied from the same house.   This is applied
to the tar, and soon the Clavie is ablaze, and the cheers
literally become howls of excited glee.   The first to put his
head under this mass of flames is usually some one of their

PLATE II

Photo : Gloyer.

The Burning of the Clavie at Burghead.

number who has recently been married. The first lift of the Clavie is an honour, and is bought in the orthodox fashion—a round of whisky to the workers. And now the strange procession hurries along the streets. He who carries the tar-dripping and flaming Clavie does not walk, he runs, and the motley crowd surges round him and behind him, cheering and shouting . . . along the same streets where similar processions have gone year after year. At certain houses and at certain street-corners, a halt is made, and a brand is whipped out of the Clavie and hurled on his flaming errand of good luck among the crowd. He who seizes the brand shall be the favourite of fortune during the . . . coming New Year. Near the head of the promontory is the Doorie Hill, the only remaining ' Baillie '. To this mound the Clavie is finally carried. A stone altar stands on the summit of the Doorie, with a hole in the centre into which the spoke of the Clavie is inserted. In this position it is visible from all parts of the village. . . . Another barrel of tar is emptied in the fire, and the great flames leap up into the black night and roll down the sides of the altar and of the hill. The daring ones of the band jump on the altar and stir up the flaming mass, or hit the sides of the barrel. The spoke of the Clavie is rescued from the flames and sold, while the charred sticks are eagerly snatched up by the villagers and set up in the ingle neuk, to be bringers of good luck and averters of evil in the coming year. [*The Evening Dispatch* (Edinburgh), Jan. 16, 1889, quoted in *F.-L. J.* VII (1889), pp. 11-14.]

On the evening of the last day of December (Old Style), the youths of the village [of Burghead] assemble about dusk, and make the necessary preparations for the celebration of the ' Clavie '. Proceeding to some shop they demand a strong empty barrel, which is usually given at once, but if refused taken by force. Another for breaking up, and a quantity of tar are likewise procured at the same time. Thus furnished they repair to a particular spot close to the sea-shore, and commence operations. A hole about four inches in diameter is first made in the bottom of the stronger barrel, into which the end of a stone pole, five feet in length, is firmly fixed : to strengthen their hold a number of supports are nailed round the outside of the former, and also closely round the latter. The tar is then put into the barrel, and set on fire, and the remaining one being broken up, stave after stave is thrown in until it is quite full. The ' Clavie ', already burning fiercely, is now shouldered by some strong young man, and borne away at a rapid pace. As soon as the bearer gives signs of exhaustion, another willingly takes his place ; and should any of those who are honoured to carry the blazing load meet with an accident, as sometimes happens, the misfortune incites no pity even among his near relatives. In making the circuit of the village they are said to confine themselves to its old boundaries. Formerly, the procession visited all the fishing-boats, but this has been discontinued for some time. Having gone over the appointed ground, the ' Clavie ' is finally carried to a small artificial eminence near the point of the promontory, interesting as being a portion of the ancient fortifications, and spared probably on account of its being used for this purpose, where a circular heap of stones used to be hastily piled up, in the hollow centre of which the ' Clavie ' was placed still burning. On this eminence, which is termed the ' durie ', the present proprietor has lately erected a small round column, with a cavity in the centre for admitting the free end of the pole, and into this it is now placed. After being allowed to burn on the ' durie ' for a few minutes, the ' Clavie ' is most unceremoniously hurled from its place, and the smoking embers scattered among the assembled crowd, by whom . . . they were eagerly caught at and fragments of them carried home and carefully preserved as charms against witchcraft. At one time superstition invested the whole proceedings with all the solemnity of a religious rite, the whole population joining in it as an act necessary to the welfare and prosperity of the little community during the year about to commence. . . .

The ' Clavie ' has now, however, degenerated into a mere frolic, kept up by the youngsters more for their own amusement than for any benefit which the due performance of the ceremony is believed to secure. [*N. & Q.* 2nd S. vol. ix, p. 38 ; see also *N. & Q.* 2nd S. vol. ix, pp. 106, 169, 269.]

In 1875 the Clavie was duly carried to one vessel just ready for sea. Handfuls of grain were thrown upon her deck, and amid a shower of fire-water she received the name of *Doorie*. The modern part of the town is not included in the circuit. [E. J. Guthrie, *Old Scottish Customs* (1885), p. 225.]

Cf. In several of the fishing villages of the north-east coast it was customary to sow corn or barley over a new boat and to break a bottle of whisky over the prow. [Greg. p. 196.]

In Burghhead, when they burn the Clavie . . . one can hear a murmur here and there from some of the old inhabitants : ' There go the witches! ' All the ills, the malefic influences, the witchcraft of the year are being consumed by the fire. [Isabel Cameron, *A Highland Chapbook*, p. 33 (1928).]

It was lucky to keep the flame from the Clavie burning in the house-fires of Burghhead all the year. [L. Gomme, *Ethnog. Survey of the U. Kingdom*, 4th Report, p. 36.]

Summary. ' Unwritten but unvarying laws ' regulate every action, one of which laws is that every article is borrowed, nothing bought. . . . Although the long nail which fastens the staves of the clavie is iron and is made specially for the purpose by the village smith, the hammer used for the purpose must be a round stone. . . .

Details in shape of a formula.

(*a*) The fire is made by a group of men connected by a common descent, that is, a kindred.

(*b*) The original inhabitants of a village form the unit from which common descent is traced.

(*c*) The flame for the fire is obtained in a sacred manner.

(*d*) Continuous life of the fire (symbolised).

(*e*) The house-fire is derived from the village fire.

(*f*) The possession of an ember is the means of good fortune.

(*g*) The bounds of the village have the fire carried round them.

(*h*) Welfare and prosperity of the community dependent upon the performance of the ceremony.

(*i*) The bearers of the fire are honoured.

(*k*) Early economic conditions are enforced in the performance of the ceremony.

(*l*) Stone-age implements are used. [*Ibid.* p. 27.]

Clavies in Earlier Times

In the first allusion to the superstition (the burning of the Clavie) in the existing Records of the Presbytery of Elgin (January 11th, 1655), the word ' Clavie ' does not occur. The ceremony is described as the carrying of fir torches about the boats. It is often spoken of much in the same way, both in these records and in those of the Kirk-Sessions of Drainie and Duffus, even when the word ' Clavie ' occurs. For instance, it is called (December 23rd, 1705) the ' practice of carrying lighted clavies or torches about ye boats '. The people are charged with burning ' their clavies about their boats ', or carrying ' a torch off candles about the boats ', or with kindling ' a clavie of firre ', or a ' candle ', and going about the boats. In one entry the ceremony is described as ' burning torches—crossing the boats therewith ', but I do not find anything to show that the use of the word ' crossing ' in this entry had any special significance.

It appears from these records that the burning of the clavie took place on ' ye new yeires even ', or on ' ye last day of Decr ', or on ' new yeires day '. It is often spoken of in these records—that is about 200 years ago—as an ' old ' custom, and is called a ' heathenish and idolatrous custome ', a ' superstitious, Idolatrous and sinfule custome ', an ' abominable heathenish practice ', and a ' great and gross scandall and Idolatrous custome '.

The religious character of the ceremony is brought out by a statement in one of the entries (February 3rd, 1689), that, in addition to carrying fire round the boats, the people ' did carrie meat and drink to the boat side, and did cast drink upon the boat '. One man is accused of having ' hade a burning clavie, paying a superstitious worship, and blessing the boats, after the old hethnish custome, contrarie to all rules of Christianitie '.

Extract from the Kirk-Session Records of the Parish of Inveravon, August 16th, 1704. ' Ane Act against Clavies : That whereas it hath been the custome and practise of many in this parish of Inveravine, to goe about ye folds and cornes with kindled Torches of firr, superstitiouslie and Idolatrouslie asscribing y^t power to the fire sanctifieing ye cornes and cattell qch is only proper and peculiar to the true and living God. . . . Therfor the Session did and hereby doth enact that whosoever shall be found guiltie of the fors^d superstitious and heathenish practises shall be proceeded ags^t as scandalous persons . . . and if it shall be found that they be children not capable of Church censure that in y^t case their names be kept in record and they declar'd incapable of any Church-priviledge when arrived att the years of discretion or any testimoniall from the Session till they remove the scandall. . . .'

The Presbytery and Kirk-Session Records of Elgin, Drainie, and Duffus show that the Burning of the Clavie was customary, not in Burghead only, as is generally supposed, but in many, if not in all, of the fishing villages on the Morayshire coast, where the object was ' the blessing of the boats '. But this extract from the Inveravon Records presents the ceremony to us under the same name, in a Banffshire parish far inland, and with a similar object—namely, the blessing of the corn fields so as to secure fertility or good crops. . . . From more than one source, indeed, I have heard that the Inveravon practice was common in some districts of Scotland till quite recent times. . . .

Those who were found guilty (of this custom), were required to ' make publick acknowledgment off the same before the congregāne in sackcloath, and to stand as many days as the Sessions should Judge fitt ' ; on ' accepting and submitting to discipline ', they were ' sharply rebuked and exhorted to serious repentance '. Others were required to satisfy the discipline ' in sacco ', to ' testify yr Repentance by standing at yᵉ pillar ', or to stand ' in the Joges two dayes '. . . . Thus . . . ' The burning of the Clavie ' . . . was openly declared to be, in the opinion of the Church, a worship of Fire which was ' only proper and peculiar to the true and living God '. [Sir Arthur Mitchell, *The Past in the Present*, Appendix, xiii, pp. 260-3 (1880).]

Scene of the burning of the Clavie. At Burghead may be seen the remains of ancient fortifications of immense strength. . . . Recent excavations shew the antiquity of the place. The few objects found are some of them pre-historic and some of them Roman, and the construction of the ramparts is of the type of the Gaulish Oppida as described by Caesar. These ramparts are twenty-four feet thick, faced with stone on both faces, and joined by oak beams, crossed by planks and nailed together with huge nails. [Hugh W. Young, F.S.A. (Scot.), in *The Reliquary & Illustrated Archaeologist*, new series, vol. I (1895), p. 22.]

Blazing Tar-Barrels

At Newton-Stewart there is a fire-procession which starts from ' The Angle ' on Hogmanay exactly at twelve o'clock at night. A tar-barrel is fixed on two long poles by means of two cross-bars. The barrel is well filled with tar and paraffin. The whole is mounted on the shoulders of four men, and the contents of the barrel are set on fire. The procession marches along the street past the bridge over the Cree that leads to Minnigaff village. When the end of the street is reached the processionists retrace their steps till they come to the bridge. This they cross and march through the village of Minnigaff to the green, where the bonfire is now in full blaze. Here they get their barrel replenished if need be. They then retrace their steps through the village and over the bridge to Newton-Stewart, and then along the street to ' The Angle ', the point from which they started. Here the poles and barrels are thrown down and the whole burned. During the procession the carriers of the blazing barrel are changed every now and again. [Rev. W. Gregor, *Ethnog. Survey of the U. Kingdom*, 4th Report, 1896, p. 16.]   Newton-Stewart, Wgtn.

It has long been customary in Campbeltown for the youth of the town to collect quantities of tar-barrels and pile them at certain centres such as the Cross, the Quay head and other conspicuous points throughout the town. The work of collecting goes on for several days previous to Hogmanay. Shortly after nightfall on Hogmanay, parties start from several parts of the town, headed by one carrying a burning tar-barrel on his head. These run along the public streets making their way to the centres of conflagration, and it is a point of honour which party can reach it first. If the person carrying the barrel is able to hold by it until he has reached the general heap, he casts it among the rest, which has already been set on fire. Sometimes an old boat can be secured, and when this is the case, perhaps more than one barrel is placed inside of it, and a willing party of supple fellows line themselves on both sides, and run along dragging the boat on its keel, the barrels burning in it, until they reach the centre, where their charge is devoted to the general burning. The town-cross is the main scene for these demonstrations. [Mlan MS.]   Kintyre, Ar.

On Hogmanay a deputation of the villagers waited on my grandfather to request the favour of a tar-barrel, which having been lighted shortly before midnight, and preceded by a brass band, was carried on men's shoulders by means of spokes blazing round the village and set down opposite his door to burn to ashes. [*The Gallovidian*, X, 23.]   See also **d.**, *Ashes in divination*, below.   Garlieston, Wtn.

Bonfire and Blazing Barrels

As the clock strikes twelve at night on Hogmanay a large bonfire is kindled on the Green of the village of Minnigaff. For some weeks before the boys are busy collecting brushwood and pieces of fallen trees from the neighbouring woods. . . . By the last day of the year a goodly quantity of material has been gathered. On that day everyone is busy in erecting the pile to be burned. . . . There is no ceremony before or at the kindling, and there is no special person set apart to apply the fire. The pile burns through the night, and commonly through part of next day. It is always erected on the same spot. About seventy years ago the bonfire was composed of different material. For months before the bones all round the district were collected and stored in a little hut built by the boys with rough stones in a corner of the village green. The bones of any animal that had died and been buried for a considerable time were dug up and stored. For about a fortnight previous to Hogmanay the boys went the round of the village and laid all the peat-stacks under tribute. The peats were all carefully stowed away till required. On the last day of the year the peats were first piled up, and then the pile was covered with the bones. At twelve o'clock at night the whole was set on fire, and the younger part of those present ran round the blazing pile, but no words were repeated. My informant (eighty-three years of age) has engaged in all this. He also said that he as well as others used to get empty tar-barrels, put a little tar in them, place them on their heads, have the tar in them set on fire, and, with them blazing on their heads, parade the village. [Rev. W. Gregor, *Ethnog. Survey of the U. Kingdom*, 4th Report, pp. 15 f.] Minnigaff, Galloway.

But the grand sight of all is the procession of young men which parades the village on New Year's Eve. By an unwritten law they must be young men—namely, those who have not ' ranged ' themselves ; and every one vies with the other as to which shall present the most bizarre appearance. Red Indians, giants, dwarfs, demons (assorted, and of all sizes) and fishwives pass in procession, carrying at intervals flaming tar-barrels, and finally gathering in a wild dance round a flaming bonfire. [Miss E. M. Johnstone, *The Graphic*, January 7th, 1893.] *Ibid.*

The burning of a crate of combustibles dragged to the cross at Dingwall, Ross and Cromarty, and a procession of swinging fireballs at Stonehaven, Kincardine, is reported by J. M. McPherson, in *Prim. Belfs, in N.E. of Scot.* (1929), pp. 23, 24.

Bonfires

At Biggar the villagers collect a large quantity of fuel, and about 9 o'clock on the last day of the old year the pile is lighted, each member of the crowd ' thinking it a duty to cast into the flaming mass some additional portion of material '. It is necessary to maintain the fire until New Year's Day is far advanced, and if the house fire has been allowed to become extinguished, recourse must be had to the village pile. [L. Gomme, *Ethnog. Survey of the U. Kingdom*, 4th Report, 1896, p. 27.] Biggar, Lnk.

A bonfire kindled at twelve o'clock at night on the last day of the year. [Rev. W. Gregor, *Ibid.* p. 16.]   Invergordon, Rs.

Huge bonfires were kindled (at Hogmanay) at the Townhead and the Common Loan. [*Ibid.*]   Auchterarder, Bf.

V d. *Rites of divination. Silver coin.* In order to ascertain whether the coming year is to be prosperous or otherwise, the master of the house, ere he retires on New Year's Eve, places his smallest silver coin on the doorstep. If it be missing in the morning, poverty will haunt the year ; while, if the coin be untouched, prosperity will crown his fortunes for the same period. [*Old Times*, p. 150.]

Coolin cheese. A slice (of the *Calluin* or Coolin cheese), cut off at this feast (Hogmanay), or a piece of the rind, if preserved, and with a hole made through it, has strange virtues. It was called *laomachan* [the gleaming?], and a person losing his way during the ensuing year, in a mist or otherwise, has only to look through the hole and he will see his way clearly. By scrambling to the top of the house, and looking through it down the *fairleus* (the hole in the roof that served in olden times for chimney and window), a person can ascertain the name of his or her future husband or wife. It will prove to be the same as that of the first person seen or heard named. [Cf. *Hallowe'en*, **V d.**] A piece of *laomachan* is also valuable for putting under one's pillow to sleep over. [*Wcrft. & Sec. Sight*, pp. 232 f.]   Hghlds.

Divination by shoulder-blade. The remnant of Haruspicy which has come down to us has come through . . . divination by the shoulder-blade. This was called *Slinnairachd* [*slinnean-achd*], from *Slinnig* [*slinneag*], the shoulder-blade. In Badenach, a . . . district of Inverness-shire, until lately there were men skilled in this sort of divination. I mention the custom here because the sacrifices offered on *Nollig* [*Nollaig*] and *Callaiwn* [*Calluin*], that is Christmas Eve and New Year's Eve, were those from which the knowledge of future events could properly be drawn. The last man in the parish of Laggan who was skilled in *Slinnaireachd* died about 70 years ago. His name was MacTavish, and he had been many years *Aireach* (the superintendent of the chief's cattle) to Mr MacDonald of Gallovie. The following I have often heard related, and once by a man worthy of credit, who averred he had been an eyewitness to it. The fame of MacTavish had travelled to distant parts of the country, and, having come to the ears of a rival diviner, the latter determined to have ocular proofs of his proficiency. For this purpose he took a journey of many miles, and on his arrival at Gallovie announced his errand, and was directed to the house of his brother soothsayer. . . . Mr MacDonald invited several of his friends to dine with him on New Year's night [Eve?], and took care to have the two diviners of the company.

After dinner a shoulder-blade was presented to the stranger, and he was requested to declare the result of his inspection, be it good or bad. After having pored over it for a certain time he was observed to change colour, and at first he refused to tell what had so affected him ; but, when pressed, he positively asserted that some one should be hanged on that domain before morning. Some believed it . . .; some did not, but had good manners enough not to turn it into ridicule. They however agreed in one thing, to let MacTavish re-inspect the blade. He did inspect it, and declared his satisfaction at the skill discovered by the stranger, but added that he had made a slight mistake, for that the ill-fated creature that was to be hanged could be no other than the devil himself, for that it had horns and hoofs. . . . Early on the next morning, as MacTavish went his rounds, he found a favourite yearling bull hanged and quite dead. He had put his head through between the bars of a ladder, and, as he was struggling to free himself, the heavy ladder fell across a deep foss, over which the animal was left suspended.

Before the shoulder-blade is inspected, the whole of the flesh must be stripped clean off, without the use of any metal, either by a bone, or a hard wooden knife, or by the teeth. Most of the discoveries are made by inspecting the spots that may be observed in the semi-transparent part of the blade ; but very great proficients penetrate into futurity through the opaque parts also. Nothing can be known that may happen beyond the circle of the ensuing year. The discoveries made have relation to the person for whom or by whom the sacrifice is offered. ['Mr Donald McPherson of Chelsea', by W. J. Thoms, *F.-L. R.* (1878), vol. I, p, 177.] Iness.

V e. *Customs of farm and byre.* The last thing done by those who possessed a cow or a horse was to visit the byre or stable, and I have been told that it was the practice with some, twenty years before my recollection, at the end of the 18th cent. to say the Lord's Prayer during this visit. [Napier, Appendix, p. 159.] W. Scot.

V f. *Household,* see under **V a** and **b.**

V h. *Water custom.* The actual ' creaming ' or skimming of the well is performed in most places immediately after the stroke of midnight and is described as a New Year rite. (*New Year*, **V h.**) But the going to the well and the preparation is carried out in the last hour of the old year ; the ceremony is therefore one of the ' straddling ' rites. [Ed.]

Creaming the well. It was a custom to cream the well at 12 o'clock at night on Hogmanay. [*Ethnog. Survey of the U. Kingdom*, 5th Report, 1897, p. 456.]   Kirkmaiden, Galloway.

Such as were envious of their neighbours' success, and wished to draw away their prosperity, creamed the well they drew water from. This act was believed to be particularly efficacious in ensuring a rich supply of milk and butter to the one who had cows, and performed the act on the well of those who also owned cows. All the utensils used in the dairy were washed with part of the cream of the well, and the cows received the remainder to drink. This ceremony was gone through in some districts on the last night of the year. In a fishing-village on the north-east coast of Aberdeenshire it was performed on the last night of the year, and a handful of grass was plucked and thrown into the pail containing the water. [Greg. pp. 159 f.]   Ab.

V j. *Blood shedding.* (At Hogmanay) a boy, whipped with a branch of holly, may be assured that he will live a year for every drop of blood he loses. This scratching and assurance were bestowed by boys on one another, and were considered a good joke. [*Wcrft. & Sec. Sight*, p. 232.] Cf. *January 1st*, **V j.**   Hghlds.

V m. *Food and drink. Bannocks.* On Hogmanay evening . . . an oat bannock was baked for each child : it was nipped round the edge, had a hole in the centre, and was flavoured with carvey (carroway) seed. Great care was taken that none of these bannocks should break in the firing, as such an occurrence was regarded as a very unlucky omen for the child. . . . It denoted illness or death during the year. (The bannocks eaten on New Year's morning.) [Napier, Appendix, p. 159.]
                                    Partick, Lnk.

Cake, buns, wine and whisky. Every visitor was, on that evening (Hogmanay), treated with wine and cake, or with whisky, buns, and shortbread, or cheese and bread. [*Time's Telescope* (1824), p. 2.]

Haggis. A day or two before Hogmanay a haggis has been cooked and set aside to cool. On Hogmanay it is laid out on a table with a knife beside it . . . (for consumption on New Year's morning). [*Ethnog. Survey of the U. Kingdom*, 4th Report, p. 14.]   Minnigaff, Galloway.

Cheese, càise calluinn. Cheese was an important part of the refreshments (given to Hogmanay revellers), and was known as . . . *Càise Calluinn.* [*Wcrft. & Sec. Sight*, p. 232.]   Hghlds.

Many of her neighbours would have been miserable if the Lady (of Dunalbin) did not eat of the cheese of the Coolin (*Calluinn*). [*Clan-Albin* (1815), I, p. 122.]

Hot pint. Towards the closing hour of the 31st December each family prepared a *hot pint* or wassail bowl of which all the members might drink to each other's prosperity as the new year began. Hot pint usually consisted of a mixture of spiced and sweetened ale with an infusion of whisky. [Rogers, *Social Life in Scotland*, II, p. 336.]

The last glass. The last glass of wine or spirits drained from the last bottle on New Year's Eve or Day is called the ' lucky glass '. It brings good fortune to whoever comes in for it, and if an unmarried person drinks it he will be the first to marry among the company. [Henderson, *F.-L. of the Northern Counties* (1879), p. 73.]   Borders.

V k, m. *Gifts of food and drink.* Sir Walter Scott, writing to Miss Joanna Baillie on Jan. 1, 1819, says he wishes she could have seen about a hundred children dancing to the pipes, and getting a piece of cake and bannock and pennies in honour of *hogmanay*. . . . [*N. & Q.*, 11th S., VI, p. 506, Dec. 28, 1912.]

The children, particularly in villages, go from house to house to seek their ' hogminay '. They commonly get something—' a piece ', or ' sweeties ', or an apple, or a halfpenny. Boys before going their rounds blackened their faces and put on petticoats. [Rev. W. Gregor.]   N.E. Scot.

Hogmanay . . . was the grand festival of all varieties of mendicants, daft folk, and children generally. . . . Among those who secured a respectable dole on such occasions was the town piper, dressed in a red uniform and cocked hat, as befitted a civic official ; . . . and it was understood that, besides his dole at Hogmanay, he was entitled to receive at least a groat annually from all well-disposed householders. [R. and W. Chambers, *Memoirs* (1884), p. 18.]   Edin.

Jollity and feasting noted also from Glasgow.

(On Hogmanay) the villagers, men and boys, went from house to house, preceded in many cases by a piper, and drown-

ing the animosities of the past year in hilarity and merriment.
[*Wcrft. & Sec. Sight*, p. 233.]　　　　　　　　　　　Hghlds.

The visitors never failed to receive their Hogmanay, which
consisted usually of bun, shortbread, and wine or whisky.
[D. MacRitchie, *Scottish Review*, Dec. 21, 1905.]

V 1, m.　*Begging for food and drink with rhymes and singing.*

> My feet's cauld, my shoon's thin ;
> Gie's my cakes, and let me rin!

It is no unpleasing scene, during the forenoon, to see the children going laden home, each with his large apron bellying
out before him, stuffed full of cakes.　[*Pop. Rhymes*[3], pp. 295 f.]

Another version :

> Get up goodwife, and be na sweer,
> But deal your bread as lang's yer here,
> The day'll come when ye'll be deed,
> And neither care for meal nor bread.
> Up stocks, down stools,
> Dinna think that we are fools,
> We are bairns come to play,
> Get up and gie's our hogmanay.

[J. E. Cr.]　　　　　　　　　　　　　　　　　　　N.E. Scot.

Some added :

> Gin ye dinna gie's our Hogmanay,
> We dunner a' yer doors the day.

[*Ethnog. Survey of the U. Kingdom*, 4th Report (1896), p. 14.]
　　　　　　　　　　　　　　　　　　　　　　　Galloway.

I have heard children in the North singing at house doors
on Hogmanay night :

> Here comes in a guid New Year
> A guid New Year, a guid New Year,
> Here comes in a guid New Year,
> An' awa b' soothin' toon.

> The back o' yer hous is thackit wi' rye,
> Thackit wi' rye, etc.

with three verses following, corresponding to those quoted
above.　[*Sc. N. & Q.* I (1888), p. 162.]　　　　　　Ab.

On the last night of the year the children, particularly in
the villages, went into the houses asking their ' hogminay '.

Sometimes they joined in companies and sang the following ditty :

> Rise up, aul wife, an shack yer feathers ;
> Dinna think it we are beggars ;
> We're only bairnies come to play—
> Rise up an gee's wir hogminay.
> Wir feet's caul, wir sheen's thin,
> Gee's a piece an lat's rin.
> We'll sing for bread, we'll sing for cheese,
> We'll sing for a' yir orra bawbees,
> We'll sing for meal, we'll sing for maut,
> We'll sing for siller to buy wir saut.

Something was usually given to the children—' a piece ', sweeties, or a bawbee. [Greg. p. 162.]   N.E. Scot.

The first six lines quoted also from Ab.

Begging while singing a *rann* noted also in Iness.

In Perth, and I believe in most towns in Scotland, Hogmenay songs are still in common use, the children beginning on St Sylvester's night [Dec. 31st] at six o'clock, and never ceasing till after ten, ringing at every bell and singing their songs as soon as the door is opened. [Henderson, *F.-L. of the Northern Counties* (1879), p. 77.]

Tiny toddlers in Scotland go from door to door at Hogmanay, singing :

> Hogmanay ! Hogmanay !
> Gie's my carol, and let's away !

[*Carol*, northern pron. of *carle*, cake. Ed.]

The ' carol ' is not a song, either secular or sacred, but a cake, which was, and still is, in some primitive parts, only prepared at this season. . . . Latterly other . . . dainties took the place of the ' carol '. [Newspaper cutting, prob. from the *Manchester Guardian*.]

The following rhyme was appointed for all who had nothing else to say :

> I do not dislike cheese,
> And have no aversion to butter ;
> But a little drop from the cask
> My throttle is in quest of.

[*Wcrft. & Sec. Sight*, p. 236.]   Hghlds.

> Here come the guisers,
> Never been before,
> Not to beg nor to borrow,
> But to drive away your sorrow.

. . . There were usually refreshments offered and accepted, consisting of bread and cheese, currant loaf, hogmanays (or three-cornered biscuits), and, in some houses, whisky to those who were grown up. As a finish-up, the guisers would all join in the following refrain :

> God bless the master of this house,
>   And mistress also,
> Likewise the little bairnies,
>   That round the table go,
> May your purse be full of money
>   Your cellars full of beer,
> We wish you many a Hogmanay,
>   And many a good New Year.

[A. Stewart, *Remin. of Dunfermline*, pp. 151-3 (1886).]

> Blinking Jock the cobbler,
>   He had a blinking e'e ;
> He selt his wife for a hunder pounds,
>   And that was a' his gear.
> His pockets fu' o' money,
>   His barrels fu' o' beer ;
> Please to help the Guisers,
>   And I wish you a happy New Year.

[*County F.-L.*, VII, p. 144.]   Dunfermline.
A native of Aberdeenshire says that the boys there had the custom of going about singing on Hogmanay night, and soliciting entertainment. He says that they would throw their *brochan* (porridge) on the doors. [Mlan MS.]   Ab.

> Hogmanay, Troll-ol, Troll-oll aye,
> Gie us a piece o' your white bread
> And eke a bittoc o' your grey,
> Wi' brown laif dawds, for Hogmanay.

[Senex, *Glasgow Past and Present*, III (1884), p. 464.]   Glasgow.
The guisers chanted in chorus :

> Rise up, guidwife, an' shak' yer feathers, [bestir yourself]
> Dinna' think that we are beggars ;
> We are guid folks come to play,
> Rise up an' gie's oor Hogmanay.
> Hogmanay, Trol-lol-lay.

Like all other customs of this kind, these visits have been increasingly abandoned to children, and indeed a late version of the rhyme substitutes the words, ' We're girls and boys come out to-day ' for the third line quoted above. [D. MacRitchie, *Scot. Review*, Dec. 21, 1905.]

Quoted with ' We are bonnie boys and girls ' from Kintyre, Ar. [Mlan MS.]

It is still customary in retired and primitive towns for the children of the poorer class of people to get themselves up in the morning swaddled up in a great sheet doubled up in front so as to form a great pocket and then to go along the streets in little bands, calling at the doors of the wealthier classes. Each child gets one quadrant of oatcake . . . and this is called their *hogmanay*. . . . The children on coming to the door cry ' Hogmanay ' . . . or :

> Hogmanay, Trollolay,
> Give us of your white bread and none of your grey, etc.

Singing of Hogmanay rhymes reported also from Lochbroom and Applecross. [Mlan MS.]   Rs.
Children in Skye sing :

> A Christmas, A Christmas,
> A happy New Year,
> A pocketful of money
> And a barrelful of beer.
>
> God bless the master of this house,
> God bless the mistress too,
> And all the children
> That round the table go.
>
> Hogmanay, Hogmanay,
> Give us a penny and let us away,
> If you haven't a penny, a ha'penny will do,
> If you haven't a ha'penny, God bless you.
>
> As I went down the river side,
> The river gave a jump,
> If you've anything within the house
> Give us a big lump.

A Gaelic rhyme followed which was not collected. [(Mrs) Mary Julia MacCulloch, *F.-L.* XXXIV, pp. 89 f.]
         Skye, Iness.

The following New-Year's rhyme . . . consists probably of several separate rhymes tagged together, and the allusions it

contains to the ' big clerk of the street ', etc., make it highly
probable the ceremonies of the evening were remains of the
Festival of Fools. . . . The rhyme is given as it came to hand.

Bless this cheerful dwelling,
With a musical voice,
That it be like a royal palace,
Without being wasteful.
Bless each man
Who surrounds this gathering,
From the one grown grey with seniority
To the one of infant's age.
Bless our gentle men,
And our young children,
All who chance at this time
To come to Donald's.
Men! this begins my tale
And I must tell it.
Ho! each black, black generous one!
Ho-go! each generous one,
Divide this portion
My servant harrowed!
  More produce!
Then it was that Margaret said,
' O dear! more produce! '
Then said Mary,
' My dearest dear!
Martin is behind the door,
Listening to us.'
' That is his excuse,' said she.
Hei fudar! hei fedar!
Up with you, you cajoler!
Fierce icinesses rose
  On Donald,
He levelled at Margaret
  Fair abuse!
He gave a rap to the harp
And the strings sounded
He quickly drew a *crambat*
And tried to tune it.
' You have done mischief,' said the clerk,
' That I don't regret!
Utter ruin has come upon you,
With your broken stick! '

‘ You have a healing vessel,’
Said the harper.
‘ When you tried with it a second time,
’Twill make the stick whole ;
So your share be yours of the healing cup.
O dearest Sir !
May that stick of many virtues
Be full of produce ! ’
I went on candle night to hold New Year revel,
In the house of fat puddings,
I asked admittance at the door
Coaxingly with fair words ;
The big clerk of the street spoke
A senseless word,
‘ If my gold crook were in my hand
I would not let your head whole from the door.’
I took the north turn to the door,
[1] That was a north turn of mischief to me ;
I struck the big toe of my foot
In the face of a stone,
The pin fell, the pan fell,
They made a clang clang clattering !
Rise down, young wife,
And honest dame, that has carried praise,
Be womanly as thou wert wont,
And bring our Christmas gifts to us,
The smooth-faced cheese,
And entrails prepared with juice ;
But if these are not convenient
Bread and cheese will suffice.
It was not greed with open mouth
That brought me to the town
But a hamper
On my servant’s back !
A white servant catch me,
Fatness burns me !
Open and let me in !
‘ True for him,’ said the goodman, ‘ let him in.’

[*Wcrft. & Sec. Sight*, pp. 234 ff.]   Hghlds.

---

[1] No interpretation of these lines can be offered here ; the ‘ north turn ’, ll. 57, 58, is a characteristic Highland prelude to disaster—and injury to the big toe is referred to in other ranns. [Ed.]

The following is recited on Hogmanay night :

Three men to-night
As on Easter night.
[The next line is unintelligible, probably half forgotten]
To-night is the night of the hard hangman,
The hard cruel tree to which Christ was hung ;
Christ, the Clerk above us.
[Another obscure line follows.]
High is the cake, and high the poor,
And high is He of to-night's night.
Brigid went upon her knee,
The King of the elements sat on her breast.

[A. Goodrich-Freer, *F.-L.* (1902), vol. xiii, p. 46.]   Hdes.
From those whose musical powers are not of a high order
the following rhyme, which sets both music and grammar at
defiance, is occasionally heard :

Round the midden I whuppit a geese ;
I'll sing nae mair till I get a bit piece.

These ditties are part of the life of the people . . . though the
festival is now mainly the province of the young. . . . [*County
F.-L.* VII, p. 143.]   Ffe.

Gaelic Begging Songs

On Hogmanay night a party of men from every township
visited every house in the vicinity, the furthest removed houses
being visited first. When they would come to any house,
before they would get to enter, they had to call out in a loud
voice the following *Rann Colluinn*. They would then sit down
to a sumptuous repast consisting of oatmeal bannocks, home
made cheese, and a drop of real Highland whisky to wash it
down. Before leaving two Gaelic songs were sung. Trans. :

I have come out on the night of the Colluinn
From a homestead of the moorland,
Here I stay till I get a bannock
From each village I know.

I shall go to the bridge-head of Lusadh,
Where is the cask of the Mackintoshes,
That I may get from Nic Mhorran
The dregs left in the stoups.

There is another thing I should like,
A crumb of bread, and a bit of mart-flesh,
A scrap of the ' fruit of summer ', [butter]
To spread on with my thumb ;

A little of the flesh of the swarthy goat,
Dragged along choked by the tether ;
For fear of her roaring
It was the mother herself cut her throat.

Let each give me the bannock,
That the New Year may go well with you.
May he who gives no bannock
Have his reward from Donald the dark and bad.[1]

[Mlan Ms.]   Skye, Iness.

The original, *bonnach*, is here translated ' bannock ', scone
or cake, but, as said elsewhere in the notes, it seems to mean
the portion due at this season. The threatening character of
the begging is strongly marked in these rhymes.   [Ed.]
In the following *rann* the curse comes from the man in the
house :

I rose early in the morning
And betook me to stirring of the porridge,
Calling upon John and upon Finlay.
I am not the door-keeper for your [way of] asking ;
If you break open the door
Master Donald will avenge it on you.

[Mlan Ms.]   Barra, Hdes.

Here is a rhyme which lads used to sing as they went from
house to house on Hogmanay evening :

> *Gabhaidh sinn an aran gun an im,*
> *'S gabhaidh sinn an im gun an aran,*
> *Gabhaidh sinn a' chaise leis fein,*
> *'S thig sinn 'ris nur a bhios sinn falamh.*

Trans. :

> We will take bread without butter,
> We will take butter without bread,
> We will take cheese alone,
> And we will come again when we are hungry.

[Mlan MS.]   W. Isles.

[1] A well-known name for the devil.

Another version. Trans. by Dr Alex. Carmichael :

> We are come to the door,
> To see if we be the better of our visit.
> To tell the generous women of the townland
> That tomorrow is Calenda Day.

After being entertained the guisers go sunwise round the fire singing :

> May God bless the dwelling,
> Each stone, and beam, and stave ;
> All food and drink and clothing ;
> May health of men be always there.

Should the guisers be inhospitably treated, they file round the fire withershins and walk out and raise a cairn in or near the door, called ' carnan mollachd ', cairn of malison, ' carnan cronachd ', scathe cairn. They tramp loudly, shaking the dust of the place off their feet, and intoning with a deep voice the following and other maledictions :

> The Malison of God and of Hogmanay be on you,
> And the scath of the plaintive buzzard,
> Of the hen-harrier, of the raven, of the eagle,
> And the scath of the sneaking fox.

> The scath of the dog and of the cat be on you,
> Of the boar, of the badger, and of the ' brugha ',
> Of the hipped bear and of the wild wolf,
> And the scath of the foul foumart.

[*Car. Gad.* I, p. 157.]   Hghlds and W. Isles.

If nothing is given them they show their displeasure in various ways. This is shown sometimes by erecting a heap of stones outside the door ; this cairn, called *Carn nam Mollachd* [cairn of the curses], is much feared, upon it the guisers pronounce their ill-wishes for the niggardly matron before taking their departure. [Mlan MS.]   Skye, Iness.

In some parts of the Outer Hebrides the following custom prevails. On the night before the New Year a number of lads go in company, perhaps as many as twelve together, taking with them an empty sack. They go to a neighbour's house, where they get a sheep-skin, and, a leader having been chosen, he carries the sack on his back, and spreads the sheep-skin over his shoulders. The whole company then form themselves into a line, each holding by the coat tail of the one before him, and in this manner they march from house to house, singing. When they enter a house, *the fire being in the middle of the floor*, they march round the fire three times, singing :

Trans. :

> I went about the fire
> Till that caught around my hide.
> I got a tumble in the hole,
> Such as was a heavy tumble.
> I would rather the size of my fist in butter
> Than the size of my head in gold.

While thus marching, the one who is next to the leader, . . . has a stick with which he keeps striking the dry sheep-skin. This done, they receive a gift from the people of the house, . . . a bannock, a piece of cheese or butter, always something to be eaten, which is put into the sack and placed again on the leader's shoulders, and away they go to the next house, where the same performance is gone through and something more is contributed to the sack. . . . Finally they go to a house where they wind up by holding festival, in which others join them ; all that was gathered is turned out and eaten and the company indulge in the usual sports. [Mlan MS.]   Outer Hdes.

Other *ranns* from the Hebrides have the lines about a *Cailleach* (old woman) :

1. *Cailleach's a' chuil, is bior 'n a da shuil,*
   Cailleach eile an cois an teine,
   Is bior 'n a goile, 's i breabadh.
   Eirich suas a bhean an tighe, agus na gearr t' órdag. . . .

2. *Cailleach 's a' chuil, is bior 'n a da shuil,*
   Is i garachdaich. [sic.]

Trans. :

1. An old woman in the corner, and a spit in her two eyes,
   Another old woman beside the fire,
   With a spit in her stomach, and she kicking.
   Rise up, O woman of the house, and don't cut thy
        thumb! . . .

2. An old woman in the corner, and a spit in her two eyes,
   And she clattering, (or murmuring) . . .

Neil A. R. Mackay of Lewis, who is an accomplished speaker of Gaelic and thoroughly acquainted with the customs and speech of the W. Isles, interprets these lines as riddles, ' The old woman beside the fire, kicking,' is the pot of porridge, the

stick for stirring in the middle of it, and the porridge boiling
and bubbling. The old woman in the corner refers to some
other kitchen process which he was unable to explain. Gaelic
rhymes are full of riddles of this kind which are not always
easy to guess, for much has been forgotten. He writes : ' Lewis
is curiously devoid of old customs and traditions. . . . There
is much in the lives and ordinary doings of the people which
is of remote origin, but it is so closely blended with that which
is new, that it is only under extraordinary circumstances that
they can be separated.'

These rhymes have been interpreted as alluding to sacri-
ficial rites of pagan times and it is pleasing to have enlighten-
ment which removes the misinterpretation.

Other rhymes mention ' an old woman in the corner ; an
old woman in the *cill*, churchyard or grave ; another beside
the fire, a spit in her stomach '. These are often incorrect and
disguise the meaning. If *cill* is in the older rhymes, ' the old
woman underground ', or ' in the grave ' may be a potato?
[Ed.]

N. A. R. Mackay writes : ' I think myself and all to whom
I have mentioned the matter . . . agree, that the reference to
the *cailleachs* in these verses is merely an example of the exceedingly common Gaelic habit of describing everyday objects
in figurative language. This sort of thing is best seen in the
Gaelic riddle, when some common objects are given a fanciful
description and the listener has to penetrate the disguise, e.g.
" *bodach beag is crios air, agus bidh na cearcan 'ga ruith.*"—A little
man with a belt and the hens chase him. That is the form of
the riddle and the answer is " A sheaf of corn ". This is a
very simple example—others are more elaborate and far-
fetched. A *cailleach* or a *bodach* is frequently brought into
them.'

Though no reading of the lines :

>   An old woman in the corner, a spit in her two eyes,
>   And she clattering . . .

was forthcoming, descriptions of querns used in the Highlands,
of which some had two and even three holes in the upper
stone, led to a guess that the lines quoted might refer to that
useful instrument. ' The quern or handmill was worked by
two women.' [*Supers. of Hghlds.*, p. 35] The two sticks worked
by the two women in turning the upper stone would be the
two spits, and the clattering or grumbling the noise made by
the grinding. This turns out to be the answer to the riddle.

It is noted in A. Nicolson's *Gaelic Riddles and Enigmas* (1938), pp. 44 f.   The third riddle of the Old Woman in the *cill* is still unsolved and seems to have been forgotten in the north.   We may remark that these Cailleachs appear in a triad, grouped in three like the Mother Goddesses known throughout Europe.[1]

J. Gregorson Campbell says : 'To keep away the fairies who were supposed to steal querns . . . they were turned *deiseal* (clockwise).   In the Hebrides the quern was rubbed every Saturday evening with a wisp of straw, " for payment " of its benevolent labours.'   [Ed.]

Here are two verses of a *Rann na Coluinn* which a native of Islay says he has often heard lads singing at Hogmanay :

> *Thainig mise 'nar ceann*
> *Mar mhaide cham a bhiodh ann coille ;*
> *Ma's direach mi, cumaibh ann mi,*
> *Ach ma's cam, cuiribh uaibh mi.*

[1] Oats were ground fresh for the Hogmanay bannock, hence the quern in Hogmanay riddles.   The third riddle should also refer to an article of food. The upper stone of the quern was, of course, commonly turned by one person only and the second spit would be the central pivot which went through the upper stone to the lower.

The illustration is after Pennant, 1772.

Thainig mi gun cuireadh,
Suidhidh mi gun iarraidh,
Ma phaigheas mi mar h-aon de chach,
Air leam gur cearr mo chuir a mach.

Trans. : I have come among you
As a crooked stick that would be in a wood.
If I am straight, keep me,
But if crooked, put me out.

I have come without invitation.
I shall sit—without a bidding.
If I pay like any other,
To my mind 'twere wrong to put me out.

[Mlan MS.]   Islay, Ar.

Commentary by Neil A. R. Mackay, M.A. of Lewis : ' The "*maide càm*" is the bent bough which suddenly strikes the passer by who does not notice it,—the meaning here is literal, but in the next two lines : " *Ma's direach mi*," etc., the words are used figuratively, " *cam* " being used to indicate a cunning, deceiving disposition, while " *direach* " indicates an honest, straightforward nature.   So that the sense of the whole verse appears to be :

" I have come on top of you like a bent bough in the woods: if I am crooked (i.e. a trickster), put me away, but if I am ' straight ' keep me.   I came without invitation and I shall sit without being asked.   If I pay my share like one of the others, I think it would be wrong to put me out."

' The words   " *Thainig mi gun chuireadh,*
                 Suididh mi gun iarraidh "

are an echo of a proverb : " *Fear a thig gun chuireadh, suididh e gun iarraidh.*" (He who comes without being invited will sit without being asked.) . . .   The *rann* contains much that is interesting and obscure.   One would like to know how it was recited in olden times.   I remember going into a house where there was a very old lady, and she made us walk " *deiseil* " round the fire (which was in the middle of the floor) while reciting the *rann*. She said that it was customary to do that when she was young.

' The following lines form the first half of the *Rann* used in the Breascleit district of Lewis about twelve years ago (1920) :

(*Hiribhi Horibhi, 'nochd oidche nam Banag*) This line not
        always used.
Thainig mi gu modhal, eòlach,

'N am tòiseachadh na Calluinn,
Cha 'n 'eil nàir 'orm 'ga inns'
Bha i ann o linn mo sheanair.
Gabhaidh mi an t-aran gun an t-im,
'S gabhaidh mi an t-im gun an t-aran.
'S gabhaidh mi a' chàis leatna féin,
Is c'uige 'réisd a bhithinn falamh?
Cha n'eil nì 'sam bith 'n ad'fhàrdaich
Nach gabh mi pàirt deth 'na m'ealach :
Ach aon rud tha mi 'g àicheadh,
'S e suileagan a bhuntata charraich.
Tha iad cudthromach r'an giulan,
'S cha n'eil iad luachmhor no fallan
'S 'cumaidh iad seachd tràthan gun éirigh
Am balach a's treun'a th'anns a' bhaile.

Some lines here forgotten.   Concluding lines :

Gearr cul càis, 's na gearr barr d'ordaig,
Thoir a bhiadh a dh'fhear an tigh'
'S thoir a' bhanag [1] dhomh-sa.

Trans. :

I have come, friendly and civil,
At the time (beginning) of the Calluinn.
I am not ashamed to speak of it,
It has existed since my grandfather's days.
I will take bread without butter,
And butter without bread :
I will take cheese by itself.
And why then should I go empty-handed?
There is not a thing in your house
Of which I wont take a part in my hand:
But one thing I do refuse,
And that is—small lumpy potatoes.
They are heavy to carry,
And they are not valuable or healthy,
And they would prevent for days from getting up
The sturdiest youth in the village.

Last lines :

Cut the back of the cheese and do not cut (the top of)
    your thumb,
Give the goodman his food,
And give me the share for Calluinn.

[1] Banag, literally = bannock.

' (This is) as much as I can remember of the form I used myself on the only occasion on which I took part in the house-to-house visitation. The second part of the *Rann* (or *Rabhd* as we called it) was, as far as I can remember, different in structure and ideas from the piece I have quoted. It appeared to be an older passage and it began with the stating of the different names which could be used for Hogmanay night. As I failed to remember it myself I tried to get in touch with those who might still have it, but I failed to find anyone who could give it. . . . In my native village the night of Calluinn is mostly referred to as " *Oidhche nam Banag* "—*banag* seems to be from Bannock—but I have some doubts as to its meaning.

' A verse of thanks was always recited after the boys had received the share of food or money given. In the event of the householder being stingy and refusing to give anything, there was a special verse used invoking anything but a blessing upon his head. I heard it used only once. [Curses expressed are quoted in other references. Ed.] In the olden days (up till 80 years ago) the night of Calluinn marked the end of a period of festivity extending over a fortnight.[1] My grandmother has often given me an account of the revels.'

Companies of young lads, about a dozen together, go about on *Oidhche na Coluinne* seeking their Hogmanay. Housewives prepare extra bannocks to have ready for them. One lad carries a poc into which all gatherings are deposited. On coming to a house they sing a *duan* (song) at the door, if welcomed they go in to receive their gifts, and so on from house to house. Here are some of the *duan* they sing :

> Chaid mi timchioll an tigh mór,
> Bhuail ordag mo choise
> Ann an aodann nan clach ;
> Fhuair mi leigeil anns a'pholl,
> Gu'm b'e sud an leigeil trom!
> Chaidh coin a'bhaile air mo dhruim,
> Thug iad bideag as mo shdil.
> B'fhearr leam uiread mo dhuirn a dh'im
> Na uiread mo chinn a dh'óir.

Trans. :

> I went round about the big house,
> The big toe of my foot struck [2]
> On the face of the stones.

[1] Cf. The Yules.

[2] Note.—This line occurs in the long extract above, ll. 59, 60, and below in a hide-beating song.

I got a tumble in the mud ;
Sure that was the serious tumble!
The dogs of the homestead were at my back,
They took a nip out of my heel.
I would rather the size of my fist of butter
Than the size of my head of gold.

Then they all shout : *Mise's dorus fosgailte!*, ' I am here and
the open door!,' and go into the house to receive the Colluinn.
[Mlan MS.]   Barra, Hdes.

Also from Barra, trans. by Dr Carmichael :
I am now come to your country,
To renew to you the Hogmanay,
I need not tell you of it,
It was in the time of our forefathers.

I ascend by the door lintel,
I descend by the doorstep,
I will sing my song becomingly,
Mannerly, slowly, mindfully.

The Hogmanay skin in my pocket,
Great will be the smoke from it presently.

     *   *   *   *   *

The house-man will get it in his hand,
He will place its nose in the fire,
He will go sunwards round the babes,
And for seven verities round the housewife.

The two last verses are an appeal to the housewife. (*Car. Gad.*,
Vol. I, p. 151.]   Hghlds. and Isles.

Verse II, l. 1,   In the version of the Mlan MS. this line runs,

I go up on the wall.

Dr Carmichael explains that the walls of West Highland
cottages were from five to eight feet thick, the thatched roof
springing from the inner edge ; to repair the thatch men went
up on the wall by stones projecting from near the door and so
went round the house. The Hogmanay lads went round the
house sunwise on this wall. [Ed.]

V c. *Burning of the piece of skin.* e. *Visit to the byre.* i. *Caisean
Uchd.* l. *Begging for gifts of* m. *food and drink.* (After striking
the hide with their *camain* . . . and calling and shouting ' The
Calluinn is here ' . . .) the young men would go round the

house several times until the people within . . . would open
the door and invite them all in. On entering the house, one
of them who was the bearer of the *caisein uchd* (the piece of skin
covering the breast-bone of a sheep or cow, generally the
former with its short curly wool, which was kept as carefully
as the hide to be brought forth on *Oidhche Challuinn*) fixed to
a stick, would immediately make for the fireplace, and put the
skin in the fire for a minute or two, when he would then go
round giving every one in the house a smell of it. After which
it would be sometimes taken into the byre burning, and all
the cattle would be regaled with its fragrance. This was
believed to be a sort of talismanic against any evil for the coming year. Then the master of the house would bring out his
big decanter of real Highland whisky and treat all the party
to a glassful. When they had all got their dram their leader
gave the order to march, and here the best of the sport came
in, for the hide-bearer would make a keen effort to be out of the
house before any of the others, and could thus gain time in being
well on to the next house before any of them could overtake
him to din him with their *camain* or clubs on the hide. Sometimes the rest of them, divining his intentions, would forestall
him by being out at his heels, or even before him, and then
there was no more peace for him until they visited all the
houses, returning home in the early hours of New Year's
morning. [Mlan MS.]   Islay, Ar.

A quite recent account from South Uist. ' The observers of
New Year's Eve . . . are approaching me with the loud shouting proper to the season, and according to old custom they
will go sunwise round the house, bringing the *Callaig* or
Calluinn gift with them. At the door the *Callaig* rhyme is to
be said on entering : " This is to bless the dwelling ; may God
bless this house and its inmates all! " Going sunwise round the
fire, the Hogmanay breast-strip (*Caisean Callaig*) is to be set on
fire or lighted, that is the breast-skin of a wedder ; each person
in the house is to seize hold of it as it burns, making the sign of
the cross if he be a Catholic, in the name of the Father, . . .
the Son, . . . and the Holy Spirit. That burning strip is to
be put thrice sunwise about their heads. If the burning skin
be extinguished in the process, it is a bad omen for the New
Year's happiness. Then they will get their Hogmanay
portion, each one according to his opportunity ; with good will
they then disperse with the words : " the blessing of God and
of the Hogmanay be with you all ; if well to-night, seven
times better may ye be a year to-night." ' [Trans. from a

letter quoted by George Henderson in *Surv*[s]. *of Belief among the Celts* (1911), pp. 263 f.]

The *caisean-uchd* is the strip of skin from the breast of a sheep killed at Christmas, New Year, and other sacred festivals. The strip is oval, and no knife must be used in removing it from the flesh. It is carried by the carollers when they visit the houses of the townland, and when lit by the head of the house it is given to each person in turn to smell, going sunwise. Should it go out, it is a bad omen for the person in whose hand it becomes extinguished. The inhaling of the fumes of the burning skin and wool is a talisman to safeguard the family from fairies, witches, demons and other uncanny creatures during the year. Two such strips were placed face to face to form a bag ; probably this was the *uilim*, the sacred bag for alms. [*Car. Gad.* II, p. 239.]

Dr Alex. Carmichael's description is authoritative for the Highlands ; other accounts vary in small details as quoted from different sources.

On the evening before New Year's Day it is usual for the cowherd and the young people to meet together, and one of them is covered with a hide. The rest of the company are provided with staves, to the ends of which bits of raw hide are tied. The person covered with the hide runs three times round the dwelling-house *deiseil*, the rest pursue, beating the hide with their staves and crying, ' *A' cholluinn so, a'cholluinn so, 'cholluinn a'bhuilg bhuidhe bhoicinn ; buail an craicionn!* ' [The Calluinn is here . . . the Calluinn of the yellow bag of hide. Strike the skin!] They then come to the door of each dwelling-house, and one of them repeats some verses composed for the purpose. When admission is granted one of them pronounces within the threshold the *beannachadh-urlair* [the benediction of the house-floor]—verses by which he pretends to draw down a blessing upon the whole family. . . . Then each burns in the fire a little of the bit of hide which is tied to the end of the staff. It is applied to the nose of each person and domestic animal that belongs to the house. This, they imagine, will tend to secure them from diseases and other misfortune throughout the ensuing year. . . . It is the principal remnant of superstition among the inhabitants of St Kilda. . . . It is most common on the West coast. [Alex. Allardyce, *Scot. and Scotsmen in the 18th Century*, II, pp. 438 f.]   St Kilda, Hdes.

On New Year's Eve, they surrounded each other's houses, carrying dried cow-hides, and beating them with sticks, thrashing the walls with clubs, all the time crying, shouting, and repeating rhymes. This is supposed to operate as a charm against fairies, demons, and spirits of every order. They provide themselves with the flap, or hanging part of the hide on the cow's neck, which they called *caisean-uchd*, and which they singed in the fire and presented to the inmates of the family, one after another, to smell, as a charm against all injuries from fairies and spirits. Rhymes quoted wish good luck to family, house and its contents, the stock and every friend. [Rev. Alex. Macgregor, *Highland Superstitions, etc.*, pp. 42-3 (1901). First appeared in Vol. II of the *Celtic Magazine*, and afterwards as an appendix to the later editions of *The Prophecies of the Brahan Seer.*]   Hghlds.

A native of Uist, referring to the old custom, which she says is still kept up to a considerable extent by the lads of the place, gives the following description of how it is done :

The breast part of a dried sheepskin is selected, and after removing the wool from it, the skin is rolled up into the form of a large cigar. Armed with this, to which they gave the name of *Càise a'Choluinn*, and a sack in which to carry whatever they might get from such friends as they might call upon, the company set out, one carrying the sack, and another the *Càise a'Choluinn*, but these might change hands two or three times in course of the expedition. When they came near enough to a house to be heard by its inmates, they started to sing a duan for the occasion (there are several duans in use). By the time the duan is finished the door is usually opened for them, and they are invited to come in. They may go through certain performances in the house, such as rehearsing the business on which they have come, which is usually done in a kind of singing style, and in words more or less extemporised, to suit the circumstances. If they get anything it goes into the sack, no matter of what description, bread, cheese, butter, tea, fish or flesh, all goes promiscuously together. And then . . . they light the *Càise a'Choluinn* and swirling it three times round the head of the mistress of the house, and perhaps the master's head also, performing the ceremony slowly, and observing the course of the sun's motion, the whole company say—*Ma's math an nochd sibh, gu ma is fearr bliadhna bho 'n nochd sibh* (If you are well to-night, may you be still better a year from to-night). They then retire with a blessing on the house, and the benediction of the season is pronounced, *Beannachd na Coluinn leibh.*

The reciter says these forms of expression may be varied or added to, according to the tastes of the party, or their appreciation of the reception they have got.

Having gone over many houses in this way, they then retire
to a house—usually such as they can have the largest measure
of freedom for carrying out the night's fun, and the feast
proceeds. [Mlan MS.]   Uist, Hdes.

V l. m. *Begging with hide-beating, ' Hogmanay of the Sack.'*
Mrs Maclean informed us of an old game. . . . At New Year's
eve, in the hall or castle of the laird, . . . one man dresses
himself in a cow's hide, upon which other men beat with
sticks. He runs with all this noise round the house, which all
the company quits in a counterfeited fright : the door is then
shut. . . . They are sure soon to recover from their terror
enough to solicit for re-admission, which, for the honour of
poetry, is not to be obtained but by repeating a verse. [S.
Johnson, *A Journey to the W. Islands of Scot.* (1773), ed. 1817,
pp. 205 f.]   Hdes.

The *Gillean Callaig* carollers or Hogmanay lads perambulate
the townland at night. One man is enveloped in the hard
hide of a bull with the horns and hoofs still attached. When
the men come to a house they ascend the wall and run round
sunwise, the man in the hide shaking the horns and hoofs, and
the other men striking the hard hide with sticks. Having
descended and recited their runes at the door, the Hogmanay
men are admitted and treated to the best in the house.

The lines recited :

> Hogmanay of the sack,
> Hogmanay of the sack,
>   Strike the hide,
>   Strike the hide.
> Hogmanay of the sack,
> Hogmanay of the sack,
>   Beat the skin. (repeated several times)

[*Car. Gad.* I, p. 149.]   Hghlds. and Is.

In some places the guisers go about in small groups of twos,
threes, or fours, in other places in large groups of tens, fifteens,
or twenties. The leader trails a dried bull-hide which his
followers strike with clubs, singing and shouting, and making
all the din possible. They call at every door where anything
good is likely to be got, singing chants and announcing that
they—the good guisers—have come, that they have never
been here before, and that they are come now, not to beg nor
to borrow, not to buy nor to steal, but to bless the house, the
houseman, the housewoman, the household and the farm and
plenishing.

When the carollers arrive at a house they generally mount
on the walls and go round on them singing, shouting, stamp-
ing, and striking the bull-hide. After this they get meat, meal,
butter, cheese, crowdie, eggs, and any other good thing there
may be in the house. They place and carry these in a tanned
leather bag of lamb-skin, called ' *uilim* ', and retire to some
roomy dwelling, barn, or other building previously arranged.
There they hold a feast and a dance, to which they invite their
girl friends. [*Car. Gad.* II, pp. 268 f.]   Hdes and Hghlds.

It used to be the custom for one of the merrymakers to have
a dried hide on his back, and for the rest to smite the hide with
their shinties, saying :

> Since there is a drought in the country
> We will hope for a dram.
> A little thing of the gift of summer [butter],
> I expect along with the bread.
> If you have got it at all [lit. ' of the world '],
> If you may give, do not keep delay upon us ;
> I am in the open door, so let me in.

If they considered themselves well treated, they would pronounce the following blessing upon leaving the house :

> If it be well to-night,
> May it be sevenfold better a year from to-night ;
> May God bless the house and all in it,
> Between man and wife and children,
> Much food and plenty of clothing,
> And the wealth of men be in it.

[A. Goodrich-Freer, *F.-L.* 1902, XIII, p. 46.]   Hdes.

The same custom is reported in the Mlan MS. from Oban,
and from Lochgilphead, Ar.

From Lewis and Harris the rite is described with a circuiting
three times of the household fire while the hides were beaten,
and the whole company sang the *rann na colluinne*. The boys
or young men recited verses explaining why certain gifts were
unwelcome, as :

> Aon rud tha mi ag aicheadh ;
> Suileagan bho a' bhuntat charrach.   (the eyes of scabby
> Cha n' eil iad eutrom ri giulan,   potatoes)
> Agus cha 'n eil iad sunndach no fallain.

One thing I decline, Small and scabby potatoes.
They are not light to carry, Nor are they sound or healthy.
[*Ibid.*]

Or, *Trans.* :

> Out with the bannocks, etc.
> Man of the house, come down.
> Do not cut your finger, do not cut your thumb.
> Keep your own share and give the boys theirs,
> Or you will be driven out of the place,
> Mention of you will cease in the town.

[Mlan Ms.] Harris, Lewis, Hdes.

The hide of the mart or winter cow was wrapped round the head of one of the men, and he made off, followed by the rest, belabouring the hide . . . with switches. The disorderly procession went three times *deiseal*, according to the course of the sun (i.e. keeping the house on the right hand) round each house in the village, striking the walls and shouting on coming to a door :

Trans. :

> The *Calluinn* of the yellow bag of hide,
> Strike the skin (upon the wall)
> An old wife in the graveyard,
> An old wife in the corner
> Another old wife beside the fire,
> A pointed stick in her two eyes,
> A pointed stick in her stomach,
> Let me in, open this.[1]

Before this request was complied with, each of the revellers had to repeat a rhyme, called *Rann Calluinn* (i.e. a Christmas rhyme), though, as might be expected, when the door opened for one, several pushed their way in, till it was ultimately left open for all. On entering each of the party was offered refreshments, oatmeal, bread, cheese, flesh, and a dram of whisky. Their leader gave to the goodman of the house . . . the *Caisein uchd*, the breast-stripe of a sheep wrapped round the point of a shinty stick. This was then singed in the fire, put three times with the right hand turn (*deiseal*) round the family,

---

[1] *A challuinn a bhuilg bhuidhe bhoicuin*
Buail an craiconn (air an tota),
Cailleach 's a' chill,
Cailleach 's a' chùil,
Cailleach eile 'n cùl an teine
Bior 'n 'a da shùil
Bior 'n 'a goile
A challuinn so;
Leig astigh mi.

and held to the noses of all. Not a drop of drink was given till this ceremony was performed. The *Caisein uchd* was also made of the breast-stripe or tail of a deer, sheep, or goat, and as many as chose had one with them. [*Wcrft. & Sec. Sight*, pp. 231 f.] Hghlds.

The *rann* in this quotation is incorrect but is allowed to stand as illustrating the common misunderstanding of the meaning. The line *Cailleach 's a' chuil* should be followed immediately by the line *Bior 'n a da shuil*, and *Cailleach eile an cul an teine* should be *Cailleach eile an cois an teine*, followed by *Bior 'n a goile*. The interpretation of these lines as riddles, given above, makes the correction imperative. [Ed.]

V n. On ' Hagmanay Nicht ', the eve of the New Year, the custom throughout the country was for bands of young men to go, in guiser's dress, to the houses of the gentry and farmers, where their advent was looked for ; and, indeed, it was a point of honour to have no door locked on that night. . . . The visitors . . . claimed the right to kiss every unmarried woman in the room ; at any rate where the scene was the kitchen, and there was practically no difference in rank between hosts and guests.—It was a time of privilege and jollity. . . . [D. MacRitchie, *Scottish Review*, Dec. 21, 1905.]

The Lord of Misrule. On Hogmanay . . . this functionary, (the Lord of Misrule or Abbot of Unreason), arrayed in a livery of green, and attended by a suite, perambulated the district, performing his escapades at the cost of private householders. In 1496 the Treasurer, on a royal precept, made to Gilbert Reade, at Stirling, a payment of ten pounds ' for spilling of his house by the Abbot of Unreason '. [Rogers, *Social Life in Scot.* II, 350.] See also under **XIV. Prohibitions.**

Parts of fishing-boats and carts hidden. The last night of the year was, and is still in some districts, regarded as a time of licence for playing practical jokes, and not a few fancy that the law is to a great degree in abeyance during that night, so that if a practical joke should be of a too flagrant cast it will be allowed to pass unpunished. Young men in the fishing villages indulge in taking away and hiding parts of the fishing boats, so that when the men of the crew go to their boat in the morning to proceed to the fishing, they find something gone that prevents them. One opening the door in the morning may find a boat placed in front of it. A farmer going out in the morning may find his ploughs or harrows all piled up in front of his house, or one or two of his carts may be missing. Some-

times one evil disposed will go the length of destroying something. [Rev. W. Gregor.]   N.E. Scot.

Mortar-stone placed at a young girl's door, to show approval.
Scarcely had the chimes of the Old Year died away when the
village youths were busy at the time-honoured custom of
removing the mortar-stone to the door of the young lady
whom they wished to see joined in wedlock during the year.
[Paragraph taken by Mr David Rorie from the *Aberdeen Free
Press* for Jan. 2nd, 1909. *F.-L.* XX, p. 482.]   Fordyce, Bf.

The 'Mortar Stane' of Fordyce, Banffshire, on Hogmanay
night is carried by the youths of the village and placed at the
door of that young woman whom they wish to see married in
the course of the year. In *The Scotsman* of March 29th, 1920,
is a letter by 'R. F.' giving a fuller description of the stone
and the ceremony : Every year at Yuletide 'the young men
gather and deposit the old freestone at the door of one of the
maidens of the village, selected by vote, and there it sits till
next Yuletide. Its virtue is to bring marriage to the maiden
during the year ; or, put another way, that she is to have
preference over all the other maidens in the village. The
ceremony is old, beyond the memory of the oldest inhabitants,
and is still regularly observed. As a scholar I have partici-
pated in the scenes, which I must confess were very rough and
noisy—the stone being conveyed in a farm cart, conscripted
for the occasion, and pulled by scores of young men. Generally
a fiddler was placed on the cart, and made music for the crowd.
Fiddler, fiddle, and the stone were simultaneously dumped
down at the door of the selected house. After the ceremony
was complete, the cart was taken to the top of a steep brae
and sent down into the burn, where the unhappy owner could
find it next day. I am informed that now the ceremony is
carried through, at the sight of the village constable, with more
decorum.

The original stone was thrown into a deep quarryhole some
years ago by some youths, and a substitute had to be found ;
but the ladies insisted on the quarry being drained, and the
original 'Mortar Stane' recovered. . . . [*F.-L.* XXXIV, p.
162.] (*Yuletide* covers *Hogmanay*.)

V o. *Observances of animals, etc. Bees.* It was a belief that
bees in their hives emitted a buzzing sound exactly at midnight
on the last day of the year ; that was the hour of the Saviour's
birth. [Greg. p. 147.] Cf. *Christmas Eve.*   N.E. Scot.

Cocks and Cows. On the last night of the year at 12 o'clock,

the cock is believed to crow, and the cows are said to groan.
[J. E. C. from Isabel A. Calder.]   N.E. Scot.

Cattle groaning. The superstition of the cattle groaning at
midnight was . . . firmly believed in by many of the old
people. [A. C. R., *Sc. N. & Q.* 3rd Series, III, p. 201 (1925).]

Beasts on their knees. [Unquestionably transferred from Christmas
Eve. Ed.] An old woman who lives in Appin . . . very
tenacious of old customs and the old style of time counting,
maintains that every beast bends its knees at midnight on New
Year's Eve, Old Style. [Mlan MS.]

VI. Fairies, Witches, etc. *Fairies' Song at Hogmanay.* There
lived at Balnahard a hump-backed man. He left his house on
Hogmanay, intending to reach Scalasaig, where he meant to
buy all that was needed to hold the New Year festivities in
royal state. When passing a green knoll alone, above Killoran
Bay, he suddenly came upon the fairies dancing on a hill-side.
The tune to which they were keeping time consisted of a
rhyme on the days of the week. He looked upon them for a
time, and, having a good ear for music, he felt there was
something wrong with the reel—it was out of time and tune.
It seems that the fairies forgot the Gaelic name for Wednesday,
Di-ceudaoin, and so the rhyme was lacking and the measure
halting. Observing this, Donald chimed in with ' *Di-
ceudaoin!* ' and the fairies at once took up the time with renewed
vigour. . . . The dancing having ended, the hillock opened
and the fairies disappeared, taking Donald along with them.
There they detained him for a year and a day, and wishing to
reward him . . . they resolved to remove his hump and sent
him . . . back to the world again a straight-backed man. The
tale tells how another hump-backed man tried the same plan,
but shouted ' *Diardaoin* ', Thursday, which put the fairies all
wrong ; they take him away and put Donald's hump on his
back in addition to his own. [Henry White, *The Old Highlands*,
paper read before the Gaelic Soc. of Glasgow, 1895.] The
tale is told from other districts. [Ed.]

                                        Isle of Colonsay, Hdes.

IX. Singing with Guizing. The doings of the *guisers* or *guizards*
(that is masquers or *mummers*) form a conspicuous feature in the
New-Year proceedings throughout Scotland. The favourite
night for this exhibition is Hogmanay, though the evenings of
Christmas, New-Year's Day, and Handsel Monday, enjoy likewise
a privilege in this respect. Such of the boys as can lay any
claim to the possession of a voice have, for weeks before, been

poring over the collection of ' excellent new songs ', which lies like a bunch of rags in the window-sill ; and being now able to screech up ' Barbara Allan ', or the ' Wee cot-house and the wee kail-yairdie ', they determine upon enacting the part of guisers. For this purpose they don old shirts belonging to their fathers, and mount mitre-shaped casques of brown paper, possibly borrowed from the Abbot of Unreason ; attached to this is a sheet of the same paper, which, falling down in front, covers and conceals the whole face, except where holes are made to let through the point of the nose, and afford sight to the eyes and breath to the mouth. Each vocal guiser is, like a knight of old, attended by a sort of humble squire, who assumes the habiliments of a girl, with an old-woman's cap and a broomstick, and is styled ' Bessie '. Bessie is equal in no respect, except that she shares fairly in the proceeds of the enterprise. She goes before her principal, opens all the doors at which he pleases to exert his singing powers ; and busies herself, during the time of the song, in sweeping the floor with her broomstick, or in playing any other antics that she thinks may amuse the indwellers. The common reward of this entertainment is a halfpenny, but many churlish persons fall upon the unfortunate guisers, and beat them out of the house. Let such persons, however, keep a good watch upon their cabbage-gardens next Hallowe'en!

The more important doings of the guisers are of a theatrical character. There is one rude and grotesque drama which they are accustomed to perform on each of the four above-mentioned nights ; and which, in various fragments or versions, exists in every part of Lowland Scotland. The performers, who are never less than three, but sometimes as many as six, having dressed themselves, proceed in a band from house to house, generally contenting themselves with the kitchen for an arena ; whither, in mansions presided over by the spirit of good-humour, the whole family will resort to witness the spectacle. Sir Walter Scott . . . invariably had a set of guisers to perform this play before his family both at Ashestiel and Abbotsford. The drama in question bears a close resemblance, with sundry modifications, to that performed by the mummers in various parts of England. [Chambers, *Book of Days*, Vol. II, pp. 788-9.]

The reciter says that in his native parish of Rogart, Sutherlandshire, young lads went out in companies on New Year's Eve to ask their ' Hogmanay '. They dressed themselves in straw hats from the rim of which long ribbons of paper hung

down to their shoulders all round. Over their ordinary clothes
they put a shirt which was allowed to hang loosely upon them.
They carried a bag which was usually slung over the back of
the neck and allowed to hang down on the chest. They also
armed themselves with good sticks which were often enough
required to protect themselves from the attacks of dogs. Upon
coming to a house they marched round about it seven times
all joining in singing a rhyme beginning with these lines :

> Rise up ye wives and shake your feathers, etc.

When they had gone round about the house the statutory
number of times they knocked at the door and whatever was
received went into the bag and off they were to another house.
. . . They usually succeeded in filling up their bags pretty
well. When they had finished their rounds the spoil was
divided among themselves. [Mlan MS.] Sld.

Similar dress, with faces blackened. [Mlan MS.]
Skye, Iness.

Processions of boys go about on New Year's Eve shouting
curious rhymes, some of which are full of the names which
pervade the Ossianic poems ; curious ceremonies are performed, and the singers are rewarded with food. [J. F.
Campbell, *West Highland Tales*, new ed. (1892), III, p. 28.]
W. Hghlds.

In many parts of Scotland, particularly in the Border counties, the custom of ' guising ' on Hogmanay . . . has died hard.
The play beloved of the ' guizards ' was the ancient doggerel
tragedy ' Golaschin ', and the adventurous youths of the towns
found fine opportunity for ranting declamation, grotesquely
attired as Wallace, Wight, Golaschin, and Old Beelzebub.
At the end of the play they were wont to . . . get to the point,
by remarking, ' Oor feet are cauld,' etc. [From a newspaper
cutting.]

The guisers are dressed in very long white linen shirts and
tall white paper hats with flaps in front covering the face,
holes being made for the eyes. These guisers represent
crowned kings and queens, popes, cardinals, mitred arch-
bishops and bishops, cowled abbots and monks, priests and
veiled nuns. [*Car. Gad.* II, p. 288.] Hghlds. and W. Is.

Hogmanay, or Singin' E'en, is, however, the festival which
is most popular in Newburgh among the young. On this, the
last evening of the year, the youth of both sexes, as in other
parts of Scotland, go about disguised from house to house in
bands, singing songs in every house they visit. . . . Many

grave consultations are held by the young beforehand as to the special disguises to be worn on Singin' E'en. The young guisers, a generation back, were rewarded with a ferl (*feorth-dael*—Anglo-Saxon, fourth part) of oaten cake, many families specially baking them for the purpose. The dole is now mostly bestowed in money, which is paid to the purser of the band, and is divided equally at the conclusion of the evening's peregrinations. The songs sung are sometimes of a kind that are popular at the time, but old and enduring favourites, and old rude rhymes, which have been handed down orally for many generations, never fail to be also sung on that night. [*County F.-L.* VII, pp. 142-143.] Newburgh, Ffe.

IX. Dancing and Singing. On *Calluinn* night every one had to say a *Calluinn* rhyme. After the songs, dancing—a woman sang ' *port á beul* ', a tune from the mouth, the tune being *Cailleach an Dùdain*, the old wife of the mill-dust, and then others. [Norman Macleod, D.D., *Reminiscences of a Highland Parish* (1867), p. 354.] Hghlds.

Guising, dramatic performance. The Drama of Golishan, 'said, sung, and acted all over Scotland from Cheviot to Cape Wrath ', at Hogmanay, is described, with full accounts of the *dramatis personae*, in *Folk-Lore*, XVI, pp. 212-216 ; *County Folk-Lore*, VII (Fife), pp. 144-146 ; R. Chambers, *Pop. Rhymes*, ed. 1842, pp. 68, 69 ; ed. 1847, pp. 294 f. ; Hone, *Every Day Book*, II, and elsewhere.

XI. Cock-fighting. The schoolboys in those days were all expected to bring a game cock to the annual ' main ' or fight usually held on the earthen floor of the village school at Hogmanay. [A. Gordon, *Scotch Life in Carglen*, quoted in *E.D.D.* (1891), p. 292.]

XIV. Prohibitions. *Powers of Kirk-Sessions in Prohibitions.* Kirk-Sessions possessed, especially during the seventeenth century, extensive powers, and were something more than a mere ecclesiastical court. . . . They took charge of the Doctrines, and of the Morals of the people, and existing in every parish as a necessary part of its organisation, nothing irregular escaped their notice. [*Northern N. & Q.*, Vols. I and II, p. 15 (1888).]

Clackmannan, January 6, 1713. The which day Session mett & after prayer the Minr informed the Session that Francis Donaldson weaver in green & Wm Stirling son to Isobell Hadden in toun were going about disguised on new years Eve, caused cite them, they were this day called, Compeared

Francis Donaldson and confessed that he had on him womens cloaths night foresaid & that his face was blacked ; Compeared Wm Stirling confessed his going disguised with his face blacked & straw ropes on his legs the foresaid night, but that he went only into one house. They both confessed their sin & promised by Gods grace never to fall into the like again. The Session thought fit to dismiss them, having held forth to them the sinfulness & abominableness of their deed with certification. [Kirk Session Records, *Northern N. & Q.*, Vol. III (1889), p. 3.]   Clkmn.

PLATE III

New Year's Eve at the Tron Church, Edinburgh.
By the courtesy of Messrs. Cassell.

JANUARY
MONTH

I. Names. January. First Month of the Year. *An ceud Mhìos na Bliadhna.* Little Spring of Whelks, Gael. *Earrach beag nam Faochag* ; the period from Nollaig, Christmas, to St Bride's day. That species of shell-fish is then at its best and the soup made from it was deemed as good as flesh. [*Wcrft. and Sec. Sight*, p. 247.] Hghlds and W. Islands.

The name *Faoilleach* or *Faoilteach* is given to January in the Island of Lewis, Hebrides, but corresponds more nearly to February in S. Scotland. See *Seasons.*

II. Sayings, Rhymes.

I ope' the gate to let the New Year in,
The weather's now too cold to Card or Spin.
Yet some men at the Cards so long dare play,
Till they have carded all they have away.

[' Prognostication ' by G. F., *Philol. and Philom.*, Edinburgh (1685).]

A January haddock
A February haddock
And a Mairch pint o' ale
A' in their season never fail.

[Rev. W. Gregor.] N.E. Scot.

1-12

III. Weather Omens. The first twelve days of January indicate the kind of weather for each month of the year. [*F.-L.* II, p. 479 (1891).] Pitsligo, Ab.

The Highlanders form a sort of almanack or presage of the weather of the ensuing year in the following manner : they make observation on twelve days, beginning at the last of December, and hold as an infallible rule, that whatsoever weather happens on each of those days, the same will prove to agree to the corresponding months. Thus, January is to answer to the weather of December 31st, February to that of January 1st, and so on with the rest. Old people still pay great attention to this augury. [Pennant [2], III, p. 384.] Cf. *The Yules.* Hghlds and Hdes.

73

Another version. There is a variation, however, . . . in this form, ' The first three days of January rule the next three months, and the last twelve days of January show what the weather will be for the twelve months.' [D. Grewar, *Sc. N. & Q.*, 3rd series, II, p. 11 (1924).]

> If the grass grow in Janiveer,
> 'Twill be the worse for't all the year.
>
> [*Pop. Rhymes*³, p. 139.]
>
> A January spring
> Is worth naething.
> Under water dearth,
> Under snow bread.
>
> March in Janiveer,
> January in March, I fear.
>
> If January calends be summerly gay,
> 'Twill be wintery weather till the calends of May.
>
> If in January the sun appear,
> March and April pay full dear.
>
> If January of rain has never a drop,
> The barn'll need an oaken prop.

[D. Grewar, *Sc. N. & Q.*, 3rd series, II, p. 11 (1924).]

V. Observances, a. *Things forbidden or avoided. Marriage.* In Perthshire, January seems to be the unlucky month for marriages. It and May are avoided. In some places, the idea of having the proclamation of Bans, and the celebration of the marriage, within the same term, is applied to all the seasons of the year. It is believed to be unlucky to be proclaimed in one quarter, and married in the next. [Mlan MS.] Pth.

Quoted also by Pennant [Second *Tour* (1772), p. 382], for Pth.

Reported from Stirling. [A. Macgregor, *Hghld. Superstitions, etc.* (1901), p. 42.]

It is supposed to be unlucky to be married between the 1st and 13th of January, that is, between the first day of the New Year—New Style, and the first day, Old Style. This belief is also found in Argyllshire. [Mlan MS.] Lewis, Hdes. ; Ar.

V b. January has been noted as a time for marriage in Wigtown and Galloway. [R. C. Maclagan, *Our Ancestors* (1913), p. 104.]

V g. *Fishing custom. Boats go round clockwise.* Fishermen, the first time they went to sea after the New Year, when they arrived at the place where to shoot their lines made their boats go round in a circle sunways before shooting their nets. They formerly fasted till they shot their lines, the old men would not allow the youths to partake of food till then. [J. E. Cr.] Buckie, Ab.

DAYS

1st

I. Names. *New Year's Day. Calluinn. Nollaig Bheag* (little Nollaig). Feast of the Circumcision.

In Islay New Year's Day was called *Là Nollaig*, correctly Christmas. *Nollaig Bheag* was on the 13th January, N.S. This was the most popular day among the people generally. [Mlan MS.] Hdes.

Cake day, from the doles of cakes. Borders.

January 1st with December 31st were called the 'Daft Days' from festivities and customs then observed. [*Pop. Rhymes.*]

Night of first day. **I. Names.** *Dàir na coille*, the night of the fecundation of the trees, when the wind blows from the west. [*O.S.A.* XII, p. 458.]

Oidhche Choinnle, Candle Night. A name given to this night and to Christmas night. Cf. *Hogmanay*, **Names.** Candle Night was probably a name first given to the Feast of the Epiphany, or Twelfth Night. Further confusion came from the earlier form of *Calltuinn*, hazel, which was *Calluinn, Colluinn,* and we have *Oidhche Coille*, the night of the hazel, which has catkins out on this night. [See *Trans. Gael. Soc. of Inverness,* xxxii (1924-25), p. 33.]

II. Sayings. *Uair ri là Nollaige bhige*, a Gaelic saying meaning ' an hour of greater length to the day of little Christmas ' ; this hour is called *Uair a'ghille*, ' the hour of the fuel lad.' The meaning may be that owing to the lengthening of the day the ' fuel lad ' has to go one trip less while bringing in fuel for the fire. [*Wcrft. & Sec. Sight*, p. 244.] Hghlds.

IV. Omens, a. *Weather, wind.* On the first night in January they observe with anxious attention the disposition of the atmosphere. Their faith in these signs is couched in verses, which may be thus translated :

The wind of the south will be productive of heat and fertility.
The wind of the west of milk and fish.

The wind of the north of cold and storm.
The wind from the east of fruit on the trees.

Gael. :

> *Gaoth a deas, teas is torradh.*
> *Gaoth an iar, iasg is bainne.*
> *Gaoth a tuath, fuachd is gaillionn.*
> *Gaoth an ear, meas air crannaibh.*

[*O.S.A.* XII, p. 458.]

Reported from Bf.　[Pennant,[2] II, p. 48.]

From the way in which the wind blew on New Year's Day auguries were drawn whether the crop of beans and peas would be good or bad during the year.　[Greg., p. 160.]

N.E. Scot.

The same signs read for the fishing.　[*F.-L.* XIII, p, 40.]

Hdes.

IV b. *Fire, ashes.*　Cf. *Hogmanay,* **V c.**　The first thing on New Year's morning was to examine if there was in the ashes any mark like the shape of a human foot with the toes pointing to the door.　If there was such a mark, one was to be removed from the family before the year was run.　Some climbed to the roof of the house and looked down the ' lum ' for the dreaded mark.　[Greg., p. 160.]　　　　　　　N.E. Scot.

If the footprint or toes pointed inwards, one would be added to the family during the course of the year.　[Rev. W. Gregor.]

Black Isle, Rs.

If the fire burned brightly on this morning it was taken as a token of prosperity during the coming year.　A smouldering fire indicated adversity.　These ceremonies and notions about Christmas were transferred in some places to New Year's Day morning.　[*Ibid.*]　　　　　　　　　　N.E. Scot.

The first fire was carefully watched.　If a peat or a live coal rolled away from it, it was regarded as an indication that a member of the family was to depart during the year.　[*Ibid.*]

Keith, Bf.

IV d. *Persons* (unlucky).　To see a woman the first thing on New Year's Day.　　　　　　　　　　　　　　　　Sld.

(Lucky.)　To see a person of the opposite sex on New Year's Day.　[*F.-L.J.* VI (1888), p. 233.]　　　　　　　　Sld.

(Unlucky.)　To see a number of persons together on New Year's Day betokened a death, either of the person who had seen it or someone connected with him, before the year was out.　[Mlan Ms.]　　　　　　　　　　　　　W. Isles.

A visitor without a gift. Mrs McF. says it used to be a custom in Islay to read the fortunes of the new year by looking out from one's window on the morning of the first day. . . . Whatever the eye first rested upon was carefully scrutinised and an opinion formed from it. . . . Some years ago she glanced out of her window on New Year day when she saw a man without his coat coming straight towards her house. He came in and had nothing with him as a gift and was her first visitor that year. . . . She declares that that year was the most unlucky she ever had. [Mlan MS.]   Islay, Ar.

IV e. *Animals, one dead.* In the island of Eigg people were in the habit of looking out through the window on the morning of New Year's Day to ascertain whether the year on which they were entering was to be of good or bad luck for them. . . . Anything dead was held to be a sure indication of misfortune before the year was out. [Mlan MS.]   Eigg, Iness.

position. In Barra they will look out as soon as they rise on New Year's day morning, and according as they will see the first beast on which their eye falls, it is according to that, . . . the New Year will go with them. If it is the beast's head that will be towards them, they are counting that the year will go well with them, but if it is the tail, they may be certain that they will have trouble before that year goes out. Neither would they like that the beast would be lying when they see it. There is nothing they prefer than that they should see it standing or walking and its head to them. [*Ibid.*]   Barra, Hdes.

IV e. *Birds.* New Year's day was a favourite day in the Outer Hebrides for making observations. The augurer (*eun-druidh*) would look out through the window in the morning and draw his *Eun-druidheachd* from what he would see. . . . They drew auguries from the habits of birds at other times of the year as well, and the habits of the stone-chatters (*cloichrean*) were a good deal in demand. If an augurer, when drawing an augur, as they termed it, on behalf of any person, were to see a *cloichrean* flying, the inference would be that the person with regard to whose future fortunes light was being asked was to emigrate to another country ; whereas if the *cloichrean* were seen sitting on a bare stone, it was taken as a sign of something bad that was to happen to him.

The people of Barra go to inspect their fowls early on New Year's day, and should they find a hen or cock, drake or duck with which there is anything wrong, they will kill that beast on the spot, and they will give it to the dogs. Should there be

nothing wrong but a sore foot, this is done, and a bite is not
eaten of what is killed this way on that day. [Mlan MS.] Hdes.

V. **Observances.** a. *Things forbidden or unlucky: to give
anything out of the house.* Nothing was allowed to be put out of
the house this day, neither the ashes of the fire nor the sweep-
ings of the house, nor dirty water, nor anything else, however
useless or however much in the way. (Cf. V c.) [*Wcrft. & Sec.
Sight*, p. 238.]   Hghlds and W. Isles.
Reported also from Galloway. [*Ethnog. Survey of the U.
Kingdom*, 4th Report, p. 15], and from Stg. [*Ibid.*, 5th Report,
p. 457].
Something is brought into the house on the morning of New
Year's Day before anything is taken out. [*Ibid.*]
                                          Kirkmaiden, Galloway.
One New Year's day something was stolen out of our house ;
that year father and mother were confined to bed for weeks ;
the cause and effect were quite clear. [Napier, Appendix,
p. 161.]   Partick, Lnk.
Mary Ritchie was a servant in the fishing village of Findon
about forty years ago. One New Year's morning she had
some washing to do whilst her mistress was at Aberdeen
selling fish.   When she went to begin her work, washing
materials were awanting. She went to a shop kept by Mrs
Gourlay to buy some soda and soft soap. On asking for the
articles, the shop-woman asked her if she had any money.
' Na, bit ma mistress 'ill pay ye fin she comes fae Aberdeen.'
' Bit I winna gee ye them. If naething's brocht in, naething's
ge'en oot, bit gyang ye oot t' the fit o' that tree, an though ye
can get bit a single blade o' green girss, it 'll dee.' The girl did
as she was bidden, went to the foot of the tree, scraped away
the snow, . . . plucked a handful of grass, carried it in and
gave it to the woman. At the same time she asked her if the
grass was for her rabbits. ' Are ye a feel to speer sic a quystin? '
was the contemptuous answer. At the same time she said it
was all right, and she would now give whatever was asked,
' Aiven though it is a' it's i' the chop.' Mary Ritchie, Rosehearty. [Rev. W. Gregor.]   Ab.
Some would not sell even a half-pennyworth of milk on New
Year's Day. [*Ethnog. Survey of the U. Kingdom*, 5th Report
(1897), p. 457.]   Portlogan, Wgtn.
Nor give anything on loan. [*Ibid.*]   Balmaghie, Kcbt.
No creature put out. The animal first put out in a district on
New Year's Day never returned. Hence neighbours always

delayed putting out any creature. On one New Year's Day a man in Kirkhill let out a flock of geese. They flew over a hill and never returned. All search was made for them, but in vain. When the owner came back at night after searching all day for them, he said he had given enough to the devil that day. Informant 73 years of age. [Rev. W. Gregor.] Rs.

To give out fire or light. Should fire be given out of the house (on New Year's Day) it was ominous that death would occur in the house within the year. Cf. **V a.** above. [*Wcrft. & Sec. Sight*, p. 239.] Hghlds. and W. Isles.

Unlucky to give away fire on this day, the luck would go with it. [Mlan MS.] Loch Awe and W. Isles.

This belief quoted also from Ar. [*Ibid.*]

From Galloway, Ayr, Stg. [*Ethnog. Survey of the U. Kingdom*, 5th Report (1897), pp. 456 f.]

Cf. *Christmas,* **V c.**

To bring in fuel or water. It is accounted unlucky to have to bring in fuel or water on Aul' New Year's Day. [J. E. Cr.] Meiklefolla, N.E. Scot.

Breaking glass or crockery. To break a glass on a New Year day is considered unlucky by people in Islay.

Anyone breaking a dish on that day he will be breaking without a stop the whole of that year. [Mlan MS.] Islay, Ar. ; Barra, Hdes.

Sowens for ill-luck. Sowens sprinkled on the doors of persons disliked, for ill luck, at Rosehearty ; also in revenge on those who refused admittance to guisers. [J. E. Cr.] Dinnet, Ab.

Cf. *E.D.D.* VI, Supp[t]. Sowen's Night ; but see **V b.**, *Sprinkling*, below.

Lifting the spinning wheel. I obtained the following notes from a lady in the parish of Cairnie, Banffshire. . . . ' On New Year's day the spinning wheel was never allowed to be lifted across the room, as this would make all the calves club-footed.' [J. Spence, *Buchan Field Club, Transactions*, V (1898), p. 233.] Bf.

Weaving. Weavers did not weave on New Year's Day. [*Ethnog. Survey of the U. Kingdom*, 5th Report (1897), p. 467.] Dundrennan, Kcbt.

Milling. There was no milling on New Year's Day, ' except when thrang '. [*Ibid.*, p. 465.]

A corpse unlucky. It was deemed unlucky to retain in the house a dead body till the morning of New Year's Day ; hence, if a death occurred at this period, the funeral was hastened. [Rogers, *Social Life in Scotland*, III, p. 238.]

' She was removed from mine to Abraham's bosom on Christmas day, and buried on Hogmanae ; for it was thought uncanny to have a dead corpse in the house on the New Year's day.' [Jamieson.]   Ayrsh.

Unlucky on Wednesday. Wednesday unlucky, particularly for the New Year. By no chance will we keep Wednesday here. One man was telling me that he does not remember of its ever being kept on Wednesday. [Mlan MS.]

Port Charlotte, Islay, Ar.

V a and V b. The following passage from Chambers's *Book of Days* describes the hilarity of midnight before New Year in Scottish towns ; the rites are both lucky and unlucky.

Till very few years ago in Scotland, the custom of the wassail bowl at the passing away of the old year might be said to be still in comparative vigour. On the approach of twelve o'clock, a *hot pint* was prepared—that is, a kettle or flagon full of warm, spiced, and sweetened ale, with an infusion of spirits. When the clock had struck the knell of the departed year, each member of the family drank of this mixture ' A good health and a happy New Year and many of them ' to all the rest, with a general hand-shaking, and perhaps a dance round the table, with the addition of a song to the tune of *Hey tuttie taitie* :

> ' Weel may we a' be,
> Ill may we never see,
> Here's to the king
> And the gude companie! ' &c.

The elders of the family would then most probably sally out, with the hot kettle, and bearing also a competent provision of buns and shortbread, or bread and cheese, with the design of visiting their neighbours, and interchanging with them the same cordial greetings. If they met by the way another party similarly bent, whom they knew, they would stop and give and take sips from their respective kettles. Reaching the friend's house, they would enter with vociferous good wishes, and soon send the kettle a-circulating. If they were the first to enter the house since twelve o'clock, they were deemed as the *first-foot* ; and, as such, it was most important, for luck to the family in the coming year, that they should make their entry, not empty-handed, but with their hands full of cakes and bread and cheese ; of which, on the other hand, civility demanded that each individual in the house should partake.

To such an extent did this custom prevail in Edinburgh in the recollection of persons still living, that, according to their account, the principal streets were more thronged between twelve and one in the morning than they usually were at midday. Much innocent mirth prevailed, and mutual good feelings were largely promoted. Edin.

First-footing is enacted with great glee and vivacity in various parts of Scotland, but more especially so in Edinburgh. The mode and hour of visit of the first-foot was, as near as possible, just after midnight, and in some instances parties of young people would visit the favoured ones, and sometimes quite a carousal took place, drinking, eating, singing, and dancing, and sometimes ending in a fight between the jealous rivals, and thus breaking up the merry gathering.

. . . The family visited, of course, expected someone to be their first-foot, and had preparations made accordingly, in the shape of refreshments, and in some instances the household were aroused out of bed. In others the daughter or daughters were prepared for the nocturnal visitor or visitors, and thus the first-footer was not kept waiting outside for his welcome ; storms being considered of no account on such occasions, but rather added to the glee.

The first-foot, on crossing the threshold, at once announced ' A gude New Year to ane and a', and mony may ye see ', or ' A happy New Year tae ye, and God's blessing ' ; then kissing the young woman, and shaking her by both hands, they passed into the household. If the visitor had not been seen for some time, the news of the families was gone into, and other matters of that sort ; then the whisky-drinking, with health-giving toasts, eating of shortbread, currant loaf, scones, oat-cakes, and cheese were all heartily consumed, then song-singing, sometimes a dance, then more drinking, and at last came the parting, in much hilarity and glee, the ' toozling ' (or hugging) and kissing of the young woman or women, and then off went the nocturnal visitor or visitors for other calls, until daylight appearing stopped their fun ; or else the first-footers kept on making their calls, drinking and carousing all through New Year's Day, and even on, far on, New Year's Night. . . . The first-footing only strengthened the courtship, the regular visiting continuing, and generally ending in marriage on a subsequent New Year's Day.

In ' Auld Reekie ' (Edinburgh), the custom of first-footing (' first-fittin' ', in Scots) dates from time immemorial ; generally, the preparations for the midnight orgies of New

Year's Eve begin to show themselves in the early part of the evening in the stir and bustle of the leading thoroughfares of the city ; groups of young men moving listlessly about, as evidently wearying for the fun to begin. The church of the *Tron Men*, or labourers of the city, has long been the gathering-place or rendezvous of the first-footers. Some sixty or seventy years ago, first-footing in Edinburgh required ingenuity and courage on the part of young men who went first-footing from the Tron Church, owing to the danger and rioting and fighting amongst the first-footers ; the whisky-shops, as they were then called, being open all night (and any amount of whisky to be had cheap) . . . enabled the revellers to keep up continued supplies in their bottles. Then there were the ' Baxters ', or ' Batchies Bow wow wows ' (as they were termed then, bakers), and who were known by their peculiar trade-signal or whistle (and who were a powerful body of men, requiring great strength of neck and head to carry, say, forty or forty-five loaves on a large board or tray, placed on the head) ; they, leaving off their work, would sally forth into the streets, and join in the revelry. Then the students attending the University would likewise turn in and join the crowds, and if perchance a wrong expression or slighting word crept from one of the students towards a ' batchie ', then woe betide all : bottles and glasses were smashed, blows were exchanged freely, a regular *mêlée* occurring, and everyone fleeing his or her own way out of the shindy, until the row dwindled down or was fought out, leaving many a cut and scar to be accounted for.

This mode of procedure of first-footing is as followed now in Edinburgh. . . . Towards evening, the thoroughfares become thronged with the youth of the city, and by ten o'clock, in the neighbourhood of the Tron Church, small crowds of young men begin to gather, and to grow impatient for the midnight hour of carousal, first-footing, and general welcoming in of the New Year, say 1893. Next, as the midnight hour approaches, drinking of healths becomes frequent, and some are already intoxicated ; the crowds become denser, the police are moving actively about regulating the traffic, which is fast becoming congested at this point, namely, the North and South Bridge Streets crossing the High Street at the ' Tron '. The public-houses are now closed, it is past eleven o'clock, the streets have become darker, the crowds very dense, and the hum of the voices louder and louder, when suddenly a great coloured light appears from some elevated point in the

High Street. One after another of these coloured lights continue, then the bells or tubes of bronze of St Giles now begin to ring for the midnight service, when, altogether, the scene is one of a most awe-inspiring nature. The eyes of the immense crowd are ever being turned towards the lighted clock-face of the ' Auld and Faithfu' ' Tron, the hour approaches, the hands seem to stand still, but in one second more the hurrahing, the cheering, the hand-shaking, the health-drinking, the swaying to and fro of the immense throng, is all kept up as long as the clock continues to ring out the much-longed-for midnight hour. The crowds slowly disperse, the much intoxicated and helpless ones being hustled about a good deal, the police urging them on out of harm's way. The first-footers are off and away, flying in every direction through the city, singing, cheering, and shaking hands with all and sundry ; ' A gude New Year and mony o' them '. [Many similar greetings quoted.]

The first-footing has thus begun in real earnest throughout the city, the windows of some of the houses are all ablaze with light, and, to add zest to all, away far up on the ramparts of the grand historical pile, the Castle, stand the band of the Highland Regiment therein stationed at that time ; then shaking hands and wishing each other ' A gude New Year ', you hear the strains of ' A guid New Year in Scotia yet ', ' For auld lang syne ', ' God save the Queen ', and a final round of cheers, then all is still.

The old Scots families who keep up the old customs encourage their domestics to come in and first-foot them for good luck in their home, wishing them ' a lucky gude ' New Year, generally accompanied with a gift of money or dress. Then again, grandparents are pleased to have their grand-children first-foot them, and in many, many cases this rhyme was sung or said by the children visiting the old people :

> ' Get up, guid wife, and shake yere feathers,
> An dinna think that we are beggars,
> For we're yere bairns come oot the day,
> So rise and gie's oor Hogmanay ; '

which was accordingly done with great glee. The older children sometimes were given ' ginger cordial ', now called wine, with shortbread, currant loaf, scones, oat-cake, cheese, and sometimes an orange or an apple added, with of course the New Year's *penny* for ' guid luck '. This, then, was a child's first-footing to grannie. Then, in the case of the seniors, as before described, there was the nocturnal welcome, the love-making, the health-drinking, the song singing, the dancing, the toozling, the ' pairtin' ' (or leave-taking), and at last the ' first-fittin' is ower ' (is over).

Then out on the streets all is bustle and commotion, hurrying to and fro of young people, cheering and singing, some drinking and health-toasting, every possible and conceivable portable musical instrument brought into play ; cheer after cheer, chorus after chorus, rend the air of the early morn, and not until daylight sends them home do the streets of Edinburgh resume their usual wont and quiet ; and thus all this stir, all this commotion, all this hubbub, over the old, old custom of 'first-fittin' ', the first lucky foot to cross a threshold on the New Year's morn, and to be sure and not to go in ' empty-handed ' (without a gift), to some one, and especially the loved one, else bad or ill luck or poverty thereafter.

Since the passing of the Forbes MacKenzie Act closing the public-houses at eleven o'clock, the increase of our police forces, the action of the Early Rechabites and total abstainers, in conjunction with temperance societies of every grade, and the evangelistic workers in all our churches, all uniting in one grand endeavour to stay the forces of the evil of intoxication at such a time as New Year, and now the inducements of recreation and amusements of every description instead, are fast bringing into disuse and distaste the ' auld, auld custom of " first-fittin' " in Guid Auld Scotia '.—G. HASTIE.

[Mr Hastie's account of First-Footing in Edinburgh is valuable as giving the actual experience of an old resident of the town, and has therefore been left untouched.—ED. *F.-L.*]
[*F.-L.*, vol. IV (1893), pp. 308-314.]

See also *F.-L.* III, 1892, pp. 257 f.

Of course the first foot is always actuated by kindly feelings. He only visits such as he respects, and wishes by his presence to testify to his esteem and goodwill. Those visited look upon it in the same light and it is held to be an honour to have this attention, and in cases where several rival first-footers visit the same family, the honour is often measured by their number.
[Mlan MS.]   Kintyre, Ar.

V. Observances. *First Foot.* **a.** *unlucky,* **b.** *lucky.*

In the north of Scotland and especially in Orkney and Shetland, where the change of Style came much later as a regular custom than in the south, the date was usually January 12th or 13th.

The First Foot, the name given in Scotland to the person who first enters the house in the New Year ; this is regarded . . . as influencing the fate of the family, especially the fair portion of it, for the ensuing year. [R. T. Hampson, *Med. Aevi Kalend.* (1841), p. 98.]

The following quotation explains how an ill-favoured First Foot is looked upon with aversion.

The attributes of the first-foot were held to cling to the house all the year, e.g. a woman whose husband (a miner) had ' slept in ' one morning and ' lost a shift ', explained it by saying that ' they had a' been sleepin' in ever since that dovey-heidit (sleepy-headed) cratur had been their first-fit '. [D. R. Rorie, M.D., in *County F.-L.* VII, p. 146.] Ffe.

Much excitement and interest attached to the appearance and character of the first visitor to cross the threshold after the advent of the New Year as upon him the happiness and prosperity of the household was supposed to depend for the ensuing twelve months. If by any stroke of luck the ' first foot ' was a woman, nothing but calamity could be expected. But such an event could only happen by some rare accident—as it was not the custom for women to go ' first footing '. Moreover, maidens of the house generally arranged beforehand that some favoured and ' weel-fawiet ' youth of their acquaintance should be their first visitor. Several physical types were deemed unlucky. Thus no good came with a flat-soled ' first-foot ', or with one whose character was conspicuously sanctimonious. [David MacRitchie, ' Christmas and New Year Customs,' in *The Scot. Review*, Dec. 21, 1905.]

V a. *Unlucky.*

> Ere New Year's morn begins to peep,
> Wi' glee, but little din,
> At doors the lassies sentrie keep,
> To let the *first-fit* in.
> Nae auld, camshauchel'd (crook-legged), warlock loun,
> Nor black, wanchaunchie carline,
> Sall cross ae threshold o' the town,
> Till ilk lass gets her darlin'
>   To kiss that night.

[Rev. Js. Nicol, *Poems, etc.* (1805), I, p. 33.]   S.E. Scot.

V a. and V b. ' Great attention was paid at all times to first-footing, but especially at the New Year, and the first Monday of every quarter. In a number of the *John O'Groat Journal* for

August, 1840, there is a curious article on this subject, from which we extract the following paragraph :

' Indeed, no one ', says the writer, ' would go on a journey, begin a job, or even run a message, without observing who was first-foot—that is, the first individual or animal one met. When fishermen went to sea, they wished no one to meet them, or to ask them where they were going, in case such a person should be a bad foot, and ill-luck follow. A hare, a pig, a mouse, or a cat, were considered to be very " bad feet " ; and a crow—time out of mind an ominous bird—was an exceedingly sinister sign. A dog, a cow, a horse, or a moorfowl, were, on the contrary, looked upon as " good feet ", as good, indeed, as could be desired. If a dog barked fiercely at the swain going to see his Dulcinea, it betokened bad success ; but if he fawned on the lucky man, it was regarded as an infallible mark of his proving a fortunate wooer. If any one put on the stocking and shoe, and tied the garter and shoe-tie before putting anything on the other foot and leg, it was firmly believed that no one would have success in his undertaking that day who had this person for his first foot.'—Calder's *Sketches from John O'Groat's*, Wick (1842), p. 224. [Contributed to *John O'Groat's Journal* (1911) by Rev. D. Beaton.]   Cths.

V a. A pious, sanctimonious person.   West of Scot.
One who had met with an accident on the way.   *Ibid.*
A flat-soled person.   *Ibid.*
A plain, solid person. [Napier, p. 160.]   *Ibid.*
A flat-footed person. [Mlan Ms.] Arran, Ayr ; Islay, Ar.
A flat-footed or ' plumb-soled ' person.   Stirling, Ffe.
People not fully dressed, especially if they have bare feet.
[Mlan Ms.]   Kintyre, Ar.
Persons carrying a knife or a pointed tool. [*F.-L.* III (1892), p. 256.]   Ffe.
A woman. [*Wcrft. & Sec. Sight*, p. 239.] Hghlds. and W. Isles.
Ditto. [Mlan Ms.]   Arran, Ar.
Ditto. [*F.-L. J.* VII (1889), p. 53.]   Sld.
Ditto. [*Ethnog. Survey of U. Kingdom*, 5th Report (1897), p. 458.]   Fisherfolk of Drumore, Ab.
A fair woman. [Mlan Ms.]   Coigach, Rs.
A decrepit old woman asking kindling deplorably unlucky.
[*Wcrft. & Sec. Sight*, p. 231.]   Hghlds. and W. Isles.
(But a woman as first foot is not unlucky in Fife or Forfarshire. [*F.-L.* III (1892), p. 256.])   Angus.
A person of fair complexion. [Rev. W. Gregor.]
                                        Achterneed, N.E. Scot.

A person of dark complexion. [*Ibid.*] Portnockie, N.E. Scot.
Red-haired persons unlucky. [*F.-L.* III (1892), p. 256.] Ffe.
Persons with red hair.   West Brough, Thurso, Selkirk, Tar-
land, Nether Lochaber, Nairn,
Banff (see also below).
With eyebrows that meet.   West Brough, Thurso, Selkirk,
Banff.
With a lame leg.   Thurso, Sld.
With a blind eye.   Thurso, Sld.
With splay feet or toes much turned out.   Banff.
With toes turned inwards.   West Brough, Cths. ; Nether
Lochaber, Iness ; Thurso, Cths.
Wearing mourning or black clothes.   Nairn.
A bearded woman.   Rosehearty, Ab.
Immoral persons.   Tarland, Ab. ; Thurso, Cths.
Stingy persons.   Tarland, Ab.
Flat-footed persons.   Achterneed.
A false pretender in religion.   Tarland, Ab.
Midwives, Gravediggers, a Hangman, a Thief, a Woman
with a reputation for Witchcraft, Persons generally with
defects or impaired faculties not acquired accidentally ; no
special places quoted. [J. E. Cr.]   N.E. Scot.

A red-haired person. If it was known that one with such (red)
hair intended coming as ' first fit ' means were taken to forestall him. [Rev. W. Gregor, *Ethnog. Survey of the U. Kingdom*,
4th Report (1896), p. 15.]   Galloway.
For one, on his way to market, to be met by a red-haired
person, would be considered as an indication that he might
prepare himself for almost any misfortune : and for the same
reason, a red-haired person is an unwelcome ' first foot '.
[Mlan MS.]   Rs. ; Sld.

Extremes unlucky. A man preferred as first foot, neither very
badly dressed nor too well dressed. If either one or the other
it was a token of unhappiness to people visited by him in the
course of the year. [Mlan MS.]   Lewis, Hdes.
Doctor or minister. Either a doctor or a minister an unlucky
first foot on New Year's day—for they being a kind of magis-
trate would bring domestic dispeace for the whole year thereafter. [Mlan MS.]   Ffe.
An empty-handed person. An empty-handed first foot was
looked upon as a bringer of bad luck in all parts of Scotland,
' tantamount to wishing a curse on the family.' [Napier,
Appendix, p. 160.]

Bad luck for first-footers. Persons going first footing believed it to be very unlucky to meet :

a bearded woman.	West Brough, Cths.
an intoed man.	*Ibid.*
man with knees twisted inwards.	*Ibid.*
rabbit running across the path.	*Ibid.*
cat running straight before one.	*Ibid.*
to hear the cry of a crow.	*Ibid.*
to meet a cat, a hare, a rabbit, a frog, a toad, a deformed person.	Thurso, Cths.
to meet a black cat (very unlucky).	Rosehearty, Ab.
to meet a cat.	Nether Lochaber, Iness.
	[J. E. Cr.]

V b. *First Foot. Lucky.*

A barefooted woman.	Banff.
A dark-haired person.	Thurso, Cths.
Persons of generous disposition.	*Ibid.*
Children.	*Ibid.*
Those in good circumstances.	Selkirk and other places.
Kind persons and good-looking persons.	Selkirk, Tarland, Ab., and elsewhere.
A man or woman with red hair very lucky.	Rosehearty, Ab.
People who spread out their feet.	Nether Lochaber, Iness.
People born feet foremost.	*Ibid.*
Persons free from suspicion of witchcraft.	Place not named.
	[J. E. Cr.]

A hearty, ranting, merry fellow. [Napier, Appendix, p. 160.]   W. Scot.

A hearty, merry fellow. [W. Nimmo, *The Hist. of Stirlingshire* [3] (1880), II, p. 387.]   Stg.

A man of good character. [*Ethnog. Survey of the U. Kingdom*, 4th Report (1896), p. 15.]   Mochrum, Galloway.

One with dark hair. [*Ibid.*]   *Ibid.*

A dark-complexioned man. [*F.-L.*, 1893.]   Edin.

One of fair complexion. [Rev. W. Gregor.]
                                                              Portnockie, Ab.

' Sonsie ' (well-favoured) folk welcome. [*E.D.D.* II, p. 367.]
                                                                        Dfs.

A young man entering as first foot with an armful of corn was an excellent sign of the year's prosperity. [*Wcrft. & Sec. Sight*, p. 239.]   Hghlds.

Dog lucky. A dog is a very lucky first foot on New Year's Day. [Mlan Ms.]   Skipness, Ar.

Enjoined. To avert ill-luck at first footing. To avert ill-luck

from the call of a person regarded as unlucky. When address-
ing the person bring in the name of the Supreme Being three
times. West Brough, Cths.

Throw salt in the fire when you see such a one coming.
Rosehearty, Ab.

Two twigs of rowan crossed and tied with a red thread.
Tarland, Ab.

Roman Catholics cross themselves.

Be sure to have the first word with him.
Nether Lochaber, Iness.

Ditto. Nairn.

Rowan tree and woodbine fixed on the door, with the words

> ' Rowan tree and woodbine
> Haud the witches on come in.'

Banff.

People regarded as bringing ill-luck were sometimes shut
up in their houses on New Year's Eve. [J. E. Cr.]

If a person going first-footing met an unlucky animal it was
sometimes the custom to spit. Thurso, Cths.

The custom was to make a cross on the road and spit ; the
first-footer would spit three times. Rosehearty, Ab.

If the person or animal was considered very dangerous the
first-footer would turn once with the sun.
West Brough, Cths.

The first-footer would turn and walk in the opposite
direction. [*Ibid.*] Stonehaven, Kin.

†*Ember put in a dish of water.* Should a person that they did
not like come in, as soon as he would leave, the people of the
house would put a burning ember in a vessel of water, and
they are saying that this will make those who have gone away
that it will not be in their power to leave any bad behind them.
This is done on New Year's day. I have never seen it done
at any other time.

Note.—The significance of this, as a Barra superstition, is
that, according to the reciter, the putting of the ember in the
dish of water is confined to New Year's day. From other
parts of the Highlands we learn that it is done at any time
when the circumstances, as stated, may take place. [Mlan
MS.] Barra, Hdes.

Cf. **V** b. *Water retains luck*, below.

Bible over the door. On the last day of the year the Bible was
placed above the door, so that the evil one could not come in
next morning with an unlucky first foot, of whom the most

undesirable was a flat-footed, red-haired woman. [A. Gunn and J. Mackay, *Sutherland and the Reay Country* (1897), p. 132.]
Sld.

Burning straw up the chimney. If one reputed to have an ' ill-fit ' entered first, it was looked on as a harbinger of evil. To counteract the evil, something, as a little straw, was set on fire, and thrown up the chimney. [Rev. W. Gregor.]
St Combs, N.E. Scot.

A man on horseback. Those going first-footing believed it lucky to meet a man on horseback. [Note by John Philip, Fordoun.]
Kin.

Luck with drams and ' het pints ' at first footing. New Year, one of the principal customs held on that day is first-footing. Young men visit their neighbours, carrying with them black bottles full of good cheer, wishing them health, happiness, and prosperity for the year to come. [M. Manson, *John O'Groat's Journal*, Dec. 15, 1911.]

The first footer brought a bottle of whisky with him, and where accompanied by a friend, or it might be two, or even three, each might have a bottle. The inmates had to be treated to the contents of each bottle, of course, and they returned the compliment in ' a dram from my bottle ', accompanied with bread and cheese. [Mlan MS.] Islay, Ar.

Het Pint, the name given to that hot beverage which it is customary for young people to carry with them from house to house on New Year's eve, or early in the morning of the new year. . . .

This is made of spirits, beer, sugar, and eggs. It is called a pint, most probably from the vessel, or measure of liquids, in which it had been formerly carried about, containing a Scots pint, or half a gallon. [Jamieson.]

Drams reported also from Iness.

Among old customs still remaining in Gairloch are those connected with . . . the New Year, which is the only festival observed in the parish. . . .

New Year's eve and New Year's day are kept according to the old style, on the 12th and 13th of January, and both days are general holidays. There is always a keen contest for the ' first-footing ' at midnight on New Year's eve ; the one who succeeds in first entering a neighbour's house claims the inevitable dram. [J. H. Dixon, *Gairloch in North-West Ross-shire : Its Records, etc.* (1886), pp. 115-6.]
Rs.

Drams, rules for drinking. It was necessary for luck that what was poured out of the ' first foot's ' gift, be it whisky or other drink, should be drunk to the dregs by each recipient, and it was requisite that he should do the same by theirs. It was against rule for any portion to be left, but if there did happen to be an unconsumed remnant, it was cast out. With any subsequent visitor these particulars were not observed. [Napier, Appendix, pp. 160 f.] W. Scot.

It was a well-established custom in Islay, when lads went to first foot on the New Year, they brought a bottle of whisky with them out of which they gave the first dram to the man of the house, or to his wife, and if neither of them emptied the glass, none of those served after them should. [Mlan MS.]
Islay, Ar.

First-footing is still practised in some parts of this county on the morning of the New Year ; but, as a rule, little, if any, importance is attached to the first-foot. It is generally engaged in merely for the ' fun of the thing ', and sometimes, perhaps, for the sake of the dram, which is generally offered and shared on those occasions, and which it would be unlucky to refuse. The drinking is, however, by no means a recent introduction. One of my informants, the Rev. Dr. Cock of Rathen, a parish in the north-east of the county of Aberdeen, where he succeeded his father as minister, tells me that about sixty years ago, when he was a boy, he recollects that spiced ale was generally carried by the first-foot, and shared with all whom he met, or at whose houses he visited. The whisky-bottle has nowadays entirely superseded the . . . wassail-kettle, mentioned by Chambers, though the reason which prompted the carrying of either on these first-footing visits was identical. Everywhere it seems to have been considered most important for luck in the coming year to the family on which he calls that the first-foot should not make his entry empty-handed. [J. E. Cr. in *F.-L.* IV (1893), p. 315.] Ab.

A dram with eatables. A visitor must bring in his hand some eatable ; he will be doubly welcome if he carries in a hot stoup or ' plotie '. [Henderson, *F.-L. of the Northern Counties* (1879), p. 72.] Borders.

Our custom is to carry in food and drink when first-footing.
Leuchars, Ffe.

The favourite thing to take (first-footing) is a red herring, but it is regarded somewhat as a joke, and if you arrive before the family is up, which is very probable, as the first-foot sets out usually soon after twelve, you may tie the red herring to the door-handle. [*F.-L.* III (1892), p. 256.] Angus.

Sometimes instead of a whisky-bottle, the first-foot carries shortbread, oatcakes, ' sweeties ', and last, but not least, sowens. [*F.-L.* IV (1893), p. 316.]   Ab.

Oats with whisky. At 12 o'clock on New Year's Eve, the ' foreman ' entered the master's bedroom as ' first fit '. He carried with him a sheaf of oats and a bottle of whisky. He cast the sheaf on the bed over the master and his wife. A glass of whisky was then poured out and health to the family and prosperity to the farming operations were drunk to. [*Ethnog. Survey of the U. Kingdom*, 4th Report (1896), p. 15.]
                                                   Minnigaff, Galloway.

A wheat-sheaf. When I arrived, I carefully explored every door and window, lest some one might have anticipated me : but all was silent. I hastened to the barn yard, procured a sheaf of wheat as a first-footing present.

I sought my way to the bed of the gudeman, wished him a happy new year and tossed into the bed above him the ample and welcomed wheatsheaf. . . . A light was speedily procured, and rapidly did servant after servant appear, each bearing some rough offering. [Donald Walker, *Sports and Games* (1837), pp. 331-2.]   Rural districts.

Rowan wood. My informant's mother always went on New Year's Day morning to the wood to get a branch of ' Rawn Tree '—the rowan or mountain ash. She cut it into small pieces, and placed one piece over each door and window. [J. E. Cr.]   Pennan, Aberdour, Ab.

The houses were decked with mountain ash. [*Wcrft. & Sec. Sight*, p. 242.]   Hghlds. and W. Isles.

The piece of rowan tree was wound round with a piece of red thread, on which seven knots had been cast. The knots were cast on the thread about half a finger-length apart. It was then tied round the piece of rowan tree from one end of it towards the other. The two ends of the thread were then tied together by a ' weaver's knot '. The whole was placed without any one seeing it done over the door in the evening. [Rev. W. Gregor.]   Aberdour, Ab.

Water and peats. Water from the ' dead and living ford ', *uisge coisrigte.* See **V** h. below.

The Rev. Mr Skinner tells me that in the Tarland district of Aberdeenshire it used to be customary to bring water from the well and peats from the stack the moment the New Year came in. [J. E. Cr., *F.-L.* IV (1893), p. 315.]   Ab.

Grass and water brought in. The common practice in many places in days long past was to go outside and bring in grass and water before taking anything out of the house.

This was to ensure plenty of food all the year round for man and beast. [J. E. Cr., *F.-L.* IV (1893), p. 316.]   N.E. Ab.
A green sod was brought in and laid on the grate cheek. [*Ibid.*]   Stonehaven, Kin.
Sea-weed. On New Year's Day sea-weed was among the first things taken into the house. It was placed over the door. [*Ibid.*]   Buchanhaven, Ab.
On New Year's morning ' belly-waar ' (Fucus nodosus) was placed over the lintel of the dwelling house inside. [*Ibid.*]
     Broadsea, Ab.
It was a custom to go to the sea on the morning of the New Year and draw a pailful of water and take it along with a little sea-weed into the house. [*Ibid.*]   Portessie, Bf.
Water retains luck. It used to be thought unlucky to give a burning peat to anybody out of one's house on New Year's day. It was supposed to carry the luck away from those who gave it. A remedy was known however and practised in cases where the kindling could not be refused to a neighbour who might ask it. It was this :—When the peat was given away a corresponding one was thrown into a pail of water in the house, which was supposed to retain the luck still in the house. [Mlan MS.]   W. Isles.
     Cf. **V b.** *To avert ill-luck at first-footing* †, above.
Smoke of the fire. When the dottle or hesp of lint was being fixed on the rock, if a man of dark complexion or ' close-broot ' came in it was not spun till put through the ' reek ' three times. [J. E. Cr.]   Rosehearty, Ab.
Sprinkling. In Glenlyon a landlady on the morning of New Year's Day sprinkles urine upon the whole family, as they are getting out of bed. [Alex. Allardyce, *Scot. and Scotsmen in the 18th Cent.* (1888), II, p. 455.]   Pth.
The door-posts and walls, and even the cattle, were sprinkled with urine. [*Wcrft. & Sec. Sight*, p. 242.]
     Hghlds. and W. Isles.
The qualified Highlander, early on New Year's morn, . . . takes a large brush, with which he profusely asperses the occupants of all beds with *Uisge Coisricht'*, from whom it is not unusual for him to receive ungrateful remonstrances. [*Pop. Superstitions.*]   Hghlds.
The practice of carrying sowens by the first-foot on the morning of Old Yule [later at New Year] to sprinkle on the doors of persons he wishes well to, was common enough. [Communicated by Dr Jamieson.]   Old Machar, Ab.
From Tarland and Fintray I get further confirmation of the

carrying of sowens by the Old Yule first-foot. My Fintray informant tells me how the aspersion was made : ' The man gets a pail like what we use to water horses with. This he fills with sowens, and then having procured a brush, similar to those painters use for whitewashing walls, he goes round the houses of those he wishes well to, sprinkling doors and windows with the concoction.' [J. E. Cr., *F.-L.* IV, p. 317.] Ab.

Sowens sprinkled for luck also at Stonehaven and Nether Lochaber, but not known further north. [J. E. Cr.] But cf. **V** a. *Sowens for ill luck.*

Plenty and good cheer. It is lucky for the whole of the year following to have one's house well supplied on New Year's Day—also to be happy and cheerful on that day. [Mlan MS.]
Bf.

Should it happen that a man or woman who would be under a bad name would come in the people of the house would give to that one anything that would be in their power, with the view of sending him away with cheerfulness, for they are saying should such a person as that leave a house on New Year's day and him under grief, that there would be a cause of grief to the people of that house the whole of the year. [Mlan MS.]
Barra, Hdes.

Greeting and kissing for luck. It was the universal custom in Scotland, till of late, for every male to salute, by kissing, every female of his acquaintance, the first time he met her in the new year. [James Anderson, *The Bee*, I, p. 103. (1791).]
Edin.

On the last night of the year the young women walk about the streets without fear, as nobody thinks of interfering with them in the way of salutation, till the town clock warns the approach of twelve. Within a few minutes of that hour young women of all ranks may be seen creeping along close to the wall, thinking to gain their houses without being discovered, young men may also be seen moving after them, only waiting for the warning clock, in order to make that salute which may not be rejected.

When men meet women, neglect of the salute on the part of the men would be deemed not merely ungallant but stupid, and its refusal on the part of the women as ungracious as unavailing.

Even a lady who passes in a sedan chair or a carriage, submits, with the best grace she can, to pay the forfeit she has incurred. [Donald Walker, *Games and Sports* (1837), pp. 327-8.]

First to rise. It is a family custom in Barra, as soon as the one who is first out of bed on New Year's day morning, gets up, he or she gives a dram to all the others still in bed, and they drink to the family health all round. The honour of being first up on that morning is matter of competition, not only within the family circle but near neighbours also strive for the credit of being first aloft to welcome the New Year. [Mlan MS.] Barra, Hdes.

New clothes. Everybody should wear a new dress on New Year's Day, and if its pockets contain money of every description they will be certain not to be empty throughout the year. [Henderson, *F.-L. of the Northern Counties* (1879), p. 72.]
Borders.

It is also deemed wise that all the members of the family, old as well as young, should have something new to wear on that day. [Contributed to *John O'Groat's Journal* (1911), by Rev. D. Beaton.] Cths.

New clothes for luck. [Mlan MS.] Easter Ross.

Also from Mochrum, Galloway. [*Ethnog. Survey of U. Kingdom*, 4th Report (1896), p. 15.]

A new-born child's crying. The child that is born on New Year's Day and gives three 'greets' will be a long liver. [Rev. W. Gregor.] Corgarff, Ab.

Things enjoined in work to avert ill luck. It used to be recommended, as a useful custom, which some tried to practice as far as possible, to do a little every New Year's day of the various kinds of work with which one expected to be employed throughout the year. [Mlan MS.] Deskford, Bf.

V c. *Fire, torches, candles, ashes. Bonfires.* Long before sunrise on the first of January (N.S.) the Inverness hills are crowned with bonfires, and when they burn low the lads and lassies dance round them and trample out the dying embers. The opposite coast shows no such fires till the morning of the New Year (O.S.), when it likewise awakens before daylight to greet the rising sun. [C. F. Gordon Cumming, *In the Hebrides* (1883), p. 225.] Iness.

Huge bonfires were kindled at the Townhead and the Common Loan. Auchterarder, Pth.

Squibs. The New Year was brought in with the firing of squibs, rockets, etc. [*F.-L.* XX (1909), p. 482.] Bf.

Fumigation with juniper. On New Year's eve large loads of juniper bushes were brought into the house and laid round the fire to dry till morning. The early sprinkling over, all doors and windows were carefully closed and all crevices stopped.

The head of the household kindles piles of the collected juniper in the different apartments, till the vapour from the burning branches condenses into clouds, and coughing, sneezing, wheezing and gasping ensue. The operator, aware that the more intense the *smúchan* (smothering smoke), the more propitious the solemnity . . . continues . . . to increase the fumigation, until in his own defence, he admits the air to recover the exhausted household and himself. He then treats the horses, cattle, etc. (see **V e.**) . . . . When the gude-wife . . . has regained sufficient strength to reach the bottle *dhu* (black), she administers its comfort to the relief of the sufferers. . . . [*Pop. Superstitions*, p. 176.] Hghlds.

Cow's hide burnt. Perambulating the township sunwise dressed in the skin of a cow took place until recently in the Hebrides at New Year, in order to keep off misfortune, a piece of the hide being burned and the smoke inhaled by each person and animal in the township. [J. A. MacCulloch, *Religion of the Ancient Celts* (1911), pp. 260 f.] Hdes.

For full description of the rite of the burnt hide see *Caisein Uchd, Hogmanay,* **V** above.

Ashes in divination. In the evening lines were drawn across the ashes on the open hearth for divination about sweethearts. [Rev. W. Gregor.] N.E. Scot.

Cf. **IV**, *Omens*, above.

For other rites with burning juniper, etc., cf. **V e.** below.

V c. *Fire*, and **V k.** *Water*. In Lewis after the house-fire has been newly kindled from the village-fire, ' a pot full of water is quickly set on it and afterwards sprinkled upon the people infected with the plague or upon the cattle that have the murrain '. [*Ethnog. Survey of the U. Kingdom*, 4th Report, p. 41.] Lewis, Hdes.

V d. *Divination. Castocs.* On New Year's Day the unmarried went to the kail-yard, and pulled castocs. They were placed over the door inside. From the first one that entered omens were drawn as to sweethearts. [Rev. W Gregor.]
St Combs, Ab.

Cf. *Hallowe'en,* **V d.**

Castocs over the door, the first man passing in under them would have the name of the future husband. Stonehaven, Kin.

Ditto. Name and colour of hair foretold. [J. E. Cr.]
Nether Lochaber, Iness.

By a person seen. You must take note what is the Christian name of the first person you see of the opposite sex on New

Year's Day : it will be that of the future husband or wife.
[Henderson, *F.-L. of the Northern Counties* (1879), p. 73.] Borders.
Cf. **V** c. *Ashes in divination.*

From eating scones. *Note.*—This is a favourite custom. A
small lump of dough, from which the cakes have been taken,
is reserved, and in it a small coin, usually a farthing (the
luckie fardin') is put. The dough is then rolled thin, and cut
into small scones, which, when fired, are handed round the
company. Not a moment must be lost in eating them, it
being of vast importance to get the scone with the hidden
treasure, as it is believed that happy person shall first taste
the sweets of matrimonial felicity. [Rev. James Nicol, *Poems,
Chiefly in the Scottish Dialect* (1805), I, p. 28.] S. Scot.

Candle spail. The rites of . . . New Year and the ' candle
spail ' were regarded with reverence and fear. . . . [John
Fraser, *The Humourous Chap-Books of Scot.* (1873), p. 36.]

Candle spails are little curls of tallow which sometimes
appear on a burning candle and have a meaning at certain
times, of which New Year was one. [Ed.]

V e. *Byre, farm, etc.* *Fumigating cattle.* On New-year's day
they burn juniper before their cattle. [T. Pennant, *Tour in
Scotland* [4] (1769), p. 205, ed. 1776.] Cths.
See also Js. Logan, *The Scottish Gael* (1831), II, p. 67.

New Year's Day was a great saining day, i.e. a day for
taking precautions for keeping away evil from the cattle
and horses. . . . Juniper was burnt in the byre. [*Wcrft. &
Sec. Sight*, p. 242.]

Smelling burning hide. See **V** c. *Cow's hide burnt.*

On New Year's Day, O.S., old shoes or pieces of old leather
along with green *aiteann*, i.e. green juniper, were burned in
each byre a little before sunrise. They were set on fire by a
coal from the house-fire. All holes in the byre were stopped,
and the door was closed, to prevent the smoke from escaping,
and to make it as strong as possible, in order that the animals
might ' host ' (cough) ; for, unless the animal coughed, there
would be no thrift with that one during the year, and, perhaps,
it might die. [J. E. Cr.] Corgarff, Ab.

Marking with tar. The animals were marked with tar.
[*Wcrft. & Sec. Sight*, p. 242.] Hghlds. and W. Isles.

Sprinkling with urine. The door-posts and walls and even the
cattle were sprinkled with urine (cf. **V** b. *Sprinkling*, above).
[*Ibid.*] Reported by Pennant for the first Monday of every
quarter. [Ed.]

Sea-weed for luck. Along the sea-board, in districts where sea-weed—' waar '—is used as manure, the farmers showed much anxiety on New-Year's morning to have the first load of weed that was taken from the shore. When the first load was carted home, a small quantity was laid down at each door of the farm-steading, and the remainder was cast into the fields—a portion into each field. This was supposed to bring good-fortune.—(Pitsligo. Told by one that followed the custom.) [*F.-L. J.*, Vol. II (1884), p. 331.]　　　　　Ab.

Dulse against witchcraft. Broad-leaved pondweed (*Potamogeton natans*), *Duileasg na h-aibhne* (river dulse). At one time in the Highlands this plant was gathered in small bundles in summer and autumn and kept until New Year's Day (O.S.), when it was put for a time in a tub of hot water and the infusion mixed with the first drink given to milch cows on New Year's Day morning. This was to guard them from witchcraft and the evil eye for the rest of the year ; as also to increase the supply of milk. [Rev. A. M. MacFarlane, *Trans. Gaelic Soc^tv of Inverness* (1924-25), XXXII, p. 38.]

Fire given out gives power over the stock. It was unlucky to give fire out of the house. It gave the means to witches and evilly-disposed people to do irreparable mischief to the cattle and their produce. [*Wcrft. & Sec. Sight*, p. 237.]

Hghlds. and W. Isles.

The 'flower of the well' brings luck to the farm. Cf. **V h.** *Water.* Some not content with creaming the well they drew water from themselves, creamed that of their neighbour to draw away his (or her) luck. This act among farmers and crofters was believed to have peculiar efficacy in securing a rich supply of milk and butter. All the utensils of the dairy were washed with part of the ' cream ' of the well, and the cows got the remainder to drink. [Rev. W. Gregor.] Keith, Pitsligo, Ab.

Unthreshed corn laid on the bed. After the visit to the cattle and horses my informant's father . . . came back to the dwelling-house with a sheaf of unthreshed grain, and laid a ' pickle ' of it over each bed. [*Ethnog. Survey of the U. Kingdom*, 5th Report (1897), p. 457.] Cf. also **V k.**　　　Galloway.

V f. *Household customs.* See entries under **V b.**

V g. *Fishermen's customs. About wakening others.* It is the common custom, when it is sea-going weather, to proceed to the fishing ground early in the morning. When one of a crew awakes, he gets out of bed, dresses, and goes to awake the rest of the crew as well as others. But on New Year's

morning no one will waken his neighbour in case bad luck
for the year may follow. [J. E. Cr.]   N.E. Scot.
    Seaweed brought in. See V b. above.
    Fine for bad luck on New Year's Day. Fishermen go in crews,
and each fisherman has his own lines and affords bait for them,
but the fish caught goes into a common stock and each gets
an equal share. An account of each man's catch was kept
during the year, and the one that had the smallest catch had
to pay a fine or ' pay the kyarlin ' to the rest of the crew on
New Year's Day. The fine commonly consisted of a ' dram ',
that is, so much whisky. Sometimes it might be bread and
cheese.   ·   Pitullie, Ab.
    At times a dried cod or other fish's head or something else,
a bundle of rags, an old barrel, was stuck on the chimney of
the unfortunate man's house. [Rev. W. Gregor.]
                                              Buchanhaven, Ab.
    First arrivals have luck. On the first day of the New Year
there was always great endeavour to be the first to reach the
harbour from the fishing ground and to be the first to throw
the fish ashore. [*Ibid.*]   Buchanhaven, Ab.
    The one that lands the first fish on New Year's Day has
most luck in the village during the year. Two boats were
vieing with each other which should first land fish. The one
boat was gaining on the other, and the skipper of the other
seeing that it would reach the harbour first ran his boat along-
side a rock where there was deep water. When near enough
the rock a fish was seized and thrown ashore before the other
boat touched land. [*Ibid.*]   Burghead, Ab.
    First fish spared. The first fish that falls off the line in hauling
the first shot on New Year's Day is not caught in the ' ave '
by the ' skimmer ' but allowed to fall back into the sea.
Unless this is done there is no luck. [*Ibid.*]   Avoch, Rs.
    The first to draw blood. It was a matter of great moment to
be the first on New Year's day to ' draw bleed '. Some
fishermen had the habit of taking the fish that was first hauled
into the boat when they were at sea on that morning, ' craig-
ing ' it, i.e. breaking its neck, squeezing some blood out of it
and rubbing it over their hands. [*Ibid.*] (Told by C. Sim,
who has seen it done, Pitullie.)
    To ' draw blood ' is practised in some of the fishing villages
on the N.E. coast of Scotland, under the belief that success
follows the act. This act must be performed on New Year's
Day and the good fortune is his only who is first to shed blood.
If the morning of the New Year is (favourable), there is quite

a struggle as to which boat will reach the fishing ground first, so as to gain the coveted prize, the first-shed blood of the year. If the weather is unfavourable for fishing, those in possession of guns . . . are out, gun in hand, along the shore before daybreak, in search of some bird or wild animal, no matter how small, that they may draw blood and thus make sure of one year's good fortune. [Rev. W. Gregor, *N. & Q*. IV, p. 11.] N.E. Scot.

Cf. *Blood must be shed*. The dinner on New-Year's day was always more dainty than usual. At it was served up a hen or a duck killed that morning. Among the first acts of the guid-wife on that morning was to go to the hen-house, select a victim, kill it, and make it ready for cooking for dinner. Blood had to be shed on the morning of the new year.—Pit-sligo. Told by one who has seen her mother do it. [*F.-L. J.*, Vol. II (1884), p. 332.]　　　　　　　　　　　　　　　　Ab.

V h. *Water customs. The flower of the well, uisge coisrichte.* At twelve o'clock on New Year's eve (or Hogmanay as we call it), just when the Old Year lies dying, a curious virtue comes into the wells and ponds. . . . In the mysterious crucible far below some occult elixir is liberated which floats on the top ; and so the water is eagerly drunk, with a never-dying faith in its power as a philtre. [Miss E. M. Johnstone, *The Graphic*, Jan. 7th, 1893.]

The fetching of water from the well—' creaming the well ' as it is called—appears from replies to my enquiries in different parts of the county to have been almost universally the first thing done on New Year's Day morning. [J. E. Cr., *F.-L.* IV (1893), p. 318.]　　　　　　　　　　　　　　　　　　　　　Ab.

This (skimming the well) they call ' getting the *scum* or ream (cream) of the well '. [Jamieson.]　　　　　　　　　S. Scot.

' Creaming the well ' was a custom followed by not a few when several families drew water from the same well, and in hamlets and villages where there was one or more common wells. The one that wished to get the luck of the year watched at the well till it struck twelve o'clock, and the moment the new year was begun drew water from it.

In some parts, for example in some of the fishing villages on the coast of Aberdeenshire, a little grass was plucked and thrown into the pail among the water. [Rev. W. Gregor.]
N.E. Scot.

The water first drawn . . . was called ' the floor o' the wall ', i.e. the flower of the well. Whoever was the first to draw water got all the luck of the year. [*Ibid.*]　　Dyke, Ab.

The . . . custom was to make for the nearest well in time to secure before any of your neighbours what was variously called the ' crop ', the ' floo'er ', or the ' ream ' of the water for the New Year. The custom was restricted to the women of the hamlet or homestead ; in some localities only the young unmarried women. [Haliburton, *Furth in Field* (1894), p. 29.]

The flower of the well brings marriage.

> Twall' struck—Twa neebor hizzies raise,
> An', liltin', gaed a sad gate ;
> ' The flower o' the well to our house gaes,
> An' I'll the bon[n]iest lad get.'

Note.—Upon the morning of the first day of the New Year, the county lassies are sure to rise as early as possible, . . . that they may get the *flower*, . . . or the first pail-full of water, from the well. The girl who is so lucky as to obtain that prize, is supposed to have more than a double chance of gaining the most accomplished young man in the parish. As they go to the well, they chant over the words which are marked with inverted commas. [Rev. James Nicol, *Poems, Chiefly in the Scottish Dialect* (1805), I, p. 80.]   S. Scot.

Luck in water. The girls there (Arran), always when they go up on the morning of the New Year to Mrs MacK. take a bottle of clean spring water with them.

I was getting J. C. to plough my land for me every year and he would be first footing me at the New Year. I said to him one time, ' Now, John, you need take nothing with you when you are coming here but a bottle of clean pure water.' He said, ' I'll tak stronger than that,' but I said, ' I would rather the water for it is lucky.' [Mlan MS.]   Arran, Ayr.

Cf. *Water customs* also under **V** b., **V** c. and **V** e.

Water from the dead and living ford.

A ford over which the living pass and the dead are carried. [Ed.]

The water from this ford, drawn in the most profound silence, the vessel containing it not allowed to touch the ground, and drunk early on New Year's day, preserves the Highlander from all direful calamities proceeding from the agency of infernal spirits, witchcraft, evil eye, and the like. [*Pop. Superstitions*, p. 253.]   Hghlds.

For *Legend* see **VI** below.

V j. *Scapegoat.* On the morning of New Year's Day it is usual, in some parts of Breadalbane, to take a dog to the door and drive him out, pronouncing these words, ' Get away you dog! Whatever death of men, or loss of cattle, would happen in this house to the end of the present year, may it all light on your head! ' (translation). [*Scot. and Scotsmen in the 18th Cent. MSS. of John Ramsay of Ochtertyre* (b. 1736), II, p. 439. Ed. by Alex. Allardyce (1888).]   Central Perthshire.

The custom of driving out the dog or cat, the dog with a bunch of straw bound to its tail and set alight, is reported also from Barra, Hebrides. ' Fortunately less common now than it once was.' [Mlan MS.]   Barra, Hdes.

Bloodshedding. See entry under **V g.** above. *Reminiscence of the ' slaying of the wren '.* On the morning of New Year's Day the boys used to go in companies to catch wrens. When one was caught its legs and neck were decked with ribbons. It was then set at liberty. This ceremony was called ' the deckan' o' the wran '. My informant has assisted at the ceremony. [*Ethnog. Survey of the U. Kingdom*, 5th Report (1897), p. 457.]
Galloway.

18th Century Song, *Hunting the Wren* :

' Will ye go to the wood? ' quo' Fozie Mozie ;
' Will ye go to the wood? ' quo' Johnnie Rednosie ;
' Will ye go to the wood? ' quo' Foslin 'ene ;
' Will ye go to the wood? ' quo' brither and kin.

' What to do there? ' quo' Fozie Mozie, etc.
' To slay the wren,' quo' Fozie Mozie, etc.
' What way will ye get her hame? ' quo' Fozie Mozie, etc.
' We'll hire carts and horse,' quo' Fozie Mozie, etc.
' What way will ye get her in? ' quo' Fozie Mozie, etc.
' We'll drive down the door-cheeks,' quo' Fozie Mozie, etc.

' I'll hae a wing,' quo' Fozie Mozie ;
' I'll hae anither,' quo' Johnnie Rednosie ;
' I'll hae a leg,' quo' Foslin 'ene ;
' And I'll hae anither,' quo' brither and kin.'

[D. Herd, *Collection of Scottish Songs, etc.* (1776), Vol. II, pp. 210 f.]

In Scotland the wren is called ' the Lady of Heaven's hen ', and boys say :

Malisons, malisons, mair than ten,
That harry the Ladye of Heaven's hen!

Also,

The robin and the wren
Are God's cock and hen.
[*Popular Rhymes*,[3] p. 159.]

V k. *Gifts and doles.* 1657. The first day of this yeir . . . the pepill observit the old ancient, bot beggerlie, custom, in seeking, craving, and begging handsell ; many superstitiouslie believing that thai could not thryve all that yeir except thai haid gottin a New Yeir's gift. [Nicoll, *Diary* (Bannatyne Club) (1836), p. 191.]

Cattle and horses have a special meal. My informant was in the habit of giving a small quantity of unthreshed grain to each of the horses and cattle on the farm on the morning of New Year's Day, and wishing each a happy New Year, and saying to each as the fodder was given : 'That's your hansel.' [*Ethnog. Survey of the U. Kingdom*, 5th Report (1897), p. 457.]
Galloway.

Burns refers to this practice in ' The Auld Farmer's Address to his Mare ', when presenting her on New-Year's morning with an extra feed of corn :

> A guid New-year I wish thee, Maggie!
> Hae, there's a ripp to thy auld baggie!

[Chambers' *Book of Days*, vol. ii, p. 752.] Stg.
The cattle were not forgotten on New Year's Day as a good extra sheaf of unthreshed corn given to them was supposed to insure plenty throughout the coming year. [A. Gunn and J. Mackay, *Sutherland and the Reay Country, etc.* (1897), p. 132.]
Sld.

An old custom that used, long ago, to be pretty general among Islay people. . . . In cases of farmers who would have cottars living on their farm, every New Year day morning, the farmer's wife would come to the door of every cottar on the farm with a sheaf of corn—*sguab arbhair*—which she would leave for the cottar's cow. At that time nearly every cottar had a cow ; and the corn sheaf was greatly valued as a token of friendship and goodwill at the beginning of a New Year. [Mlan MS.] Islay, Ar.

Gifts at Court. Gift-bestowing on the morning of New Year's Day obtained generally. On the first of January, 1489, the Treasurer presented to James IV a personal ' offerande ' ; he also handed the king, while still in bed, ten angellis, that is £12, that he might therewith make gifts to his royal household.[1] The existence of a custom remembering first-foot is, in the Treasurer's Account, . . . ' The X of Januare 1496 giffin to Sandi Ellem Patrick Homes man, that brocht tithingis

---

[1] Treasurer's Accounts, i, pp. 127, 171.

to the King of the first bargane in the new yere, five Scottis Crownis, an vnicorne, and half a ridare ; summary, £4 . 16 . 2.[1]   [Rogers, *Social Life in Scotland,*, II, pp. 336-7.]

On the first of January, 1664, New Year's Day, my husband (Sir Richard Fanshawe), as Privy Counsellor, presented his Majesty with ten pieces of gold in a purse ; and the person that carries it hath a ticket given him of the receipt thereof, from the cupboard of Privy Chamber, where it is delivered to the Master of the Jewel-House, who is thereupon to give him twenty shillings for his pains, out of which he is to give to the servants of the Master of the Jewel-House eighteen pence. We received, as the custom is, fifteen ounces of gilt plate for a Privy Counsellor, and fifteen ounces for Secretary of the Latin Tongue ; likewise we had impost of four tuns of Wine, two for a Privy Counsellor, and two for a Master of Requests. [*Lady Fanshawe's Memoirs*, ed. 1830, p. 162.]

V k. and V m. *Food, etc.* The water-carriers and milk-women, in their daily visits to their customers, were treated (at New Year) with a dram and cheese and bread or buns. [*Time's Telescope* for 1824, p. 3.]   Edin.

In some places the well-to-do farmer's wife left a little (of the sowens) overnight (New Year's night), at the house of every poor man on the farm. [*Wcrft. & Sec. Sight*, p. 238.]
                                                                Hghlds.

The custom of giving *noor-cakes* (New Year's cakes) to children of those . . . in the lower walks of life is . . . generally practised. . . . The Cottagers' children go to the doors of those who are in more opulent circumstances, chaunt over the *hogmoney* song, filled with wishes for prosperity of the family, and receive . . . a cake made of oatmeal, called a *hogmanay* or *noor cake*. [Rev. James Nicol, *Poems, Chiefly in the Scottish Dialect* (1805), Note to poem on the Daft Days, I, p. 27.]   S. Scot.

Fish. It was looked on as lucky to receive a present of fish on the morning of the New Year. [Rev. W. Gregor.]
                                                                N.E. Scot.

V 1. *Begging.* Very often on New Year's Day companies of young men in twos, threes, and fours set out shortly after breakfast to ' thigg ' for an old woman, or an old man, or an aged couple, or an invalid that might be in narrow circumstances. Carrying a sack to receive the alms of meal and a

---

[1] Treasurer's Accounts, i, p. 307.

PLATE IV

Burnet Pinx.ᵗ   Stewart & Burnet Sculp.ᵗ

AULD FARMER'S SALUTATION.

A GUID NEW-YEAR I WISH THEE MAGGIE,

HAE, THERE'S A RIPP TO THY AULD BAGGIE:

R. BURNS.

small bag for the money, they travelled over a good many
miles of the district of the country in which they lived, getting
a ' bossiefu ' of meal from this guidewife and a contribution
of money from this other one. They usually sang the following
song :

> The guide new year it is begun,
>   B' soothan, b' soothan,
> The beggars they're begun to run,
>   An awa b' mony a toon.
> Rise up gueedewife, an dinna be swear,
>   B' soothan, b' soothan,
> An deal yir chirity t' the peer,
>   An awa b' mony a toon.
> May your bairnies n'er be peer,
>   B' soothan, b' soothan,
> Nor yet yir coo misgae the steer,
>   An awa b' mony a toon.
> It's nae for oorsels it we come here,
>   B' soothan, b' soothan,
> It's for . . . sae scant o' gear,
>   An awa b' mony a toon.
> We sing for meal, we sing for maut,
>   B' soothan, b' soothan,
> We sing for cheese an a'thing fat,
>   An awa b' mony a toon.
> Fess neither cog nor yet the mutty,
>   B' soothan, b' soothan,
> Bit fess the peck fou' lairge and lucky,
>   An awa b' mony a toon.
> The roads are slippery, we canna rin,
>   B' soothan, b' soothan,
> We maun myne oor feet for fear we fa',
>   An rin b' mony a toon.

Then came the question : ' Are ye gueede for beggars? '
' Sometimes,' was the answer, followed by the question, ' Fah
are ye beggin' for? ' ' For so-and-so.' The alms was then
given, and then came the words of thanks, which were often
improvised in a kind of doggerel.

The young men were invited to sit down, and partake of the
New Year's hospitality. The invitation was refused with the
words, ' Na, na, sittin' beggars cunna speed.' The whisky
bottle and the Yeel kebback were forthwith produced ; or, if
whisky was refused, ale. The thiggars partook of the good
things, and set out again.

When the bag of meal became too heavy to be carried conveniently, it was left in some house, and another bag was substituted. By such an action as much meal and money were collected for many a poor old worthy as, supplemented by a small sum from the ' peers' box ', kept want from the door.

' *Thiggars* ' were people who beg in a genteel way, who have their houses they call at in certain seasons. See *The Gallovidian Encyclopedia* (1824), p. 445. [Greg., pp. 160-162.]
N.E. Scot.

(When a case of distress occurred about New Year) it was a common practice for sympathisers to go round among the neighbours soliciting charity, accompanied by some one who could play an accompaniment on the fiddle or bagpipes to the following ditty :

[Shortened form of song quoted above.]
[*Sc. N. & Q.* I (1888), p. 163.]   Ab.

†In the beginning of the present century the following verses used to be sung as a New Year's greeting by a Collieston fishwife to her customers in Udny :

> Here begins a gweed New Year,
>   Be soothin', be soothin',
> An' joy an' peace an' a' be here
>   An' awa' by Lunnon toonie.
>
> By Baerniesdell and Coventree
>   Be soothin', be soothin',
> An' up and doon the hail countree
>   An' awa' by Lunnon toonie.
>
> Rise up good wife an' binna swear,
>   Be soothin', be soothin',
> An' gie's a dram to grace the year
>   An' awa' by Lunnon toonie.

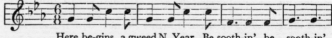

Here be-gins a gweed N. Year, Be sooth-in', be   sooth-in',

Joy an' peace an' a' be here, An' a- wa' by Lunnon too-nie.

[*Sc. N. & Q.* I, p. 140.]   Ab.

Thigging Rhymes :

1 She has neither coo nor hog,
    Be soothin', Be soothin',
  Bit a bonny dame and a dainty dog
    An' awa' to soothin' toon.

The above song was sung at Braco. (Dainty was the dog's
ame.)

2 Rise up guid wife and dinna be sweer,
  An' deal yer charitie to the peer ;
    Be soothin', be soothin',
  An' gin ye dinna lift yer han',
  We'll mak ye sure, o' a verse o' wir sang,
    An' awa' be soothin' toon.

Iere's the threat—

3 The maiden o' Millegin she gangs sae braw,
    A' soothin', A' soothin',
  Till never a penny had she awa'
    An' awa' be soothin' toon.

4 For the tailor he ance geed ower the score
  An' put the back o' the breeks afore,
    An' awa' be soothin' toon.

Rev. W. Gregor.]   N.E. Scot.
In this part of the country (Dinnet, Ab.) those carrying
owens from house to house were generally a band of young
olks of both sexes ; they approached each house in turn
there was no first-foot among them), chanting this ditty :

Rise up, good wife, and shake your feathers,
  Rise up and be na sweer,
For here we've come wi' our Yule sowens,
  And fain would taste your cheer.

f they were refused admittance, the door was liberally
espattered with sowens in revenge.—Communicated by Rev.
Ir Michie of Dinnet. [J. E. Cr., *F.-L.* IV, p. 317.]   Ab.
  Cf. **V a.** above.
[Others consulted by J. E. Crombie did not agree that
owens were sprinkled in revenge.]
  Dr Moresin tells us that in Scotland it was in his time the
ustom to *send* New Year's gifts on New Year's Eve, but that
on New Year's Day they wished each other a happy day, and
sked a New Year's gift. [J. Brand, *Pop. Antiquities of Gt.
Britain*, Ellis's ed. (1849), p. 15.] Cf. **V k.**

V m. *Food and drink.   Sowens.*   On getting up in the mornin
the head of the family treated all the household to a dram
After that a spoonful of half-boiled sowens, the poorest foo
imaginable, was given for luck. . . .   The custom of having th
dish of sowens was known in the central Highlands, and in Lorr
but does not seem to have extended to Mull, Morvern, or th
Western Islands.   [*Wcrft. & Sec. Sight*, p. 238.]   Hghld

Sowens is a concoction something like gruel, but is mad
from the dust of the oatmeal, mixed with the husks of th
corn, which are left to steep till they become sour.   [J. E. Cr.

Whisky, bread and cheese.   My informant's father was in th
habit of bringing whisky with bread and cheese into eacl
sleeping apartment and of giving each one a ' dram ', i.e.
little of the whisky, along with some of the bread and cheese
[*Ethnog. Survey of the U. Kingdom*, 5th Report (1897), p. 457.

For the entertainment of the ' first fit ' on . . . New Year'
Day and of other friends that may call during the day, i
prepared ' chittert ', i.e. pressed and cooled so as to be cut i
slices.   This, along with bread and cheese, is placed on a tabl
all ready for use.   [*Ibid.*]   Galloway

Feasting.   The reciter says that he remembers when he wa
young, they commenced their feasting on Hogmanay, an
kept it up, going backward and forward to each other'
houses till Handsel Monday (*Di-luain an t-sainnseil*)—that wa
the second Monday after the New Year's day.   [Mlan MS.
                                                    Islay, Ar

Clubbing for drink.   On the morning of the New Year, it i
common for neighbours to go into each other's houses, and t
club their money in order to send out for drink, to welcome i
the year.   This is done in private houses.   [Jamieson.]   N. Scot

Haggis.   A day or two before Hogmanay a haggis has beer
cooked and set aside to cool.   On Hogmanay it is laid out or
a table with a knife beside it.   When the ' first fit ' ha
finished his congratulations he helps himself to a slice of th
haggis, and walks away.   Each one that calls afterwards doe
the same.   The custom still exists, but not to such an extent
as in days of old.   [*Ethnog. Survey of the U. Kingdom*, 4th Repor
(1897), pp. 14, 15.]   Minnigaff, Galloway

Eaten with oaten cakes.   [*Ibid.*]   Inch, Galloway

Treacle bannocks.   A kind of bannocks, called ' treacle
bannocks ' used to be made for use about the New Year
They were composed of oatmeal with treacle added.   Sometimes carraway seeds were added.   [*Ibid.*, 5th Report (1897),
p. 465.]

In the morning we children got our bannocks (baked on
Hogmanay) to breakfast. They were small, and it was un-
lucky to leave any portion of them. [Napier, Appendix,
p. 160.]   Partick, Lnk.
Cross on bannocks. Before women bake their bannocks, or
oatmeal cakes, they form a cross on the last they make. [Th.
Pennant, *Tour in Scot.*[4] (1769), p. 115.]   N. Scot.
Fish. Fish in some form or other used to be served up as
part of the breakfast on the morning of New Year's Day.
Ethnog. Survey of the U. Kingdom, 5th Report (1897), p. 457.]
See also entries under **V k**. *Doles and gifts*, above.

V n. *Tricks and pranks. Indoor games.* Next morning (New
Year's day) when some of the people tried to open their doors,
they would find their egress barred by a collection of carts
and wheelbarrows, or by a fishing-boat drawn up from the
beach. Others had their windows boarded or built up with
bricks, while signboards would be removed and re-erected
elsewhere. . . .   [*The Gallovidian*, X, p. 23.]
                                                 Garlieston, Wtn.
Early in the morning all the principal streets were rendered
impassable by boats stolen from the beach and turned bottom
uppermost, most of the doors were barricaded from the outside
with props and pieces of wood, to furnish which almost every
temporary structure in the village was demolished . . . ; house-
roofs were climbed for the purpose of dropping stones and
mud into the ' Sowens '. . . .   Young Burgheadians . . . tried
the experiment of fishing with hook and line out of the pot
from the chimney. [Alex. Jeffrey, Junr., *Sketches from the
traditional Hist. of Burghead* (1928), pp. 12 f.]
                                            Burghead, Morayshire.
Scarcely had the chimes of the Old Year died away when
the village youths were busy at the time-honoured custom of
removing the mortar-stone to the door of the young lady
whom they wished to see joined in wedlock during the year.
[F.-L. XX (1909), p. 482.]   Fordyce, Bf.
The day is terminated with . . . card-parties. [*Time's
Telescope* (1825), p. 5.]
Creeling. (The day after the wedding in former days) it
was customary to *creel* the bridegroom. Having procured a
creel or wicker basket, they tied it to the back of the young
gentleman and placed a long pole with a broom affixed to
the top over his left shoulder. Thus equipped he was forced
to run a race, followed by his young gudewife with a knife to

cut the cords. About forty or fifty years ago . . . the custom
was deferred to New Year's day. Accordingly on this morning
the young men of the village assemble, provided with a wicke
hamper or crockery crate filled with stones with which they
visit the houses of all those who have entered the bonds of
matrimony during the preceding year, and compel the young
gudeman to bear the creel to his nearest neighbour who may
have qualified himself for the honour. [*N.S.A.* V. i.]

Dalry, Ayr

' Creeling ' is reported as enacted ' once a year or oftener
at Eccles, Berwick. The unmarried men try to fill the married
man's basket with stones as he runs. The wife follows, armed
with a knife, and attempts to cut the rope attaching the baske
to her husband's shoulders. [*Ibid.*, II, iii, p. 59.] Berwick

In the W. Highlands women filled the basket with stones
the wife cuts the cord. [Pennant,[4] p. 206.]

VI. Beliefs in the Supernatural, Witchcraft, etc.

Will o' the Wisp. There is a light yonder that is sometimes
seen about the time of the New Year. The name they have
on it is Willie Wisp. It is not carried by any person, but it
just comes to lead people astray. [Mlan MS.]   Islay, Ar

Sac ban. The *sac ban* was something in shape like a large
bag stuffed with wool. It was white, and would be seen
rolling along before people on the ground. When it wanted
to play tricks on anybody it got about his feet and tripped
him, and if it tumbled a man it would roll over him and this it
might repeat several times. It was always at night it was seen
and an old Islay-man adds that it was mostly about New Year
day time. [*Ibid.*]   *Ibid.*

Water turned into wine. On the first of the year, says an old
legend, did Christ at Cana of Galilee turn water into wine.
And as Christ blessed the waters on that day, so now, when
the midnight hour peals forth, do all the waters of the earth
become wine. [*Old Times*, p. 150.]

IX. Mumming, Guizing, etc.
During Christmas week a
band of boys go from house to house and act a drama in the
various kitchens. These boys are locally known as White
Boys, a name of Irish origin. In the border counties they are
called Guizards or Galatians, the last name being the name of
the play which they act. From the structure of its verse I
believe it dates back to the time of Ralph Royster Doyster.

The boys are dressed with large hats decorated with
coloured paper, supposed to be a ludicrous copy of the Bishop's

mitre, long white shirts and wooden swords complete their costume. Alexander of Macedon sometimes appears, ornamented with curtain-rings in nose and ears, which is supposed to surround him with a pleasing Oriental atmosphere. The devil appears at the close with a broom and a sooty face, and sweeps bad luck in or out, with a guileless impartiality, according to the douceur which he receives. [Miss E. M. Johnstone, ' New Year's Customs,' *The Graphic*, Jan. 7, 1893.]
Galloway.

When gloamin' gray comes frae the east,
Through a' the *gysarts* venture.

Note.—A company of boys, generally about half a dozen, blacken their faces, put on their shirts uppermost, and with a helmet and sword, armed cap-à-pie, go to the neighbouring houses, and personating the characters of Alexander, Caesar, etc., act a certain interlude, which is handed down from father to son. A few pence reward their . . . endeavours to please. [Rev. James Nicol, *Poems, Chiefly in the Scottish Dialect* (1805), I, p. 29.]
S. Scot.

Guizing amongst the younger portion of the community was largely in evidence.
N. Berwick.

Bands of youngsters were out ' guizanting '. [D. Rorie, *F.-L.* XX, p. 481.]
Kelso, Rxb.

XI. Games, racing, mock combats. For X see pp. 117-8.

Shinty. The chief game in Scotland at New Year was Shinty, or Shinny, the second probably the oldest form of the name. Played with a bent or curved stick, the *caman*, its Gaelic name was *Camanachd*, shortened to *Cammock* ; it was also known as *Iomain*, driving, though this name applied as well to football, or any game in which a ball was driven forward. It is honourable as a game for heroes in early Irish as well as Gaelic legend, and may be introduced by two references from *Waifs & Strays of Celtic Trad.*, Argyll Series, II (1890). In the Herding of Cruachan, the youngest son of the herdsman plays *camanachd* with the wizard-champion (*gruagach*) three times, using a golden ball and a silver shinty (stick), on the enchanted hill. This Cruachan is the Roscommon Cruachan, the ancient palace of the kings of Connaught, pp. 97 *et seq.*

In the tale of Young Manus, son of the King of Lochlann, after being thrown over the cliff by his nurse, Young Manus plays shinty on the shore with a silver ball and a golden shinty, p. 343.

The Rev. J. Ninian MacDonald, of St Benedict's Abbey, Fort Augustus (1932), quotes an ancient training school for young heroes at Skye, where *camanachd* was part of the curriculum. Specially of Scottish interest are, Deirdre watching Naoise play shinty (Doug. Hyde, in *Zeit. f. Celt. Phil.*, II, p. 138) ; Finn playing the game (*Rev. Celt.*, V, p. 197), and references to it in J. F. Campbell's *Tales of the W. Highlands.* Conall Gulban, son of the great Niall, played with a club of elder.

The game of shinny is usually played at this season. . . . New Year's Day old style. . . . To drive the ball from one goal to the other is called *leth bhair*, a half hale (goal) ; to drive it back again is called *bair*, a hale ; and to win a goal at a man's game is nearly as great a feat as to gain a battle. In some parts of the Highlands hundreds used to be engaged, all excited to a degree. [J. F. Campbell, *Tales of the W. Highlands*, New ed. (1892), III, p. 28.]

The first New Year's Day game was ' club and Shinty '. The method we observed was this—two points were marked out, the one the starting point, and the other the goal, or ' hail '. Then two leaders were chosen by a sort of ballot, which consisted in casting a club up into the air between the two ranks into which the players were divided. The leaders thus chosen stood out from the rest, and from the number present, alternately called a boy to his standard. The Shinty or Shinny, a ball of wood, was then inserted into the ground, and the leaders with their clubs struck at it till they got it out again. The heat of the game, or battle as I might call it, then began. The one party laboured hard, and most keenly, to drive the ball to the opposite point or ' hail ', the other to drive it across the boundary to the starting-point ; and which party soever did either carried the day. In my younger years the game was universal in the north. Men of all ages among the working classes joined in it, especially on old New Year's day. I distinctly recollect of seeing, on such joyous occasions at Dornoch, the whole male population, from the grey-headed grandfather to the lightest-heeled stripling, turn out to the links, each with his club ; and, from 11 o'clock in the forenoon, till it became dark, they would keep at it, with all the keenness, accompanied by shouts, with which their forefathers had wielded the claymore. It was withal a most dangerous game, both to young and old. When the two parties met midway between the two points, with their blood up, their tempers heated, and clubs in their hands, the game then assumed all the features of a personal quarrel ; and wounds were inflicted, either with the club or the ball which, in not a few instances, actually proved fatal. [Rev. D. Sage, *Memorabilia Domestica* (1889), edited by his son, p. 158.]

Dornoch, Sld.

Rules of the Game. Rules have differed at divers times and in divers places, but the leading features have remained untouched. A modern account is :

It was played with a ball (*liathroid*) about four inches in diameter, made of some light elastic material, such as woollen yarn wound round and round and covered with leather. Sometimes a rounded piece of wood, a ball of twisted hair, a cork, or even part of the vertebral bone of a sheep, or a gnarl or knob from the trunk of a tree, carefully fashioned into a globular shape (and later termed a ' nag, not, cad, gad, cor, coit or golley ') was substituted. . . . Each player had a wooden club with which to strike the ball ; it was frequently made of ash, about three feet in length, carefully shaped and smoothed, and with the lower end flat and curved, and it was usually called a caman (cammoc, or camman), though we also find in the old writings, lorg . . ., bunsach and bachall, later a shinny, shinty, hurlay, hurlett, doddart, etc.

In a regular match the players on either side were equal in number. It was played on a more or less level and grassy field or plain. At each end of the delimited ground the boundary or objective was clearly designated. Sometimes the objective consisted merely of a gap (berna, for beàrn?) in a hedge or wall ; sometimes it was the space between two trees, bushes or other fixed objects. The length of territory between the objective of one party and that of the other varied considerably—from a hundred yards to several miles.

The game was begun by throwing up the ball in the middle of the field of play ; this was done by some neutral person, alternately the ball was buried in the sand. The players endeavoured to drive the ball with their camans towards their objective. Whichever party succeeding in first reaching a boundary or goal was adjudged to have scored a ' leth-baire ' (lit. half a goal) ; the teams then made an . . . *about turn*, and exchanged objectives. If the previous scorers succeeded in driving the ball again to the objective, they were deemed to have scored a ' baire ' [for *bàir*] (full goal), and the contest came to an end. . . .

In Scotland we also find another term employed instead of baire [*bàir*] to denote **a** scoring hit, viz. hail. . . . *Leth-thadhaill*, and *tadhall* correspond to the older terms . . . and

H   C.C.S. II meant ' half a visit ' and ' a visit '. [Rev. J. Ninian Macdonald, *Shinty* (1932), pp. 57-59.]

Towards midday (on New Year's day) the men gathered in some suitable place, the largest and most level field in the neighbourhood, for the great Shinty match. . . . A match was formed between adjoining districts and villages, or, if the village itself was populous, by two leaders, appointed for the purpose, choosing one alternately from those present till the whole gathering was gone through. It was decided who was to choose first by one of the leaders holding his shinty stick (*caman*) vertically, or up and down, and throwing it to the other, who caught it somewhere about the middle. The two then grasped the stick alternately, the hand of the one being close above that of the other, and the one who grasped the end, so that he could swing the stick three times round his head, had the first choice. Sometimes to decide the point quickly, one asked the other which he would have, ' foot or palm ' (*cas no bas*), meaning which end of the shinty stick he made choice of, the ' foot ' being that by which the stick is held, the ' palm ' that with which the ball is struck. On a choice being made the club was thrown into the air and the matter was decided by the point of it which pointed southwardly.

In the game a wooden ball was used in the day time, when men could guard themselves against being struck by it, but when the game was played at night, in the dusk or by moonlight, a ball of hair or thread called *crìod* [*cneut*] was used. The object of the game was to drive this ball a ' hail ' (*tadhal*), that is between and beyond certain marks at the two ends of the field. Of course the two parties had opposite ' hails '. The play commenced by setting the ball in a suitable place, and giving the first blow . . . to the chief, proprietor, priest, minister, or other principal person present. A player stood opposite to him, and if the ball was missed at the first blow, as sometimes happened, whipped it away from him in the opposite direction, and without further ceremony every person ran after it as he chose, and hit it as he got opportunity. Two or three of the best players on each side were kept behind their party, ' behind hail ' (*Air chùl tahail*), to act as a guard when their adversaries too nearly sent the ball ' home '. A piper played before and after the game. . . . At the end the chief, or laird, gave a dinner, or, failing him, a number were entertained at the house of a mutual friend. In the evening a ball was given, open to all. [*Wcrft. & Sec. Sight*, pp. 239-241.]

Hghlds. and W. Isles.

In some parts of the country the Shinty, called in Gaelic *Caman*, was long and played with both hands, but in Kintyre it was always short, and played with one hand. It was made of any suitable wood, ash and elder being much in demand, especially elder for its lightness and good wearing qualities. The part which lay to the ground, and with which the ball was struck was called the ' Bass ', and, in the making, great care was taken to give that part a proper bevel with the view of lifting the ball well from the ground. A good shinty was an object of ambition and pride.

The ball was made of elder usually, but sometimes of harder wood, and was about the size of an orange. [*Trans. Gaelic Soc. of Inverness*, II, p. 39.]

Till late in the 18th century shinty used to be played to and from the church. [*Ibid.*, XXX, p. 47.]   Hghlds.

The rules of the game were unwritten ; . . . but universally well known, and generally strictly adhered to. [Mlan MS.]   Kintyre, Ar.

The game was called Knotty in the northern counties. [J. S. Mackay, *Stirling Nat. Hist. and Archaeol. Soc.*, March 1912, p. 92.]   N. Scot.

Cuaill. The young men engaged in a game of Ball on New Year's Day. The ball was driven by crooked sticks called ' cammocks ', and the game went by the name of ' *cuwaill* ' [*cuaill*, club]. [J. E. Cr.]   Kingussie, Iness.

Clubbing. The game of Ball was played at New Year's Day. It was driven by a ' club ' or ' scuddie '. Some weeks before the New Year those intending to play went to the woods to cut suitable sticks, so that they might have them dried and suitably prepared. On the day the players met . . . two were selected as chiefs, and they chose their party man by man. When all were chosen they arranged themselves in two lines facing each other with a space between sufficiently wide to play the game. At one end of the course was the ball, and at the other a jar of whisky or ' a pigfou ' [*pig*, a small pot or jar, *pigfou*, a potfull]. The chief of the party that had to drive the ball to the other end sent it off. The aim of his men was to catch it up and drive it along the open space between the line of players. The aim of the opposing party was to drive it back and to prevent it from reaching the goal. Thus backwards and forwards went the ball between the two companies till it reached the goal where the jar of whisky lay, when all partook of the whisky. This game went by the name of ' clubbing '. [J. E. Cr.] Fodderty, Contin, Rs.

Kyles, ' *a bawbee she kyles* '.† At Kirkcaldy ' the ruins of Ravenscraig Castle and adjacent grounds were, in accordance with an old custom, thrown open by the new proprietor of Dysart House. . . . There the ancient Scottish game of " She Kyles " was played.' ' She Kyles ', Mr. Mackinlay tells me, is nine-pins. . . . [M. Peacock, *F.-L.* VIII (1897), p. 174.]   Ffe.

Kyles, from the French *feu de quilles*, the Fr. game of nine-pins. [*Sc. N. & Q.*, 3rd Series, V (1927), p. 53.]

Cf. also the German game, called *Kegel*. [*Ibid.*, p. 71.]

It was long a wont of the inhabitants of Pathhead to have the entry of Ravenscraig Castle on Auld Hansel Monday. They amused themselves with a variety of games, one of which is at least worthy of being recorded as a contribution to folk-lore. An iron ring was stuck into the ground so as to stand upright ; a player then took a heavy iron ball, and, retiring to a distance, rolled it towards the hoop. The spectators, ranged in lines up the ground, immediately formed bets, generally of a penny, as to whether the ball would pass through the ring or not. When it *did* go through, the ball was said to ' kyle '. The players were in the custom of throwing their stakes on the ground—crying out ' A penny it kyles! '—' A penny it doesna'! ' and so on. Of course, if the ball missed, the players betting on its kyling lost, and *vice versa*.

                                                                                 Pathhead, Ffe.

Another Account.—This game is played annually on the first day of the year on the rough sward in front of the castle, a number of holes—nine, I think—being roughly scooped out, and while the player, who has an iron ball, endeavours from a stipulated distance, to kyle—or coil?—it into a certain hole, spectators line the course and bet on the result in the words ' A penny she kyles! ' ' A penny she doesna'! ' [*C. F.-L.* VII, pp. 149 f.]

The game played also at Wemyss with a metal ball and a leather thong. [*F.-L.* XX (1909), p. 481.]

Bowls. The all but obsolete game of ' bowls ' was indulged in (on New Year's day) on the links, by about fifty people. [*F.-L.* XX (1909), p. 481.]   Dornoch, Sld.

Mock combats. *Cock-fighting.* The day of the cock-fighting was a great day in Uist in olden times. The reciter says it was on New Year's Day and her father said they used to collect the cocks carefully and feed them on special food for some time beforehand. When the day came they repaired to the beach where there would be a great gathering of people. The gentry of the place ... gave prizes to the best fighting cocks. [Mlan MS.] Cf. *cock-fighting at Hogmanay*.]

Uist and W. Isles.

†*Shooting*. One of the village tailors used to have a shooting competition on the sands (on New Year's day), the prizes being waistcoats. [*The Gallovidian*, X, p. 23.]

Garlieston, Wtn.

Sailing toy boats. Boys and young men construct boats and ships, commonly fashioning them with a knife. They rig them with much neatness. They are named and launched with due ceremony, and it is a source of much amusement to sail these boats and ships (generally round the coast). In many of the villages (Macduff, Pennan, Rosehearty) sailing matches or regattas were common, and betting was rife (Macduff). At the village of Pennan, not many years ago, there was a regatta on New Year's Day for some years in succession on the mill-pond of the farm of Clenterty, when many from the village, as well as many from the neighbouring farms, met to witness the race. Prizes were awarded for the victors. In Rosehearty, New Year's Day was specially devoted to the sailing of their ships by the boys. [Rev. W. Gregor, *F.-L.* II, p. 93.]

N.E. Scot. ; Ab.

Merrymaking. Upon such occasions (New Year visiting), the gravest is expected to be merry, and to join in a cheerful song. [*O.S.A.*, V, p. 48.]

Angus.

Men who kept sober all the year round would not have thought New Year's Day properly observed unless they got tipsy. [*The Gallovidian*, X, p. 23.]

S.W. Scot.

New Year was signalised by various domestic festivities. [R. and W. Chambers, *Memoirs*, p. 19.]

Edin.

One day if not more was observed as holiday ... by tradesmen and labourers of all kinds. [Greg., p. 156.]

N.E. Scot.

The first day of the New Year is their only holiday, which they spend in friendly visits and mutual congratulations. [*N.S.A.*, XV, p. 75.]

Bothwell, Lnk.

For a ball on this evening open to all, see p. 114, two bottom lines.

X. Processions. †Dec. 30, 1556. The provost, bailies and Council order all merchants, craftsmen and other inhabitants of this burgh in time coming, to send their servants with torches to the conveying of the provost all the festival days of

Yule, New-yeir-mes, and Vphellymes from the evensong to his own lodging, under pain of XL s. from each person that fails herein. [Ext^t from the *Rec^{ds} of the Burgh of Edinburgh*, 1528-57, p. 260.]   Edin.

Wapinshaw. See section *Wapinshaws*, Vol. I.

1st Monday After New Year

I. Name. Handsel Monday or Monanday. Gael. *Diluain an t'sainnseil.*

IV. Omens. *Weather.* †From (this day), in Skye, the twelve days, corresponding in weather to the twelve months of the year, are computed. [*Wcrft. & Sec. Sight*, p. 245.]
                                                        Skye, Iness.

V. Observances.

A full description of Handsel Monday in Fife is given in *C. F.-L.* VII, pp. 146-149. The rites resemble those quoted for New Year's Day, for owing to the change of style, this day was in many parts of Scotland observed on January 12th, later 13th, which day then fell together with Handsel Monday, and popular customs were transferred to this old time holiday. Where the New Year observances had been banned they were transferred to the later date. The main features of the observance in Fife were :

V b. *Lucky or prescribed.* First-footing, with food and other gifts for luck ; dark-complexioned visitors preferred.

V c. *Fire or torches.* Torches carried.

V m. *Special food and drink.*

V n. *Pranks.* Hornblowing.

In extract sent by Mr MacRitchie items noted are :

V c. Torches and bonfires.

V l. Calling on neighbours for buns and a dram.

V m. Cakes and fruit won by raffles ; sow's head supper ; festive drinking.

V a. *Unlucky or forbidden. To get out of bed too early.* People did not get out of bed early on Hansel Monday. This was to protect themselves from fairies or witches, who were abroad in full force on that morning but had all to disappear . . . before sunrise. The first Monday and the first Friday of

each quarter were days on which fairies and witches held
revel. [Rev. W. Gregor.]   Dyke, Moray.
    As at New Year not even the smallest thing was given away
nor was money spent. [Greg., p. 164.]   N.E. Scot.

V c. and V i. *Visiting a well with torches.*   †There are two
caves at the bottom of a cliff immediately under the ruined
castle of Easter Wemyss . . . one, which has a narrow entry,
is very spacious within, and contains a well of good water.
It is visited on the first Monday of January, old style, by the
young people of the neighbourhood, with torches, but the
origin of the custom is unknown. [*C. F.-L.* VII, p. 151.]   Ffe.

V e. *Farm and byre. Feeding cattle.* Some were in the habit of
giving, on the morning of that day, a small quantity of unthreshed oats to the cattle and the horses on the farm. [Greg.,
p. 164.]   N.E. Scot.

V e., V l. and V m. *Food and drink.* The farmers used to treat
the whole of their servants on that morning to a liberal breakfast of roast and boiled, with ale, whisky and cake. . . .   Even
now, when most old customs are much decayed, *Auld Handsel
Monday* continues to be the holiday of the year to the class of
farm labourers in Scotland. [Chambers, *Bk. of Days*, I, p. 52.]

V k. *Doles and gifts.* Handsel Monday, the first Monday of
the New Year, O.S. ; so-called because it has been the custom,
from time immemorial, for servants and others to ask, or
receive, *handsel* on this day. [Jamieson.]
    Postmen, scavengers, and deliverers of newspapers look for
their little annual guerdons (on Handsel Monday). [Cham-
bers, *Bk. of Days*, I, p. 52.]
    The distinction between the friendly gift of ' Hugmanay '
and the more material bestowal of money on Handsel Monday,
the first Monday of the year, must be kept in mind ; the
latter being a kind of wage still expected and received by
those in service. [Dav. MacRitchie, *The Scottish Review*, Dec.
21, 1905.]
    Gratuities to schoolmasters. Scholars commonly give a hansel
to their master or mistress on this day. The boy who gives the
largest sum is called the king, and the girl the queen, and the
king claims the right of demanding at least that day as a holiday. Cf. *Shrovetide*, Vol. I. [Henderson, *F.-L. of the Northern
Counties* (1879), p. 77.]   Borders.
    In some districts . . . children brought a gratuity (in

money) to the schoolmaster. In other districts this was not the case till Shrovetide. [*Wcrft. & Sec. Sight*, p. 245.]

Hghlds. and W. Isles.

Gifts especially to children and visitors quoted in *Pop. Rhymes* (1870), p. 161 ; and *Wcrft. & Sec. Sight*, p. 245.

†*Chap-books given*. The first Monday in the year was marked by tossing a profusion of ballads and penny chap-books from windows among a crowd of clamorous youngsters. [R. and W. Chambers, *Memoirs*, p. 19.]   Edin.

V k. and V m. *Gifts of food.   Pies and porter.*

> Hansel Monday's comin' on,
> We'll get pies and porter.

[G. Setoun, *Sunshine* (1895), p. 1. (E. D. D. s.v. Handsel).]

E. Scot.

V m. *Food and drink.* On Hansel Monday it was customary for the tacksmen (landlords in chief) to make a large feast for the occasion, to which all their cottars were invited, along with their servants. These feasts consisted chiefly of potatoes and mutton. Tables were laid according to the number that were to sit, including the host and hostess with their family. Basins of *Buntat' Breac*, as the potatoes and mutton were called, were placed in a row on the long tables, and each, armed with a long spoon, was expected to help himself from the basin nearest. Of course the ' square bottle ' would be in evidence. After supper the usual games were indulged in, and perhaps a dance. *Di-luain an t-sainnseill* has gone almost entirely out of keeping in the Highlands now. [Mlan MS.]   Islay, Ar.

V n. †*Pranks.* The most remarkable feature in the observance of Handsel-Monday in Newburgh, and which seems peculiar to the town, is the blowing of horns in the street by the boys the moment that the clock strikes the twelfth hour on Sunday night. They continue this unmelodious music until daylight, kindle bonfires, and a generation back removed tradesmen's signs to private dwellings, and perpetrated other mad pranks. The adherence of the boys to these old usages is a striking instance of the toughness of long-descended customs. [A. Laing, *Lindores Abbey*, etc. (1876), pp. 393 f. ; quoted in *C. F.-L.* VII, p. 149.]   Ffe.

XI. Games, merrymaking. *Throwing up thistles or crowns.* 'Tis well known that the first Monday of the year is always observed with uncommon Gaiety and Mirth, and in Con-

PLATE V

Photo: Cowper.

'A Bawbee She Kyles,' as played at Kirkcaldy on New Year's Day.

sequence becomes a Holiday to Apprentices and Servants. (Some) went to divert themselves with a common amusement among Boys, by throwing up Thistles or Crowns. . . . [From a cutting in Jos. Haslewood's copy of Brand's *Pop. Antiquities* . . ., dated by him 1740.]   Kirkcaldy, Ffe.

Kyles. For Kyles played on Hansel Monday see *January* 1*st*, **XI**, above.

†*Yettlings.* At the foot of this cave [the Court Cave] lies a flattish reach of red sandstone of fully a quarter of a mile in length and from 60 to 80 yards in breadth, terminating on the east at the Round Doocot, and on the west near the village burn. These smooth-topped Skerries have clearly been the higher playground of the tidal waves (they are barely covered during the neap tides) since ever the Forth receded to its present coast line, or perhaps we may say, since Scotland last rose a few hundred feet out of the sea. This rocky floor is peculiar to the Fife shore, and it is curious to note that a singular and primitive-looking game has been played over it during the New Year's holidays from time immemorial by the youths and young men of Wemyss. The local origin of the game is not known, but some think that it may have been introduced by Baltic traders as a game named ' Klotschassen ', played in the Low Countries in winter over ice-bound courses, is identical, save in the minor differences of the balls, which are made of wood loaded with iron ; while at Wemyss, at the present time, the balls, locally called ' Yettlins ', are wholly of iron. The probability that the game was carried from Wemyss to the Low Countries is as likely. . . .

Over sixty years ago, however, I have seen the game played on Old Hansel Monday with whinstone bullets, which had been picked up along the shore after heavy storms. There was nothing artificial in their form—they had been smoothed and rounded by the restless sea. Many spectators on those days, as now, lined the course and applauded heartily the player who succeeded in making a ' hail ' in the fewest number of throws from goal to goal. A given number of ' hails ' constituted a win, and the player whose scores first reached the winning number is declared the victor for the year and holds the club medal accordingly.

Although the stronger men have the advantage of winning the game, yet it does not always fall to their lot, as a good many difficulties have to be encountered, such as the lie of the rocks, the wave-worn facets of tiny ledges, and the watery state of the course—all of which have, in some degree, a diverging and retarding influence on the balls as they rattle over the Skerries, spinning every now and then a grey band of spray while darting through the abounding pools of shallow water.

A deviation in the manner of play has taken place of late years. A narrow leather belt of about a yard in length is fastened to the player's hand, and from time to time soaked in water before rolling it round the ball, which, accordingly, on delivery, receives an extra impetus by the unrolling action of the wet, semi-elastic belt. [Jn. Patrick, *The Reliquary and Illustrat. Archaeologist*, XI, No. 2, Apr. 1908. See *C. F.-L.* VII, pp. 150 f.] Wemyss, Ffe.

Raffles and shooting. At Currie . . . the early part (of Handsel Monday) is generally devoted to . . . raffles, and shooting with fire-arms . . . often old and rusty. [*N.S.A.* I, p. 550.]
Edin.

Cock-fighting, raffles. With Han'sel Monday, until some twenty years ago, came a week's holidays for the employés in the principal public works. . . . But now the Monday itself is alone observed as a holiday. Cock-fighting at this time was one of the chief amusements of the lower orders—a barbarous pastime which in the present day is rarely heard of, either in the nailmaking or colliery districts. ' Raffle-shooting ' for buns and other seasonable articles, was another great institution ; but it has also become obsolete. [Nimmo, W., *The History of Stirlingshire* [3] (1880), vol. ii, pp. 387-8.] Stg.

Cockfighting quoted among colliers in Falkirk. [Wm. Hone, *Every Day Book*, II. Under *Hogmanay*.]

Shooting matches with prize-giving ; Street-fighting at the Cross.

Handsel Mununday, as the old folk called it, sixty years ago was, barring the Muir Market, the one outstanding day of the whole year in ' the lang toun ' of Auchterarder . . . and the laddies might have been heard of an ' efternicht fa'in' ' as they carried pirees to their father at his loom, singing

> Handsel Monday's drawin' near,
> Ale and shortbread will appear.

. . . There were raffles for shortbread, buns, and fruit— delicacies of the season only to be seen on common folk's tables at Handsel Monday. The raffles were carried out sometimes in the holder's kitchen, sometimes in his workshop. You paid your penny and when sufficient pennies were got, you took the dice cup, shook it with a will, and threw the dice on the table. . . . Each player had his throw and the winner who stood highest marched gleefully off with his prize.

As the day wore on there were the blin' barrow competitions and the shooting matches, at both of which prizes in kind were awarded. At the blin' barrow contests a handkerchief was firmly bound over your eyes and then you caught hold of the handles of the barrow and tried to run it up against a mark some distance off. . . . The shooting matches were important events. One was held in the Muir near the Granny Stane. . . . The prizes were of various sorts, generally useful articles,—often fishing wands. . . . A 'sou's head supper' might bring the day's festivities to a close. This supper was held in some public house, these houses were then quite numerous. A few kindred spirits formed the company, and besides the pork, enjoyed the 'tappit hens' or at least their contents, for the 'tappit hen' was the half-mutchkin measure, and its contents usquebaugh (whisky).

Of course, mention of Handsel Monday would be incomplete without reference to the flambeaux and the bonfires of the Headiers and the Fittiers, and the 'fechts at the Cross' wherein the young man of mettle burned to take part. . . . [Extract from a paper, probably contributed by Mr MacRitchie himself, and sent by him. Nov. 1911.]   Pth.

Handsel Tuesday

The day after Handsel Monday was known in some parts of Scotland as Handsel Tuesday, holiday customs continuing over the second day.

6th

I. **Names.** *Epiphany. Twelfth Night.* †In Strathglass, N. Inverness, the Epiphany is called *Féille Faire*, 'the latter word having dialectically *r* for *l*' as in *Féille Faile*, festival of laving. [G. Henderson, *Survivals of Belief, etc.*, p. 217.]

Uphaliday was the old popular name for Twelfth Night, twelve days after Christmas, which saw the end of the Yuletide revels. The observance began the night before at Court, or wherever the king or queen of the Bean was recognised, the election being on the eve by the division of the Twelfth cake. In the far north the holiday-making continued till twenty-four days after Christmas, and Uphely-a was observed on January 18th.

' As the Gregorian Calendar only began to be adopted in Scotland in the year 1600 and did not receive anything like full recognition till the passing of an Act of Parliament in 1751 " for regulating the commencement of the year, etc.", there was for generations a conflict of custom between the New and the Old " Style " of reckoning, often necessitating the distinctive letters N.S. and O.S. after a date. . . . It is on . . . old Twelfth Day that the people of Shetland, ignoring the Gregorian calendar, celebrate the end of their Yule festivities, it has therefore come to be styled " Four an' Twenty Day " instead of Twelfth Day.' [D. MacRitchie, *The Scottish Review*, Jan. 11, 1906.]

The loss of these eleven, and later twelve, days was looked upon as almost sacrilegious and was for a time resented ; tales are told of messengers sent to the Pope to claim the lost days and the O.S. dates continued in observance till recent times. A transference of customs from one date to another marks the whole holiday season of ' the Yules '.   [Ed.]

V. Observances.

V d. *Divination.* (On Twelfth Night) a small lump of dough from which the New Year cakes have been taken is reserved, and in it a small coin, usually a farthing, is put. The dough is then rolled thin and cut into small round scones, which, when fired are handed round to the company. The one receiving the coin will be the first to marry. [Lean's *Collectanea* (1903), II, p. 358.]   S. Scot.

V n. *Indoor games. The twelve days of Yule.*
The king sent his lady on the first Yule day,
A papingo-aye ; (a peacock)
Wha learns my carol and carries it away?
The king sent his lady on the second Yule day,
Three partridges, a papingo-aye ;
Wha learns my carol and carries it away?
The king sent his lady on the third Yule day
Three plovers, three partridges, a papingo-aye ;
Wha learns my carol and carries it away?
The king sent his lady on the fourth Yule day
A goose that was gray,
Three plovers, three partridges, a papingo-aye ;
Wha learns my carol and carries it away?
The king sent his lady on the fifth Yule day,
Three starlings, a goose that was gray,
Three plovers, three partridges, a papingo-aye ;

Wha learns my carol and carries it away?
The king sent his lady on the sixth Yule day,
Three goldspinks, three starlings, a goose that was gray,
Three plovers, three partridges, and a papingo-aye ;
Wha learns my carol and carries it away?
The king sent his lady on the seventh Yule day,
A bull that was brown, three goldspinks, three starlings,
A goose that was gray,
Three plovers, three partridges and a papingo-aye ;
Wha learns my carol and carries it away?
The king sent his lady on the eighth Yule day,
Three ducks a-merry laying, a bull that was brown,
      (The rest to follow as before.)
The king sent his lady on the ninth Yule day,
Three swans a-merry swimming, . . .
                        (As before.)
The king sent his lady on the tenth Yule day,
An Arabian baboon, . . .
                        (As before.)
The king sent his lady on the eleventh Yule day,
Three hinds a-merry hunting, . . .
                        (As before.)
The king sent his lady on the twelfth Yule day,
Three maids a-merry dancing, . . .
                        (As before.)
The king sent his lady on the thirteenth Yule day,
Three stalks o' merry corn, three maids a-merry dancing,
Three hinds a-merry hunting, an Arabian baboon,
Three swans a-merry swimming,
Three ducks a-merry laying, a bull that was brown,
Three goldspinks, three starlings, a goose that was gray,
Three plovers, three partridges, a papingo-aye ;
Wha learns my carol and carries it away?

[*Pop. Rhymes*,[4] pp. 42, 43.]

Chambers does not describe the way the game given by
him was played, but it was probably much in the same manner
(as the games quoted for the ' Twelve Days of Christmas '
rhymes known in England). 'The Twelve Days' was a
Christmas game, played on Twelfth Day Night. . . . The
party was usually a mixed gathering of juveniles and adults,
mostly relatives, and before supper—that is before eating
mince-pies and twelfth cake—this game and the cushion
dance [not quoted from Scotland] were played, and the
forfeits consequent upon them always cried. The company

were all seated round the room. The leader of the game commenced by saying the first line. . . . The lines for the ' first day ' of Christmas were said by each of the company in turn ; then the ' first day ' was repeated with the addition of the ' second ' by the leader, and then this was said all round the circle in turn. This was continued until the lines for the ' twelve days ' were said by every player. For every mistake a forfeit—a small article belonging to the person—had to be given up. These forfeits were afterwards ' cried ' in the usual way, and were not returned to the owner until they had been redeemed by the penalty inflicted being performed. [(Lady) Alice B. Gomme, *The Traditional Games of Engl., Scot., etc.* (1894), II, p. 319.]

IX. **Guising, etc.** The Guisard appeared at Court on . . . Uphaly Day. . . . [Anna J. Mill, *Mediaeval Plays in Scot.*, p. 15.]

In 1497 the ' gysaris ' received on this day £2 . 14 . 0. They were mummers from the town who . . . were welcome at such times to the king's hall. [Thomas Dickson, in Preface to *Scottish Records*, 1473-1498, p. ccxliii.]

Clinking metal. 1636. January 15. Alex. Dunbar (sentenced) to stand at the pillar on Sunday next for clinking of basens through the town on Uphaly even. [*Elgin Records*, II, p. 230.]
Morayshire.

XII. **Festivals.** *The King or Queen of Bean.* The election of a mock sovereign to preside over the festivities of a season was practised throughout Europe and has been noted, analysed, and described by many competent students of rite and custom. Reference here is to the custom as observed in Scotland, and as it is based on Treasurers' accounts for the most part, it quotes the observances at Court, or at official festivals, or as prescribed by universities.

' The King of the Bean was regularly appointed at Uphaly day at the Scottish Court from at least the end of the fifteenth century. Occasionally his place was taken by a Queen of the Bean. Although one may assume that similar elections took place throughout the land in humbler spheres at the Epiphany, the only other trace of the custom in early times which I have found is at the University of St Andrews, where a minute, dated 1432, regulates the garment to be worn by the " Rex ffabe " and his attendants at the feast of Kings.'

1432, November 21st. Statuimus de festo regum eundem eundo ad ecclesiam et redeundo cum rege ffabe quod magistri et scolares incedant in ▪habitibus propriis hoc solo excepto quod liceat regi portare habitum dissimulatum aliqualiter statui regali congruentem.

Excerpt from the MS. Liber Conclusionum Universitatis Sanctiandree. [A. J. Mill, *Med. Plays in Scot.*, pp. 16, 17 and 284.]

Excerpts from the Accounts of the Lord High Treasurer of Scotland :

1491/2. Item, to Pringill king of bene, xxxvj s.

1502/3. Item, to the King of Bene. . . .

1531. Livery granted to Christian Rae, Queen of the Bean. [*Ibid.*, Appendix I.]

. . . Thou art bot king of Bene. [Sir Dav. Lindsay, *The Testament and Complaynt of the Papyngo*, pp. 1, 337.]

Note.—Vol. I, p. 265, ed. David Laing (1879), Bone (or Bene) referring to the popular custom of Epiphany . . . of choosing as Sovereign for that evening the person who found the Bean inserted in the cake prepared for the occasion of that festival.

On the eve of Uphaliday . . . the widely observed custom of electing a king or queen of the Bean, by the division of the Twelfth cake, to preside over the festivities of the following day, was duly honoured in the king's household. . . . [Th. Dickson, *Scottish Records*, I (1473-1498), preface, p. ccxliii.]

For the description of the Queen of the Bean elected at the Twelfth Day observance by Mary Queen of Scots at Holyrood in 1563, see Strickland, *Lives of the Queens of Scot.*, IV, p. 20.

XII. Religious Observance. On Uphaliday there appears regularly a payment for incense. To furnish this seems to have been a perquisite of the clerks of the chapel. . . . The regular occurrence of this on the Epiphany suggests that it may have been connected with the custom which prevailed and is not yet obsolete, of making an offering on that day on the part of the king or queen, of gold, frankincense and myrrh, in commemoration of the homage of the Magi. [Th. Dickson, *Scottish Records*, Vol. I (1473-1498), Preface, p. ccxliv.] Edin.

Dr Dickson's surmise is fully corroborated by an entry in a later volume of the Lord High Treasurer's Accounts (edited by Sir J. Balfour Paul), which records a payment of three French crowns on Up-Haly-Day 1506, being ' the king's offering in honour of the Three Kings '. . . . One reads further that when James IV's queen, Margaret Tudor, daughter of Henry VII of England, made her entry into Aberdeen in 1511, the procession in her honour contained the

' Orient Kings Three ', who were represented offering gold, frankincense and myrrh to the infant Christ. [David Mac-Ritchie, *The Scottish Review*, Jan. 11, 1906.]

8th, N.S. 19th, O.S.

III. Saint. St Nathalan, Nauchlan, *d.* Tullich, Ab. 679. From an analysis of his name, a compound, *Necto-launos*, ' pure-rejoicing ', or ' rejoicing in purity ', in British *Neithlaun*, *Naithlon*, ' the inference is that Nathalan was a British saint who . . . went across to Ireland, where he was known as Nechtan, stayed there for some time, and came back to Alba [Scotland].' [*Celt. Place-Names.*] His day coincides with that of Nechtan, who has commemoration in Scotland and is probably the same person. He was famed for his beneficence. Legend says that during a great scarcity he fed the starving and gave away his seed-corn. In the spring, having no seed, he sowed his lands with the finest sand which miraculously produced rich crops for the following harvest . His neighbours assembled in masses to reap the corn but storms came on with torrential rain and the flooded rivers swept away his crops. The angered saint uttered unguarded expressions, which he repented as the heavens cleared, and as a penance fastened a heavy iron chain round his ankle. The key of the padlock he threw into a pool of the Dee, still known as the ' Key Pool ', vowing not to unlock the padlock till after a pilgrimage to Rome. There he was walking laboriously along a street when he saw a boy selling fish ; he bought one and in it found his key. He returned blessed with healing powers and became patron saint of the Braes of Mar. [*Sc. N. & Q.*, IX (1895).]

Cf. the resemblance to the fish incident in the Kentigern legend and the traces of his cult in Aberdeen with a St Mungo's kirk close to one of St Nathalan. There was a cessation of work on his day, as on those of St Fillan and St Columba at Killin and Glen Lyn. In Kincardine at Cowie an old rhyme ran :

> Atween the kirk an' the kirk-yard,
> There lies St Nachlan's Hoard.

The hoard was said to be concealed in a bull's hide tied with a rope which would hang the finder of the treasure. [*Sc. N. & Q.*, IX (1896), p. 186, 5.]

Professor W. J. Watson, *Celt. Pl.-Names*, surmises that the couplet had a Gaelic original in which the word interpreted

' hoard ' meant rather a tomb, such ' grave-verses ' being well known in Old Gaelic and in Welsh.

XI. Outdoor Games. *Football.* In a number of the *Reliquary and Illustrated Archaeologist* (vol. iii., p. 48), Mr J. M. Mackinlay says, . . . that at the hamlet of Tullich, near Ballater, is a ruined church standing in a circular graveyard. ' Outside the ruin, but within an iron railing, is a collection of five or six ancient sculptured stones, some showing a cross incised on them, and one having the curious mirror-like symbol so puzzling to antiquaries. St Nathalan, said to have been born in the district, was the patron saint of the church. His day was kept as a holiday in the parish till within the last twenty-five or thirty years. It fell on the 8th of January, and was held on or about the 19th, according to the old style of reckoning. Football was the favourite amusement on the occasion. The churchyard, which had then no wall round it, was the place selected for the game, and the ball was kicked about over the tombs, often amid snow.' [M. Peacock, *F.-L.*, Vol. VIII, p. 74.]   Ab.

9th

III. Saints. St Fáelán of Cluain, known as St Fillan ; saint of Cill Thaolan, Kilillan, in Kintail. Local tradition says that his body was taken in a galley, which lay for a night at Camus Longart on Loch Long and then sailed up to near Kilillan. Columba is said to have sent a sod from Iona to cover his grave. There are sixteen saints of this name. It was more probably St Fáelán Nemlabar (' the dumb '), whose name is associated with Rob. Bruce (see his day, June 20, II). [*Celt. Pl.-Names.*]

According to the Aberdeen Breviary St Fáelán was cast into a lake by his father immediately after his birth and lived a year in the water tended by angels. The legend relates also that while he was superintending the building of his church in Fife the ox used for drawing materials to the spot was killed by a wolf, which, moved by the prayers of the saint, returned to replace the ox and itself drew the materials for building the church. Cf. January 13th, Legend of St Kentigern, who converts a wolf to draw the plough.

Another legend. An Urisk, haunting *Beinn Doohran*, on the confines of Argyllshire and Perthshire, stayed in summer time near the top of the hill, and in winter came down to the straths. A waterfall near the village of Clifton at Tyndrum, where it stayed on these occasions, is still called *Eas na h-ùruisg*, the Urisk's cascade. The Urisk, when encountered by St Fillan, who had his abode in a neighbouring strath, was banished to Rome. [*Supers*. *of the Scot. Hghlds*., p. 196.]

. . . He spent a considerable part of his life at a monastery which he built in Pittenweem. . . . It is stated that, while engaged here in transcribing the Scriptures, his left hand sent forth sufficient light to enable him, at night, to continue his work without a lamp. For the sake of seclusion, he finally

Quigrich of St. Fillan (in its shrine) [1]

retired to a wild and lonely vale, called from him Strathfillan, in Perthshire, where he died, and where his name is still attached to the ruins of a chapel, to a pool, and a bed of rock.

Strange as it may appear, the ancient bell of the chapel, believed to have been St Fillan's bell, of a very antique form, continued till the beginning of the nineteenth century to lie loose on a grave-stone in the churchyard, ready to be used, as it occasionally was, in the ceremonial for the cure of lunatics. The popular belief was, that it was needless to attempt to appropriate and carry it away, as it was sure, by some mysterious means, to return. An . . . English traveller at length put the belief to the test, and the bell has been no more heard

[1] The illustration of the Crosier is given by the courtesy of Messrs. W. & R. Chambers, Ltd.

of. The head of St Fillan's crosier, called the *Quigrich*, of silver gilt, elegantly carved, and with a jewel in front, remained at Killin, in the possession of a peasant's family, by the representative of which it was conveyed some years ago to Canada. [Chambers, *Book of Days*, I, p. 78.]

Quigrich, Gael. *Coigreach*, a stranger, foreigner, and the chief duty of the Dewar, or keeper of St Fillan's staff, was to pursue 'stolen goods or cattle wherever they were to be found within the kingdom of Scotland. The staff ... was the effective agent in the business, conferring authority and immunity from harm. From its travels into foreign parts it was called *an Coigreach*'. [*Celt. Pl.-Names.*] It is now in the National Museum of Antiquities of Scotland, Edinburgh.

The bell, called the *Bernan*, of the Celtic square shape with a loop handle, was found in Herts, and restored to the Edinburgh Museum. Another relic was the *Farig*, a wooden mallet used for beating barley out of its husks in a stone mortar ; this, with the enshrined arm and the psalter, disappeared after the Reformation. The Dewar, or custodian of these relics, was not a cleric, but a layman, upheld by the civil judiciary. The hereditary rights of the office were confirmed by James III. In the Quigrich is a piece of rock crystal, held to have curative powers ; it also gave protection to its bearer, and victory in battle. See Hugh MacMillan, *The Highland Tay, etc.* [Ed.]

Faolan's mill was built at Killin, and it is only recently that the mill was allowed to be worked on Faolan's day. . . . Faolan's fair was established at Killin, and is still held there in the month of January. [Ch. Stewart, *The Gaelic Kingdom in Scotland, etc.* (1880), pp. 80 f.]

Healing stones of Faolan. There are eight stones so designated, which from time immemorial have been preserved at Faolan's Mill at Killin. They are preserved in a niche in the wall, and at each renewing of the mill such has been duly made for them. They are small stones in the rough, evidently taken from the bed of the adjoining river. One of these stones has two holes in the centre of it, and another, now broken, evidently had the same. . . . Peter McGibbon the village archaeologist [already referred to] tells me that he remembers when the whole inhabitants turned out on Faolan's day and put clean straw under them. [*Ibid.*, p. 89.]

At the north-west corner of the Dochart Bridge at Killin stands the meal mill, at the site traditionally occupied by a succession of mills. In this mill are preserved what are known as St Fillan's Stones. From John Shearer's *Antiquities in Perthshire* (1836), I copy this account : ' It would appear that St Fillan acted as judge as well as priest. The seat where he decreed justice is at Killin ; it is entire, and appears to have been cut out of the rock. At the side of it grows a large ash tree, which is held sacred by the natives, as no person will burn any of the branches, although fallen to the ground, nor destroy them in any manner. . . . The branches that fall lie till they rot.

There is a mill here which they call St Fillan's mill, standing about twenty yards westward, on the banks of the Dochart, which goes well all the year except on St Fillan's day, the 20th of January ; but it will not go on that day without doing a great deal of mischief. One millar had the boldness to keep it going on that day, when some of the machinery broke . . . and killed the millar. . . . The present millar would not set it going on that day although he was to be made the laird of the glen. Adjoining is an old house, where some of the relics of St Fillan lie. . . . An old gable still remains. In this gable there is a square hole, where a number of circular stones are kept for rubbing the bodies of invalids . . . troubled with pains. Each stone has its particular part assigned to be rubbed. First, one for the head, which is large, the shape similar to a skull. The old woman rubs the head three times one way, then reverse three times, then three times round the head ; she at the same time pronounces a Gaelic benediction. They are then cured. Second, one for the back, in which the old woman says you will see a resemblance of all the joints of the back, . . . while going through the same ceremony as formerly. Third, she has one for each side of the body ; on them you will see lines in shape of the ribs ; the former ceremony is here gone through. There was one of the stones taken away, according to the story it came back itself. Fourth, one for the belly, of a flat round shape ; and the above ceremony gone through. The stones have to be bedded once in the year in sand and hay, on St Fillan's day. The matron is not allowed to charge any pence, but looks for a present. . . . Her ancestors and herself pay no rent, but have kept up this ceremony these many centuries back, probably since the time of the Saint. The millar is obliged to keep a number of geese and a white cock, as an injunction left by the Saint.'

The *N.S.A.*, 1845, after describing treatment of insane people (in the Holy Pool) . . . goes on to say there was a stone at the mill of Killin called St Fillan's Chair, and seven small round stones that had been consecrated by the saint and endowed with the power of curing diseases. Each had its own peculiar merit. They got a fresh bed each Christmas eve from the straw and weeds cast ashore by the river. Five of them are still preserved at the mill.

In the *Proceedings of the Soc. of Antiquaries of Scotland*, 1880, is a report of a communication from Mr C. Stewart of Killin . . . a part runs : ' Not very long ago the villagers assembled on the saint's day [January 9th] and put clean straw under the stones. They were considered efficacious in cases of insanity and rheumatism.' Mr Stewart describes them as common stones taken from the bed of the river . . ., hard quartzose boulders, the largest weighing 8 lbs. 10 oz., saying there were seven or eight of them. Specially interesting was Mr Stewart's statement that some of them had shallow, rounded cavities or markings on them. . . .

(The quoter of this report believes these were merely the socket stones in which the spindle of the upper mill-stone used to work.)

At the present time (1912) the stones are kept in a recess in the wall of the mill, behind a locked grating, and are shown by the millar to the curious. Far from having a bed of straw they were found lying in a thick bed of soot, for the recess communicates by crevices in the wall with the flue of the kiln. Of the eight stones, seven are water-worn pebbles, the largest shows little rounding. Two are ' socket stones ' with highly polished holes in them. . . . The tradition still remains in the district that these stones were used in cases of illness, though not for a very long time. The ' socket stones ' were placed over the nipples of women's breasts, and the smaller stones were rubbed on affected parts. This rubbing may partly account for their high polish. . . .

I cannot reconcile the various numbers (of the stones) quoted . . . with the number now actually in the mill, eight. Of St Fillan's Chair we heard and saw nothing. But the mere dead stump of St Fillan's Ash-tree still stands against the south post of the mill gate. And quite near it is a young ash, said to be its descendant. This has an out-curving branch that was said to have been the gallows-branch in olden days ; but it is obviously too young and too weak. [Article quoted, not quite verbatim, from *Proceedings of Soc. of Antiq*[s]. *of Scot*., 4th series, X (1911-12), pp. 278 ff.]

In August 1931, I visited Killin (Perthshire) to see the sacred stones of St Fillan. There was only one man in the village who appeared to know anything about them. . . . His information was gained from hearsay and from the owner of the wool mill where the stones are now housed. The mill is of grey stone, and was founded in the ninth century by St Fillan, for a weaving industry. The ancient building was afterwards used as a mill, but is now once more used as a wool and weaving industry. The mill is situated by the river and bridge of Killin, and St Fillan used to stand at a corner of the bridge to preach to the people, who stood below upon the pebbles at the river's edge. These pebbles became sacred to those who had heard these sermons, and were used to massage those who were afflicted with disease. After St Fillan died the pebbles were collected and still used for massage, but in the passing of time . . . only eight remained. One of the late Lords of Breadalbane had these eight stones placed in a niche in the wall of an upper room in the mill, with an iron grille in front of them. They are grey, rough stones of irregular shape and size. . . . Only once in the year are they allowed to emerge from their prison. On Christmas Eve, quite late in the evening, they are taken out, and the ceremony of ' Bedding the Stones ' takes place. The man who described this to me had taken part in this little ceremony since 1916, with the owner of the wool mill . . . but he understood that it had been done for hundreds of years. The origin or reason of the ceremony he did not know.

The grille is unlocked and the stones are taken out. On the floor of the niche is a bed of wrack (i.e. sun-bleached grass or hay, washed down by the river). This is taken out and brought down to the water's edge, where it is scattered upon the waters, and new wrack is gathered from the bushes and rocks near the river. The stones are bedded upon the new wrack, and the grille is once more locked for another year. At the present time the stones are only used for wishing, and I could not discover when they were last used for massage. [Lilias Erskine (Miss L. M. Bosanquet), *F.-L.* XLII, 4, pp. 466 f. (1931).]

Reference follows to a visit of 1901, when only three stones were seen. These stones had been used for sick cattle, who were miraculously cured by drinking the water in which the stones had been immersed. Women also used them as specially efficacious in diseases of the chest. [Quoted from Hugh MacMillan in *The Highland Tay, etc.*, p. 30.]

For the ceremony performed at the Holy Well at Strath-fillan on the first day of the quarter for the cure of the insane, see *Movable Festivals*, Wells visited quarterly.

13th

I. Name. St Mungo's Day.

III. Saint. St Kentigern or Mungo, bishop of the Strath-clyde Britons, *d.* 603. He lives in tradition as the illegitimate son of a British princess, St Thenew [see her legend, July 18th] and was brought up in the Christian faith by St Serf, at Culross [see his legend, July 1st]. Miracles from his early years are related in his *Life* by Joceline, Cistercian monk of Furness, written in the 12th century. We first learn of him as restoring to life a redbreast, pet of St Serf, which had been killed by the rough hands of boys at play in the monastery. These boys were filled with jealousy of their companion and put out all the monastery fires on a night when it was Kentigern's duty to light the church lamps at cock-crow. He found no means to light the lamps and was on his way to escape from the monastery in despair, when he repented and returned to the church. On his way he plucked the bough of a hazel and carried it to the church, praying for help, while he signed and blessed the bough. On this a fire descended from heaven and put a flame in his hand, with which he lighted the lamps. The hazel afterwards grew into a wood, from which, according to the country folk, the greenest twig will blaze at the touch of fire and send forth a fiery haze.

Commanded by St Serf to shew his power, he raised from death the monastery cook. Envy of his powers now grew strong ; he left Culross in secret and found a passage miraculously prepared for him to pass through the river on dry ground at a place which ever after remained impassable. Arrived in Cambria, he was called to visit the anchorite, St Fergus, now near death, who longed to see one of whose fame he had heard. On the following day Kentigern yoked to a new wain two untamed bulls, and when he had laid the body of St Fergus on the wain, he commanded the bulls to bear it to its appointed place. They travelled by a straight road, where there had been no path, to the place where Glasgow now stands, many folk accompanying, till they halted at a burial ground which had been consecrated by St Ninian ; here St Fergus was buried. Over his tomb the crypt was built known to-day as Blackadder's aisle. Kentigern was now elected bishop, and consecrated by one bishop from Ireland, ' after the manner of the Britons and Scots of that period '. He was thus in charge of the ancient church of Strathclyde. He . . . began to over-throw the shrines of demons, to cast down their images and to build churches. After the custom of Scottish saints he would withdraw at times to desert places and spent . . . Lent in a cave. His pastoral staff was of wood, simply fashioned, neither rounded nor adorned with gilding and gems as were many of later date. At one time, owing to a lack of oxen, the plough-lands lay fallow, when the saint looked about for animals to draw the plough. He called to his aid the deer which he saw bounding through the forest ; these came willingly, returning each morning to the work. . . . One evening as they left the ploughs a hungry wolf made after them and caught a weary stag, which was instantly devoured. The saint summoned the wolf to his presence and commanded the penitent animal . . . to make reparation. This it did by sharing the yoke of one of the stags in the ploughing of nine acres ; after this it was allowed to depart. . . .

After the ploughing there was no seed for sowing, all grain having been given to feed the needy. The saint commanded that sand should be scattered over the ground and this sprang up into stalk, producing the richest wheat. . . .

At another time, when his barns were empty, a pagan king taunted him with a lack of corn while the royal barns were full. He challenged the saint to transfer the barns with grain to his own place. On this the saint caused the Clyde to rise in flood and bear the corn to the banks of the brook Molen-dinar (a place called Mellingdenor) where stood his wattled church ; here every blade and sheaf was delivered dry. The saint appeared before the king . . . when this ' man of Belial ' struck him with his foot to the ground ; the swelling of this foot afterwards caused the king's death and the disease of gout has been inherited by his race.

Aware of a plot to take his life, the saint escaped to visit St David (Dewi) in Wales. . . . He was invited to remain in Menevia by the king and was guided by a boar to a place where he established a monastery. . . . Later he was recalled to Cambria by king Rederech and was at work at Hoddam, Dfs., before establishing himself at Glasgow. He expelled a multitude of phantom devils, after making clear to the idolaters that these were inventions of man, based on creatures and formations destined in nature for his use. Woden he retained, not as a deity, but as a worshipful though mortal man and ' king of the Saxons '. In Annandale the ground on which he sat grew into a little hill [known to-day as Birrenswork].

At this time he restored to the queen a ring given to her by the king, which she had been unable to produce at his request till it had been recovered from the guts of a salmon caught in the Clyde [for the ring and grain-bearing sand cf. the legend of St Nathalan, January 8th.]

There came to the Court an Irish jester, who, playing on the timbrel and the harp, brought merriment to the company assembled for Christmas. After the Epiphany rich gifts were offered him, but he refused them saying there was abundance of such in his own country, and begged for a dish of mulberries as his reward. These were not at hand in winter time ; the saint, however, reminded the king of a thorn-bush over which he had thrown a cloak cast off during the heat of hunting, and advised that on this bush mulberries would be found. These were brought to the jester, who remained at the Court till he entered the service of the Church. Also new milk spilled in the water of the Clyde while being taken across to a certain artisan was not lost, but converted to cheese by the power of the saint.

When Columba visited him he knew him by a golden crown descended from heaven on his head. One of this saint's followers carried away a ram from Kentigern's herd and cut off its head ; the ram ran back headless to the flock, while the head, turned to stone, remained stuck fast on the thief's hand. The head of stone, released by favour of the saint, was to be seen till Joceline's day.

Many crosses were constructed by Kentigern, one of which is mentioned by Sir D. Lindsay in *The Monarchy*, ll. 2373-4 :

> Thay bryng mad men on fuit and horsse,
> And byndes thame to Sanct Mongose crosse.

[This was probably the cross made of sea-sand at Lothwerved, now Borthwick, Midlothian.]

He breathed his last on the octave of the Epiphany. After burial his miracles continued. Thus, near his tomb a cow was found dead and bound to the foot of the thief who had stolen it. Merlin is reported to have lived as a fool at Rederech's Court after his conversion by Kentigern ; at his death he gave himself up to extreme grief and practised his gift of prophecy in foretelling the death of the king. [This was Merlinus Caledonius—not the Merlin of Arthur's Court.][1] [Alex. P. Forbes, Bishop of Brechin, *Lives of S. Ninian and S. Kentigern*, Compiled in the Twelfth Century (1874).]

Till the Reformation Kentigern's shrine in Glasgow

---

[1] For *Merlin the Wild*, of Caledonia, see Sir W. Scott, *Minstrelsy of the Sc. Border* (ed. 1932), Vol. IV, pp. 109 ff.

attracted large crowds of pilgrims. On certain occasions his relics, bones, hair shirt, and scourge, with a red liquor that flowed from his tomb, were displayed. These were removed to France by Archbishop Beaton in 1560. Services for his day were special and ample till the Reformation. The church of Alloa, Cln., has a statue of St Mungo with a book in his hand ; according to local belief it turned a page whenever the clock struck. The seal of the university of Glasgow bears his well-known figure, with a book in one hand and in the other a fish with a ring in its mouth. He has many dedications throughout Scotland and several healing wells. His altar in the Collegiate Church of St Giles, Edinburgh, was upheld by the corporation of the surgeons and barbers of that town. [*Anc^t. Ch. Ded. N.*]

In a proverb long current in Aberdeen systematic benevolence was said to be ' like St Mungo's work, which was never done . . .'. [*Sc. N. & Q.* IX (1896), p. 187.]

The name Kentigern is explained in *Celt. Pl.-Names* as British. The name Mungo, earlier Munghu, was held by Jocelyn to be Welsh, meaning ' very dear friend '. *Celt. Pl.-Names* states : ' the formation is not clear to me,' p. 169.

To this day the country folk about Annandale point out a hill which they say rose from the lower ground as Kentigern stood preaching on it. [Ed.]

15th

I. †Name. *Oidche na Calainn,* night of the bannock. Hogmanay customs were observed on this night in Lewis, Hdes. [*The Celtic Review,* V (1909), p. 243.]

17th

III. Saint. Antony of Coma in Upper Egypt, 3rd century ; he is known generally in Europe as a patron of beasts, particularly of hogs, and is often represented with a bell, or with a pig carrying a bell at its neck. His order of Hospitallers had a Preceptory at Leith, where the common seal bears his effigy with the pig and bell at his feet. There is a hermitage of St Anthony on Arthur's Seat, Edinburgh, with his spring close by, still visited as a wishing well. He is commemorated at St Giles', Edinburgh, at Linlithgow and in Perth, also at Dundee. In Kincardineshire his fair was known as Taunton's (St Anton's) Fair. [*Anc^t. Ch. Ded. N.*]

The Preceptory, founded in 1435, was magnificent. Pilgrims who prayed at his shrine obtained relief from erysipelas,

' Sacred ' or ' St Antony's ' Fire, and his begging Hospitallers threatened those who refused to give them alms with this pest, and so earned unpopularity.

His Hospitallers at Clermont, France, had the privilege of feeding their swine gratuitously on acorns and beechnuts in the woods ; a bell hung on the neck of one or more sows in the herd and probably accounts for his emblem. Another explanation is that the sow represented gluttony which he had conquered. Sir David Lindsay describes him as ' sett up with ane sow ', the people entreating him for that animal's safety.

Vintners give portion of wine to St Anthony's Altar. April 25, 1561. The prouest baillies and counsale, vnderstanding that in the tyme of blindnes and mysknawlege of the treuth thair wes be consent of the nychtbouris of this burgh ane confrarie and bruderheid of ventaris of wyne quhilkis payit of euerye puntioun wyne ane choppoun to Sanct Anthonis alter for sustenyng of idolatrie and wikitnes, and sen at this present . . . is knawin that all sic confrareis bandis and promissis, inventit be the vngodlie sort of papistis for filling of thair belleis, ar contrair to the will and glorye of God, thairfor ordanis proclamatioun to be maid at all pairttis of this burgh neidfull, dischargeing the confrarie of Sanct Anthonis, the Hally Blude, and all vther confrareis quhatsumeuir quhilk hes bene heirtofore in tyme of ignorance, and all sic dewiteis as wes gevin thairto according to the statutis maid heiranent, to be vptaikin and applyit to the pure. . . . [*Burgh Records*, 1557-1571, p. 111. Extracts from the *Records of the Burgh of Edinburgh*, 1557-1571. Scottish Burgh Record Society, 1875.]   Edin.

20th

III. Saint. Sebastian of Narbonne, 3rd century, as ' Sanct Bastien ' is mentioned by Sir D. Lindsay, invoked for protection against death by shooting.

21st

I. Name. St Agnes's Day. ' Fruitful in love superstitions.' [R. T. Hampson, *Med. Aev. Kalend.* (1841), p. 150.]

III. Saint. St Agnes, 3rd century.

V. Observances. d. *Divination.* Formerly on the eve of St Agnes's Day the following custom was . . . observed in the northern parts of Scotland by the mountain peasantry. A number of young lads and lasses meeting together on the eve of St Agnes, at the hour of twelve, went one by one to a certain cornfield and threw in some grain, after which they pronounced the follow-ing rhyme :

> Agnes sweet, and Agnes fair,
> Hither, hither, now repair ;
> Bonny Agnes, let me see
> The lad who is to marry me. (or lass).

The prayer was granted by their favourite saint, and the shadow of the destined bride or bridegroom was seen in a mirror on this very night. [*Time's Telescope* (1832), p. 15.]

Cf. Love divination connected with cornfields and grain, *Hallowmas*, **V d.**

22nd

I. Name.   St Vincent's Day.

II. Saying.   If the sun shine on St Vincent's Day there will be more wine than water that year.   [D. Grewar, *Sc. N. & Q.*, 3rd Series, II (1924), p. 11.]

III. Saint.   St Vincent, Spanish ; 3rd century.   He has one or two commemorations in Scotland.   [See *Anc⁴. Ch. Ded. N.*]

25th

I. Name.   Conversion of St Paul.   Cf. *June 30th. St. Paul's Day.*

II. Sayings.   By the weather prophets of the older time St Paul's Day was credited with considerable influence over the rest of the year.   This finds expression in a rhyme, which is still quoted in some outlying parts of Scotland.   [*The Border Magazine*, XV, p. 31.]
Rhyme :

> Giff Sanct paullis day be fair and cleir
> Than salle be ane happie yeir.
> Giff it chance to snaw or rain
> Than salle dew all kynd of grane.
> And giff þe wind do flie on loft
> Than wer sall vex þe countrie oft.
> And giff þe clouds mak darke þe skye
> Baith nowte and foull that yeir sall die.

[Alex. P. Forbes, *Kalendars of Scot. Saints* (1872).   Quoted from page 1 of the Kalendar of Ferne, at Dunrobin ;   MS. probably of the 15th century. The rhyme occurs as a note of later date.]

The reference to snow refers the rhyme to the date of the Conversion rather than to St Paul's Day on June 30th. [Ed.]

IV. Weather Omen. See rhyme above.

29th

II. Saint. Volocus or Makwoloch : the old parish of St Walach (Glass, Ab.) bears his name.

> Wala fair in Logie Mar
> The thirtieth day of Januar.

[*Celt. Pl.-Names.*]

Ab.

How the lost eleven Days were recovered for Scotland.

The eleven days ' lost ' by the change from old style to new were believed to have been taken from January. The following tale from the Western Isles illustrates the sense of unfair loss.

Long ago a man of the name of Michael Scott volunteered to go in search of the eleven missing days. His offer having been accepted, he took a halter and waved it three times in the air, and thereupon a handsome black steed made its appearance. Michael mounted the horse and rode through the air across the straits of Dover and landed in a town in France. He intimated the object of his visit, demanding of the people the days of which he was in search, but they said they knew nothing of them. Not satisfied with their reply he, with the aid of his horse, destroyed the town. He then went on to another town and demanded of its inhabitants that they should restore to him the lost eleven days. They refused. ' One neigh and kick of a horse I have got ', said Michael, ' will send your town to destruction.' The people only laughed at him, for they saw no horse. Then Michael waved the halter in the air as he had done before leaving Scotland, and the black horse appeared breathing fire. The people trembled at the sight and gave up the missing days, when Michael returned home in triumph, and ever since Scotland has possessed ' full time '. [Mlan MS.]   Told in Islay, Ar.

From old calendars, dated 1680 to 1692, the Dismal Days were on numbers 1, 2, 4, 5, 10, 17, 19.

FEBRUARY

MONTH

I. Names. February. *Faoilleach* or *Faoilteach*, season of the wolf ravage. *Ceud mhios an Earraich*, first month of spring. †*Am mios marbh*, the dead month, N. Ar.

Faoilleach corresponds loosely to February, as far as a seasonal name can be the equivalent of a calendar term of later origin. It was sometimes divided into two halves, named, the first, the winter *Faoilleach*, the second, the spring *Faoilleach*. Cf. *Seasons*. These seasonal names begin with the *Faoilleach* and the first start of out-door life after the period of the winter solstice. [Ed.]

†Flicherin' Fevverear. If it happens while a boat is at the fishing that the wind varies much, the saying is, ' flicherin' Fevverear's come back '. [Rev. W. Gregor.]   Macduff, Bf.

II. Sayings, rhymes.

> A' the months o' the year
> Curse a fair Februeer.   Hghlds.

[James Ferguson, ' Old Scottish Sayings, etc.,' in *Chambers's Journal*, Feb. 1916, p. 108.]   Hghlds.

Upon the whole, there is a prejudice against February in the Scottish mind. The pastoral people of Peeblesshire and Selkirkshire say :

> Leap year
> was never a good sheep year.

The Aberdonians have a saying,

> The fair-day of Auld Deer,
>   (the third Thursday of Feb.)
> Is the warst day in a' the year.

[*Pop. Rhymes*,[3] p. 141.]

February should ' come in with the head of a serpent and go out with the serpent's tail '. [*Wcrft. & Sec. Sight*, p. 246.]

Februar rins nineteen times mad.

Nineteen out of its twenty-eight normal days are bad. When good weather prevails in February the succeeding months are out of joint and have to curse a fair February. [J. Spence, *Trans. Buchan Field Club*, IV (1896-8), p. 230.]

To expect black brambles in February ; said of unreasonable expectations. [*Wcrft. & Sec. Sight*, p. 246.]

Old people said, ' Better the land be plundered than a calm morning in February.' [*Ibid.*]

It was said to be as unnatural to hear thunder at this time as to hear a calf lowing in its mother's womb. Cf. *Seasons*. [*Ibid.*]

Winter's back breaks about the middle of February. [*Sc. N. & Q.*, 3rd series, II, p. 24.]

III. Omens. *Weather.* The weather of February presages that of the remainder of the year. [J. E. Cr.]

> If February gives much snow,
> A fine summer it doth foreshow.

> There will be as many frosts in June
> As there are fogs in February.

> If in February there be no rain,
> 'Tis neither good for hay nor grain.

If the cat lies in the sun in February, she will creep behind the stove in March.

> If in February thou hearest thunder,
> Thou shalt see a summer wonder.

A snowy February, a dusty March, a moist April, and a dry May,—we shall have a good year.

> February fill the dyke,
> Either with the black or white—
> If the white it's better to like.

The last line was added later. This was originally an English proverb, but became very popular in Scotland, though ' dyke ' was misunderstood by Scots peasantry, to whom the dyke was a wall. [D. Grewar, *Sc. N. & Q.*, 3rd series, II, p. 23.]

> Februar, an ye be fair,
> The hoggs 'ill mend and nothing 'pair. (impair)
> Februar, an ye be foul, the hoggs 'ill die in ilka pool.
> (hoggs, sheep in their 2nd year.)
>> Tweeddale, S. Scot.

Yet throughout the country generally good weather in February is regarded as an unfavourable symptom. [*Pop. Rhymes,*[3] p. 141.]

Twa full meens in Febberwarry
There 'ill be girs to the nowt in April.
[Rev. W. Gregor.]   Corgaff, Ab.
   In the north it was said mist in February means snow next
day.   [*Wcrft. & Sec. Sight*, p. 246.]   Hghlds.

If Feberweer be fair and clear,
There'll be twa winters in the year.   Galloway.

If February blow fresh and fair,
The meal will be dear for a year and mair.
[*Ethnog. Sur. of the U. Kingdom*, 5th Report (1897), p. 456.]
                                                  Laurieston, Stg.
   Here is a description current among old people in Islay
which shows the kind of weather they liked to see,—the
furrows three days full of snow, three days full of rain and three
days full of thatch (blown) from off the houses.   [Mlan MS.]
                                                       Islay, Ar.
   The last two weeks of the month were in parts of the
Highlands termed the ' Whulticks '.   If the weather was bad
a fine spell was expected at its termination. . . .   If it was fine
a rough and boisterous March was looked for.   [D. Grewar,
Sc. N. & Q., 3rd series, II, p. 24.]

   IV. Omens.   e. *From animals, birds, insects, reptiles.*   It is unfortunate if the heat of the season is such, and old men say they
have seen it, that the cattle run with the heat (during *Faoilleach*) ; but it is a healthy sign . . . if men go about with their
hands wrinkled with the cold till they resemble an animal's
hoof and are kept in their pockets (anciently belts) for warmth :

Wild month, wild month, hoof in belt,
Much rejoicing should be held ;
Cows and sheep running in heat,
Weeping and wailing then are meet.

[*Wcrft. & Sec. Sight*, p. 247.]   Cf. *Seasons.*   Hghlds.
   Birds.   To hear birds singing during the *Faoilleach* is taken
as a sure sign of a bad spring season to follow, and there is an
old Gaelic saying about the mavis which expresses this,—
*cha do sheinn i (an smeorach) roimh 'n fhaoilteach nach do chaoin
i 'sa' Mhart,*—she never sang in the *Faoilteach* but she wept in
March.   [Mlan MS.]   W. Hghlds.
   Frogs.   Frogs make their nests in water pools and marshes
during the time of the *Faoiltich*, and it used to be a common
belief that if the nests were near the edges of the pools, a wet
summer would follow, but if towards the centre, the summer

following would be dry beyond the average. An Islay man
says that old people used to pay great attention to this sign
and had faith in it. [Mlan MS.] Islay, Ar.

> When the poddock croaks in Febberwarry
> He'll hide his head in Mairch.

> If the poddock goggle in Febberwarry
> It'll greet in Mairch.

[Rev. W. Gregor.] Corgaff, Ab.

IV. Observances. *Marriage avoided.* In some parts of Argyll,
February is avoided nearly as much as May under the im-
pression that it is an unlucky month in which to get married.
[Mlan MS.] Ar.

†*Horse-racing.* The place appropriated to horse-racing at
Perth was the South Inch ; the course was marked by six
stakes. The first account given of a prize being run for is in
1613 ; the prize was a silver arrow. In 1631 there were three
prize silver bells. Till 1688 the race was called ' the bell
race ' (in February). Pth.

†*Bell ringing.* In the month of February, 1586, the Perth
Session ordains Nicol Balmain to ring the Curfew and workman
bell in the morning and evening. ' One space of ane quarter of
an hour at the times appointed, viz. four hours in the morning,
and eight at even,' and in the town's record, 1657, is the act
requiring obedience to the ringing of bells for putting out fires.[1]
[E. J. Guthrie, *Old Scottish Customs* (1885), p. 116.] Pth.

Guising. The guisard appeared at Court . . . even in the
beginning of February. Cf. *Uphaly Day.* [A. J. Mill, *Med.
Plays in Scot.* (1927), p. 15.]

Borrowed days. Highlanders have their borrowed or
borrowing days, but with them February borrows from January
and bribes him with three young sheep. These first three
days by Highland reckoning (that is by old style) occur between February 11 and 15. [Mrs Grant, *Superstitions of the
Highlanders*, II, p. 217.] Hghlds.

DAYS

1st

I. Names. *Imbolc*, given as *Oimelc* by Cormac, was an old
Celtic name for the beginning of spring on this day, interpreted by K. Meyer as meaning legal washing or purification.

---

[1] Not ordained for February only. [Ed.]

The day of St Bride, the Celtic Brigit. The day was known also as Candlemas in the Highlands ; *Féill Brìde*, the festival of Bride, displaced the festival of Mary. *Féill* referred in most places to the eve of the festival, its interpretation as the festival itself led to confusion in the commemoration of two different festivals, aided by the original ceremonial sense of purification attached to the day. Rites and customs belonging to Candlemas are therefore often quoted as attached to St Bride's Day. [Ed.]

II. Sayings and rhymes. As the year goes on and the temperature of the water becomes less chill, there is a saying :

> Brigid put a foot in it,
> Mary put a hand in it,
> Patrick put a stone in it.

Candlemas ... is more temperate (than St Bride's Day), and St Patrick's Day, March 17th, takes away all the venom. . . . [A. Goodrich-Freer, *F.-L.* XIII (1902), p. 39.]   Hdes.

Bride is said to preside over the different seasons of the year and to bestow their functions upon them. . . . The venom of the cold is said to tremble for its safety on Bride's Day and to flee for its life on Patrick's Day. There is a saying :

> Bride put her finger in the river (Bride, another version,
>   Mary)
> On the Feast Day of Bride
> And away went the hatching mother of the cold,
> And she bathed her palms in the river
> On the Feast Day of Patrick,
> And away went the conception mother of the cold.

Another version says :

> Bride put her palm in it,
> Mary put her foot in it,
> Patrick put the cold stone in it.

[Car. Gad. I, pp. 170 f.]

La Fhéill-Brighde thig an righinn as a toll, on St Bride's Day the nymph (or princess) will come out of her hole.

The handsome black and white bird, known in English as the oyster-catcher, is called in Gaelic *Gille Brighde*, servant of St Bride, and its reappearance every due season was regarded as a sure sign of the approach of spring. By *ribhinn* (*righinn*) or nymph referred to in the last quoted saying, there is meant the adder, the term, according to Nicholson, being a deprecatory one ;—*ribhinn* for *nimhir*, a term for the serpent, imply-

ing ' venomous one '. All adders were believed to come out
of their winter holes on St Bride's day. [T. D. MacDonald,
Gaelic Proverbs & Proverbial Sayings (1926), p. 144.]

A week previous to St Bridget's Day (February 1st, O.S.)
serpents are obliged to leave their holes under ground, and if
the ground is then covered with snow they perish. In the
popular rhyme (as above) the serpent is called in Argyll and
Perthshire ' the daughter of Edward ', but in Skye *an ribhinn*,
the damsel. In both cases the name is probably a mere
euphemism suggested by the rhyme to avoid giving . . .
offence to the venomous creature. [*Sup*[s]. *of Hghlds.*, p. 225.]

The Serpent as Ivar's Daughter. In the new volume (*Outer
Isles*, 1902) . . . we are categorically informed that ' Ivar's
daughter ' is the nettle-plant, which about St Patrick's Day
puts her head out of holes in the walls of the houses loosely
built without lime. In this Miss Freer is, I believe, mistaken.
' Ivar's daughter ' is a euphemism for a snake, not for a nettle,
The late Mr Campbell of Tiree in his *Superstitions of the Scottish
Highlands*, p. 225, mentions that in a popular rhyme in Argyllshire and Perthshire the serpent is called the ' daughter of
Edward ', but in Skye simply ' the damsel ', *an ribhinn*. As
the words Ivar and Edward have probably a common origin
it can hardly be doubted that ' Ivar's daughter ' refers to a
snake. [John Abercromby, in *F.-L.* XIV (1903), p. 99.]

Dr Carmichael also reads *nighean Iomhair*, Ivar's daughter,
as a mistake for *an nimhir*, the serpent.

> Supper and light the night of St Bride,
> Sleep and light the night of St Patrick.

[*Car. Gad.* I.] Hghlds.

For the raven's nest rhyme see Vol. I, p. 4.

Trans.—For the cold of *Calluinn* thickest woollen homespun
is right, for the cold of St Bride's day mixed stuff will do. [Rev.
A. Stewart, *Twixt Ben Nevis & Glencoe* (1884), p. 274.] Iness.

Sleep spell.

I lie down to-night with Mary and her son,
With Michael the bright-white, and with Bride beneath her
    mantle,
I lie down with God, and may God lie down with me :
I shall not lie down with Brian, and Brian shall not lie down
    with me.

[Brian, Satan. Ed.] [Isabel Cameron, *A Highland Chapbook*
(1928), p. 90.]

III. Saint. St Brigit (Bride) of Kildare on the plain of the Liffey in Ireland, *d.* about 525, ' Mary of the Gael '. The origin of her cult and its connection with the old Celtic ' Woman of Wisdom ' discussed by Cormac in his Glossary may be studied in Irish annals and in the works of Irish scholars. Dr Douglas Hyde gives details of her birth, her veiling as a nun, and her oratory, and quotes all best authorities (*Lit. Hist. of Ireland*, pp. 156 ff.) The undying fire, the oaktree, her ordination as head of all abbesses of the Scots by a disciple of St Patrick have been variously interpreted.

Professor Watson quotes fifteen saints of the name of Brigit, among whom it is impossible to discover the actual saint of many places and churches originally founded in this name. But the Brigit of Gaelic hymns and incantations is the Brigit of Kildare. In rites connected with her there are traces of an underlying pre-Christian cult. Her most notable dedication in Scotland was at Abernethy, where her church was founded by Nechtan Morbet, king of the Picts ; by her intercession he had been helped to return to his kingdom. It is pointed out in *Celtic Place-Names* that the dates of Brigit's life, *c.* 452-525, and those of Nechtan's reign, 457-481, bring this legend under suspicion ; it was however told by early historians. The seal of the church bears her image with a pastoral staff and her emblem, the cow. Abernethy was for long the seat of the metropolitan See, and from this famous centre of ecclesiastical influence the Christian cult of Brigit spread over Scotland. Her worshippers were anxious to claim her as of Scottish birth, and a legend grew that she had died at Abernethy. Caithness was stated to have been her birthplace, while a legend from Arran describes her as playing with ' her brother St Patrick ' on the banks of the Clyde and gathering cockles with him near Dumbarton. Every honour was paid to her memory ; ' by the divinity of St Brigit ' was one of the most solemn oaths of the Highlands.

She was specially invoked for the protection of the cow, and is often represented in Christian art holding a cow, standing by a barn, or with a pair of milk-pails or a bunch of corn in her hands. This seems to have been the most popular character of her cult during the Middle Ages. Hence the complaints against it :

> Preistes, pray no more
> To Sanct Anthone to saue your sow,
> Nor to Sanct Bride to keipe your cow,
> That grieues God right sore.

[*Sc. Poems of the 16th Cent.* Ed. by J. G. Dalyell, 1801], and Sir D. Lindsay attacks the superstitious pilgrimages to ' Sanct Bryde, well carvit with ane Kow '. Many of her legends connect her with butter-making.

Carmina Gadelica names seven saints of the Highlands invoked during milking, among them ' the herdsman Patrick ' and ' the milkmaid Bride '. One of her titles is ' Christ's milkmaid ' ; she is appealed to, with nine others, for the protection of cows and of sheep. Spells quoted below reflect the strong belief in her power to guard animals of the farm, and on this account her festival has been thought to have taken the place of an older milking festival. [Cf. Miss E. Hull, *Folklore of the Brit. Isles* (1928), p. 52.] Other connections are with fire and light, which make her ' St Bride of Brightness ' :

> St Bridget's cross hung over door,
> Which did the house from fire secure.
>
> [Lean, *Collectanea*, II, i, p. 417.]

Legends also typify this feature of her cult, she hangs her cloak on a sunbeam, and walks with Mary to the Temple after the birth of her Son, carrying in each hand a lighted candle ; ' these did not even flicker ' though the wind at the time was strong. She is sometimes represented with a flame at her side.

Bride was invoked in Uist as the Aid-Woman of Mothers ; for in legend she had been serving-maid in the inn at Bethlehem, and when Mary went to the stable aided her there, the first to raise the Christ-child in her arms at His birth. [Ed.]

The cult was strong in the south of Scotland. She was patron of the house of Douglas and in connection with this family had an altar at Melrose. [*Celt. Pl.-Names*, p. 152.]

There are many places of the name of Kilbride in Scotland and wells have been dedicated to one or other of the SS. Brigit. [*Ibid.*]

The appearance of the serpent with Brigit is remarkable. On her Day the serpent was cast into the ocean, ' so that the sea may swallow her up '. But the reptile will not injure a descendant of Ivor, he having made *tabhar agus tuis*, offering and incense, to it.

> To-day is the Day of Bride,
> The serpent shall come from the hole.

or :

> The daughter of Ivor shall come forth from the knoll.
> The serpent will come from the hole
> On the brown day of Bride

Though there should be three feet of snow
On the flat surface of the ground.

[*Ibid.*, pp. 169-171.] Cf. **II. Rhymes**, above, and **V c.**, **V d.**
below.

Divination by looking through a circle made by the fingers
of the hand is said to have been practised first by Joseph and
Mary when looking for the Child Christ. St Bride was
employed in this *Frith* and looked through a circle made by
the fingers of the Virgin herself. [A. Goodrich-Freer, *Outer
Isles* (1903), p. 227.]

Her patronage was much extended in Europe.

IV. Omens. a. *Weather*.

As far as the wind shall enter the door
On the Feast of St Bride,
The snow shall enter the door
On the Feast Day of Patrick.

[*Car. Gad.* I, p. 170.]   Hghlds.

See also **I a.**, above.

Good weather on St Bride's day indicates a famine or foray.
[Mlan MS.]   W. Isles.

e. *Birds*. It is a sign of the approaching spring that on this
day . . . larks sing with a clearer voice. [*Wcrft. & Sec. Sight*,
p. 249.]   Hghlds.

The observances described in the following extracts do not
fit into any scheme of classification, but belong partly to
divination.

V. Observances. c. *Ashes.* **V d.** *Divination*, and **XII.** *Religious
festival*.

On Bride's Eve the girls of the townland fashion a sheaf of
corn into the likeness of a woman. They dress and deck the
figure with shining shells, sparkling crystals, primroses, snowdrops, and greenery. . . . A specially bright shell or crystal
is placed over the heart of the figure.

This is the ' Guiding Star of Bride ', typifying the star over
the stable door which directed her as she went her way from
the inn to serve Mary. The dressed figure is carried by the
girls in procession ; it is called by pet names and the girls,
dressed in white with their hair hanging down, sing Bride's
song, ' Beauteous Bride '. They call at every house where the
gift of a shell, crystal or flower is expected, tokens of the worship
of Bride. The mothers give a bannock, cheese, or a roll of
butter. The girls retire with the offerings to a house where
windows and doors are made fast as the feast of Bride is made

ready, placing the figure where it may be seen by all. The young men of the community now assemble and ask permission to enter and honour Bride. After they are admitted dancing, singing and fun fill the hours till dawn. In the grey light the young men and girls join hands in a circle and again sing the song of ' Beauteous Bride '. The fragments left of the feast are distributed among the poor women of the place.

The older women have been busy on this eve. They make a basket in the shape of a cradle which they call the ' Bed of Bride '. A sheaf of corn, usually oats, is shaped in the form of a woman, and both the basket and the figure are decorated with ribands, flowers, shells, and coloured stones. When this *dealbh Bride*, image or figure of Bride, is so dressed, a woman standing ready goes to the door and taking her place on the step with her hands on the jambs calls to those outside, ' Bride's bed is ready! ' To this a woman standing behind replies ' Let Bride come in, Bride is welcome '. The woman at the door again addresses the figure : ' Bride, Bride, come thou in, thy bed is made ' ; the figure is then gravely placed in the bed (or cradle). A small white straight wand, peeled, is laid beside the figure. This is generally of birch, broom, bramble, white willow, or other sacred wood ; crossed or banned wood would not be used. The women then ' smoor ' the ashes on the hearth, levelling them carefully, and these are carefully examined early on the following morning. Marks of Bride's wand are welcome, but there is great rejoicing should the mark of her footstep be there, for then they know that she had been with them during the night and bestows her favour on them, insuring increase in family, flock and field during the ensuing year. If there is no sign of her presence she must be propitiated and an oblation is offered, usually a cockerel or a pullet buried alive near a place where three streams meet, and burnt as incense on the hearth the last thing before going to bed on St Bride's night. [For a fuller account see *Car. Gad.* I, pp. 167-168.] Outer Hdes.

The custom (of Bride's bed) is long extinct in the parts of the Highlands with which the writer is acquainted and the only particulars connected with it he has heard are, that on St Bride's Day a bed of birch twigs is made by the women, and that they then cried, ' Bride, Bride, come in, your bed is ready ' (*Bride, Bride, thig astigh, tha do leaba deante*). [*Wcrft. & Sec. Sight*, p. 248.] Hghlds. and Is.

The night before Candlemas a bed was made with corn and hay, over which some blankets are laid, in a part of the house

near the door. When it is ready a person goes out and repeats three times, ' *A Bridh, A Bridh, thig astigh is gabh do leabaidh!* ' ' Bridget, Bridget, come in ; thy bed is ready! ' [lit. ' take thy bed! '] One or more candles are left burning near it all night. [MS. of John Ramsay of Ochtertyre (*b.* 1736), ed. by Alex. Allardyce in *Scot. and Scotsmen in the 18th Cent.* (1888), II, p. 447.]
W. Coast and Isles.

The last sheaf used for Bride's bed. The Celts of the west country attached great importance to cutting the last sheaf. All the harvesters stood round in a circle while the youngest girl among the reapers cut a few straws left standing at the corner of the field for that purpose. This sheaf was ultimately used, as I have been assured by old people, for making Brüd's bed. [Rev. Js. MacDonald, *Religion and Myth* (1893), p. 141.]

Spreading a bed for strangers. It is said of St Bride that she spread a bed for the child Jesus, and on St Bride's Eve it was till lately, the custom to make a bed for . . . strangers or homeless persons who might be passing by. The old people speak of a custom of ' spreading the bed of Bride ' of which the details are now forgotten. [A. Goodrich-Freer, *Outer Isles* (1902), p. 226.]
Outer Hdes.

†From an old ' person '. You need not ask me about these things, they were long done before my day, . . . but I heard that they kept *Latha 'ill Bridhe* (St Bride's Day) until perhaps seventy or eighty years ago in some places. They had big feasts and a lot of merrymaking and each had on his best suit of clothes, and mind you no one thought of doing work that day. Oh, no, and then the women would take a big cloth, such as a bedcover, and they would take hold of it by each corner and then they would dance, and now and then call out together ; and at other times only one would call ' *Brie- dean, Briedean, thig an nall 's dean do leabaidh* ' (Bridean, Bridean, come over and make your bed), and at times a little bundle of straw would be thrown out in a corner as if it was meant that the saint was to come and sleep on it.

P.M.D. says, ' I could not find out how long this went on from my informant, he was so reticent and did not want to speak of it. The reason I believe was that his own mother was keeping it. I just remember seeing her as an old woman '. [Mlan MS.]
Ledaig, Ar.

†*Pounding the serpent in effigy.* Early during the day a bit of peat was taken out from the fireplace to the doorstep by a pair of tongs. Here the person performing the rite, apparently a woman, took off her stocking, put the peat into it and

pounded it well on the doorstep, repeating meanwhile a *rann* of which but a few lines have been recorded :

> This is the day of Bride,
> The queen will come from the mound;
> I will not touch the queen
> Nor will the queen touch me.

When the peat was thoroughly pounded the stocking was replaced and its owner returned to the family circle. [For a full account, the only one collected, refer to *Carmina Gadelica*, I, p. 171. For beliefs relating to the serpent, cf. serpent rhymes above.] Skye, Iness.

V e. *Farm and pasture customs.* †In Uist the flocks are counted and dedicated to Bride on her day. [*Car. Gad.* I, p. 173.] Hdes.
Cf. also **VI**. *Spells.*

V g. *Fishermen's customs.* †On St Bride's day the people of Barra meet outside the church, and, by a very old custom, ballot for the position of the boats for the coming fishing season, after which again the skipper of each boat draws lots for his crew, he himself having made his arrangements with some fish-curer who lets him have a boat and bounty for the men, while he, in return, undertakes to let the curer have all the herring taken by the boat's crew during the season. [The service in the church is referred to.] [A. Goodrich-Freer, *Outer Isles* (1902), pp. 121 f.] Barra, W. Isles.

The fishing in Barra is annually inaugurated with religious services in the church on St Bride's Day . . ., and until six years ago the fishing banks were distributed among the various crews. The ceremony of distributing the banks was carried on by means of casting lots, under the direction of the priest. As the people left the church they chanted one of their old hymns (to Father, Son and Holy Spirit, on the back of the wave or on the hillside). But the sea was regarded as the Virgin's Treasury, and when an unexpected haul of fish was landed, it was observed that it came from *Cuile Mhoire*, or the secret store of the Virgin. [*Trans. Gaelic Soc^tv. of Inverness*, XVIII, 1891, p. 2.] W. Isles.

The ballot connected with St Barr. The Roman Catholic fishermen belonging to the island continued to favour the culture of St Barr. They meet in the church on February 1, and arrange by ballot who are to occupy the boats destined for the various banks at the forthcoming long-line fishing.

After the ballot the priest holds a service in which he commends the fishermen to the care of the Holy Trinity, St Mary, St Bride, and St Barr. [*Anᵗ. Ch. Ded. N.*, p. 141.]

Barra, Outer Hdes.

V m. *Food custom. Bonnach Brìde.* That (cake) baked for the first day of spring was called *Bonnach Brìde*, bannock of Bride. [*Car. Gad.* I, p. 211.] Hghlds. and W. Isles.

V o. *Observances of animals, birds, insects, etc.*
On February 1st

> The raven goes to prepare his nest,
> And again goes the rook.
> [*Car Gad.* I, p. 178.]

The serpent or viper comes from his hole. Cf. **I a.**, above.

VI. Beliefs in charms, spells, fairies, witchcraft.

Changeling restored. It was believed that a changeling placed below high-water mark on St Bride's night would be taken away and the original child restored. [*Celt. Review*, V (1908-9), p. 162.] Lewis and Harris, Hdes.

The following spells and incantations belong to the name rather than to the day of St Bride, but throw light on her cult.
Spell :

> Bride went out
> In the morning early
> With a pair of horses ;
> One broke his leg,
> With much ado
> That was apart
> She put bone to bone, etc.
>
> . . . . .
>
> As she healed that
> May I heal this.

[Trans. by Dr Carmichael, *Car. Gad.* II, pp. 18 f.] This well-known spell, adapted from the Merseburg charm, is used with several other names, including that of Christ Himself.

Hymn-Charm. It is customary to recite the genealogy of St Bride, . . . and among the concluding lines are these :

> Each day and each night that I recall the genealogy of Brigid,
> I shall not be killed,
> I shall not be wounded,
> I shall not be struck by the Evil Eye.

[*F.-L.* (1899), Vol. X, p. 261.] Hdes.

A very old spell invoking the Torranan (figwort), was recited in the name of Bride while the plant was being plucked.

> The hand of St Bride with me
> I am now to pluck thee.
> Let me pluck thee, Torranan!
> With thine increase as to sea and land ;
> With the flowing tide that shall know no ebbing,
> By the assistance of the chaste St Bride.

SS. Columba and Michael also invoked, as in the house charm below. [*Car. Gad.*]

The crop of the plant gradually fills up with . . . dew while the tide is flowing and slowly dries up again during the ebb. You place the Torranan under one of your milk-pails, and while placing it there repeat the *Eòlas* [spell] three times ; making a circle sunwise, also three times, with the plant over the milk-vessel, repeat or chant slowly the spell (in Gaelic). [Alex. Stewart, *Twixt Ben Nevis and Glencoe* (1885), pp. 182-3.]

Hdes.

Spell of the Genealogy.

> Bride, daughter of Dugall the dark,
> Son of Aodh, son of Art, son of Conn.
> Each day and each night
> I will call to mind the genealogy of Bride.
> I shall not be killed,
> I shall not be wounded,
> I shall not be bewitched,
> Nor will Christ fail to protect me,
> Nor will the fire of Satan burn me,
> And neither river nor ocean drown me,
> If I (am) under the protection of Holy Mary
> And my dear nurse, Bride.

[See Gaelic in *Trans. Gaelic Soc^tv of Inverness*, XVIII (1891), p. 2.] Cf. *Car. Gad.* I, p. 175.

The same Society gives also a spell or incantation calling on ' gentle Bride ' with her rod and staff to use enchantment and take pledges against drowning of cattle of any kind in the stream or tricky dyke, and against harm or mischief.

Against lung-sickness in cattle. Carmen pro lonsoucht. In nomine patris, etc. . . . Deus benedicat greges istos sicut benedixit greges in deserto et per uirtutem illorum uerborum quod nocet non nocebit morbo de lonsoucht nec aliquo alio morbo caduco in uirtute et per uirtutem Sancte brigide Sicut Deus dedit potestatem ei benedicere omnia animalia in terra Amen.

Now þai sal tak a best and mak a bor in þe horn and þar in put þis forsaid charm and tak a peny and bov in þe bestis hevyd and gar a voman gan to Sanct brid and offer it in hir nam and tak haly vater and cast on þam as þai gan furth fra þe charmyng non plus, etc.

A charm against murrain found on the blank leaf of a service-book from a chapel in E. Lothian, invoking the aid of St Bride. [A. P. Forbes, *Calendars of the Sc. Saints*, Appendix I (1872), p. liv.]

Bride invoked as a guardian of the house, from a MS. dated 1684.

At night, in the time of popery, when folks went to bed, they believed the repetition of this following prayer was effectual to preserve them from danger, and the house too.

> Who sains the house the night,
> They that sains it ilka night.
> Saint Bryde and her brate, [mantle]
> Saint Colme and his hat,
> Saint Michael and his spear,
> Keep this house from the weir ;
> From running thief,
> From burning thief ;
> And from a'ill Rea
> That be the gate can gae ;
> And from an ill wight
> That be the gate can light. . . .

[George Sinclair, *Satan's Invisible World Discovered* (1789), pp. 143 f.]

IX. Dancing, Singing, etc. In Tiree in the evening it was customary to have a ball (St Bride's night). [*Wcrft. & Sec. Sight*, p. 299.]   I. of Tiree, Ar.

See also dancing as described at the ' Bed of Bride ' rites, above.

XI. Cock Fighting. Bride's Day was also called ' Day of Cock-fighting '. The boys brought cocks to the school to fight. The most successful cock was called *coileach buadha*, victor cock, and its proud owner was elected king of the school for the year. A defeated bird was called *fuidse*, craven. . . . All the defeated, maimed and killed cocks were the perquisites of the schoolmaster. In the Lowlands Candlemas Day was the day thus observed. [*Car. Gad.* I, p. 172.]

Reported also from the island of Tiree, Ar. [Mlan MS.]

2nd

I. Names. Candlemas, the Purification ; known as *Féill Brìde* in some of the Gaelic speaking districts. At one time Candlemas rather than Twelfth Day was held by many to mark the end of the Yule festivities. [D. MacRitchie, *Scot. Review*, Feb. 1, 1906.]

II. Sayings. Snowdrops now beginning to appear are known as Candlemas Bells. [D. MacRitchie.]

III. Saint. The Virgin Mary, her Purification. This festival was one of the most venerated of the older Christian festivals.

Candlemas is one of the very few (festivals) which have continued impressed upon the minds of the Presbyterian people of Scotland after all ostensible veneration for such days had passed away. . . . It is . . . remarkable that these few days are chiefly of those which are understood to have been Pagan festivals before the introduction of Christianity (Candlemas, Beltane, Lammas, and Hallowmas). [*Pop. Rhymes*,[3] p. 141.]

The correspondence between the original pagan and subsequent Christian festival . . . is among the most remarkable coincidences that have fallen under notice. [R. T. Hampson, *Med. Aevi. Kal.* (1841), p. 157.]

IV. Omens. a. *Weather.*

If Candlemas day be clear and fair.
The half of the winter is to come and mair.

[' Prognostication,' by G. F., *Philol. and Philom.*, Edinburgh (1685).]

If the wind's in the east on Candlemas day
There it will bide till the second o' May.

If you throw your coat at Candlemas
You will need your mifles in May.
(i.e. mittens without fingers.)

Corgarff, Ab.

The fisherman wid raither see his wife o' the bier
Nor a Candlemas day fair and clear. (Variant, Than
Candlemas day to be fair and clear.)

[Rev. W. Gregor.]   Ab.

The shepherd would rather see the wolf in his fold than the sun on Candlemas Day. [D. Grewar, *Sc. N. & Q.*, 3rd series, II, p. 24.]

> Where the wind is on Candlemas Day,
> There it will stick till the end of May.

> At Candlemas, if the thorn hang a drop,
> Of peas we gather a heavy crop.

> If Candlemas be fair and bright
> Winter will have another flight,
> But if Candlemas bring cloud and rain,
> Winter is gone and will not come again.
>
> [*Ibid.*]

e. As long as the laverock [lark] sings before Candlemas it will greet after it. [Ch. Swainson, *F.-L. of British Birds* (1886), p. 93.]

For other rhymes about *Candlemas* see Vol. I, p. 3.

V. Observances. b. *Things enjoined or lucky. Nothing taken out of the house.* It was a custom not long ago to bring something into the houses on the morning of Candlemas Day before taking anything out. [*Ethnog. Survey of the U. Kingdom*, 5th Report (1897), p. 459.] Galloway.

Candlemas candles. The reciter says that he has frequently seen small bits of candles worn by people as a charm to keep mischief away. He believes they were the remains of candles that were set aside for that purpose at the time of *Féill Brìde*.[1] They sewed them in a convenient corner in the inside of their coats. [Mlan MS.] W. Isles.

Sprinkled with holy water and blessed, these candles (of Candlemas) were supposed to possess the power of repelling evil spirits. [R. T. Hampson, *Med. Aevi. Kalend.* (1841), p. 156.]

V c. *Fire, torches, etc. The Candlemas Bleeze.* The Candlemas bleeze is yet another survival of the (pagan) time. [*Dumfries & Galloway, N. & Q.* I, p. 66.]

Reformation Burghers of Scottish towns and, as the custom began to die out, their children, used to walk in procession to the town cross, bearing their candles or torches in their hands; and thereafter they finished the day by lighting a prepared bonfire, or in default of that by making a ' Candlemas Bleeze ' of the nearest thicket of whins. [D. MacRitchie, *Scot. Review*, Feb. 1st, 1906.]

The evening of this notable day (Candlemas) was given

---

[1] Féill Brìde, Candlemas here, as often in the Highlands. [Ed.]

over to the Candlemas ' bleeze ', the burning of any suitable clump of broom or whins in the neighbourhood, or if this were not available, the erection of a huge bonfire in a prominent position. ' The anniversary of St Blazius is the 3rd of February ' [the 2nd was the eve of St Blaize's day, hence the custom] to light up fires in the hills on St Blayse night [for eve.?] : a custom anciently taken up perhaps for no better reason than the jingling resemblance of his name to the word *blaze.*' [From Percy, *Northumberland Household Book.*]

' Bleyvis sylver ' and ' bent sylver ' formed part of the revenue of the schoolmaster in many places as recently as 1840. [A. D. Cumming, *Old Times in Scotland* (1910), pp. 128-9.] Torches and Candles also under **X**. Cf. Cult of St Blaise, Feb. 3rd, below. Also Feb. 13th for gift to schoolmaster.

V e. *Farm and Byre. Ploughing.* The farmer, whatever the state of the weather, . . . obstinately adhered to the immemorial practice of beginning to plough on Old Candlemas Day (February 13th). [*O.S.A.* XX, p. 474.] Dowally, Pth.

Farm custom. Kettle, 1680.—There were farmers who had such a reverence for ancient customs, that they would not yoke a plough till Candlemass, while some went so far as to be unwilling to remove the weeds from the fields, believing that through Adam's fall Providence willed that weeds should grow. [*Fife Herald and Journal*, June 21st, 1905.] Kettle, Ffe.

V k. *Doles and gifts. Bleeze money,* or *Candlemas Bleeze.* That offering or present pupils make to their Dominies on Candlemas Day. Anciently it used to be a large candle, one that could give a good blaze, hence the name bleeze ; now-a-days ' hard cash ' [it] is thought gives as pleasant a light. [Mactaggart, *Encyclop.* (1824), p. 111, as quoted in *E.D.D.*]

The scholars assembled in the schoolroom. The roll was called, and as each one's name was called out, he or she went forward to the teacher's desk and laid down a piece of money. There was a contest between a boy and a girl who was to be king or queen, and the teacher knew beforehand who were to contend for the honour. Their names were called out last. They went to the teacher's desk as the others did and laid down a shilling (about). The one that laid down for the longest time was king or queen as the case might be. Whisky toddy, weak and sweet, was then given to each scholar. Sometimes oranges and other good things were added. Then followed a dance. My informant, when a scholar, used to supply the music from a fiddle, and for years after he left

school. Parents, scholars and friends were at times entertained at a dance in the evening. Next day was generally
given as a holiday to the scholars. When the custom fell out
of use a present was made to the teacher about Christmas.
The custom of making a present at Christmas continues.
The Rev. H. M. B. Reid notes upon this : ' The arrangements
were made a few days before February 2 (Candlemas). If
February 2 fell on a Sunday, the next day after was kept. In
Glenlochar School (Balmaghie) the king and queen were *not*
known beforehand.'—(Schoolmaster's widow, aged 79.)
[*Ethnog. Survey of the U. Kingdom*, 5th Report (1897), p. 458.]

Laurieston, Stg.

Given in the *Ethnog. Survey* also, with small variations, from
Kcbt. with the toast,

> Here's health, wealth, wit t' guide it,
> Over my throat I mean to guide it.

[*Ibid.*, p. 459.]   Kcbt.

The custom was very popular in the schools throughout
Kintyre. . . .

In some schools one of the boys was appointed to keep the
school clean, and light the fires in the winter season. He was
called the Scavenger, and his remuneration consisted in free
education and a Candlemas offering by the scholars, which
was contributed in the same way as the Teacher's, and ranged
from 1d. to 6d. [In this case occasionally there was no King
or Queen.]

The offerings being all taken in, the amount was announced,
and the Teacher returned thanks for himself and the Scavenger, especially for himself, taking occasion to make honourable
mention of the King and Queen, the amount of whose respective offerings were publicly intimated.

Then followed a treat provided by the Teacher. It was
usually an orange and a few sweets : the King and Queen
receiving twice as much as any of the others. Sometimes
the treat was on a more elaborate scale, and one Teacher at
least gave a glass of whisky. [Mlan MS.]   Kintyre, Ar.

The most usual present was a quarter's wages, or seven
shillings and sixpence, commonly paid by three half-crowns ;
but many of the scholars gave only five shillings, and some of
them merely two shillings and sixpence ; indeed there were
some boys whose parents were unable to give their sons even
the last-mentioned pittance to present. . . . A few of the sons
of the richer class of citizens gave ten shillings and sixpence,

always in gold ; and I remember in particular that a son of one of our mercantile magnates presented a gold guinea, and was declared *King*. [Senex, *Glasgow Past and Present* (1884), vol. i, p. 302.]   Glasgow.

A profitable source of revenue was the Candlemas offering, or ' oblation '. . . .   On that day each scholar brought a money gift to the master, who was graciously pleased to receive it, seated aloft on his chair of state.   The humblest gifts were received in silence, a gift equalling a quarter's fee with the shout of 'vivat !' and double this sum with 'floreat bis !' A higher amount evoked ' floreat ter !' while the donor of the highest gift was acclaimed with the enraptured ' gloreat !' and publicly styled ' victor ', or ' king ', or ' queen '. [A. D. Cumming, *Old Times in Scot.* (1910), p. 128.]

The ' King ' receives a football.   It was a long-established practice for the Rector of Kelso Grammar School and the other teachers to present ' the king ', that is the boy who made the most liberal Candlemas offering, with a football. [E. J. Guthrie, *Old Scottish Customs* (1885), p. 92.]   Rxb.

Candlemas Crown.   In the city of St Andrews is a grammar-school in the patronage of the town-council. . . .   The scholars in general pay at least 5s. a quarter, and a Candlemas gratuity, according to their rank and fortune, from 5s. even as far as 5 guineas, when there is a keen competition for the Candlemas Crown.   The King, *i.e.* he who pays most, reigns for 6 weeks, during which period he is not only intitled to demand an afternoon's play for the scholars once a week, but he has also the royal privilege of remitting all punishments. [*County F.-L.*, VII, p. 195.]   Ffe.

†*A Play-day claimed.*   It was usual about Candlemas for a deputation of students from the University to repair to the Grammar School at Common Hall time and to solicit a play-day for each of the four classes, which the teachers always readily granted ; and in return . . . four boys of the oldest class in the school resorted to the College and requested a like favour from the Principal for the University students, which of course was never denied. On these occasions the Latin language only was used by both parties. [Senex, *Glasgow Past and Present* (1884), III, p. 409.]   Glasgow.

V o. *Observances of animals, birds, etc.*   Larks are believed to pair about Candlemas. [Greg., p. 184.]   N.E. Scot.

VI. Beliefs in Witchcraft, etc. *The Gyrecarline.* The Gyre-carline cut a considerable figure on the stage of our northern superstition. She assumed the appearance of an old woman, and paid her visits only at a certain season of the year—namely, between Candlemas and Fasterneen. She was a noted spinster ; and during this period, it was necessary to take the band off the spinning-wheel every night, and ' sain ' it, otherwise she would disturb and frighten the whole family with her spinning. The noise she made was often as loud as that of a pair of fanners at work. If any female had the courage and presence of mind to ask from her a gift of the art of spinning, she would obtain it to such a degree that she would be able, within a given period, to spin more than any other three or four women. The Gyrecarline was always accompanied by a child ; and, as she made it a regular point to bathe the latter before retiring, it was necessary to have some clear spring water in the house for that purpose. Unless this and some other little arrangements were attended to for her accommodation, she would do some mischief to the family. In the south, the Gyrecarline was embodied into a much more distinct and palpable character and with attributes sufficiently repulsive. She was conceived to be the great hag, or mother of the witches, and often got the name of Nicneven. [Calder's *Sketches from John O'Groats*, Wick (1842), pp. 223-4.] Cths.

Witches' Candles. At first sight it would seem that the candles were naturally used only to illuminate the midnight festivities, but the evidence points to the burning lights being part of the (witches') ritual. This is also suggested by their importance in the cult of the early-spring festival of Candlemas, a festival which has long been recognised as being of pre-Christian origin.

The light is particularly mentioned in many instances as being carried by the Devil, usually on his head ; the witches often lit their torches and candles at this flame. . . . The witches of North Berwick in 1590 mention candles as part of the ritual (of the Candlemas Sabbath). [M. A. Murray, *The Witch Cult in Western Europe* (1921), pp. 144-5.]

N. Berwick.

IX. Dramatic Performances, Dancing, Singing. *Pageant with some drama*. These pageants and dramas were regulated by acts and ordinances of the magistrates and town council. The earliest of them appears in the year 1442, and the pageants and dramatis personæ are represented as follows :

(September 16th, 1442.) Yir craftes undwritin sal fynd

yerly, in ye offerand of our Lady at Cãdilmis, yir p̃sonnes undwritin ; yat is to say—

Ye Littistares sal fynd
Ye empriour and twa docteours, and alsmony honeste squiares
as yai may.
Ye Smythes and Haṁmen sal fynd
Ye three kings of Culane, and etc.
Ye Talzoures sal fynd
Our Lady, Sancte Bride, Sancte Helene, Joseph, and etc.
Ye Skȳnares sal fynd
Twa bischopes, four angeles, and etc.
Ye Webstares and Walkares sal fynd
Symion, and his disciples, and etc.
Ye Cordonares sal fynd
Ye messyngear, and Moyses, and etc.
Ye Fleschowares sal fynd
Twa or four wodmen, and etc.
Ye Brethir of ye Gild sal fynd
The menstralis, and etc.
[*Council Register*, V, p. 661.]

In the year 1505, we find another of these pageants, preparatory to the offering of the ' Play, in honour of God, and the blessed Virgin Mary '. The dramatis personæ were regulated as follows :

The Craftsmen, furnishing -	- The Pageants.
The Cordwainers - -	- The Messing.
The Websters and Waulkers	- Symeon.
The Smiths and Goldsmiths	- Three Kings of Cullane.
The Litsters - - -	- The Emperor.
The Masons - - -	- The three Knights.
The Tailors - - -	- Our Lady of St Bride and St Helen.
The Skinners - - -	- The two Bishops.

In the year 1532, another drama, which is partly scriptural, partly legendary, is particularly mentioned ; and was enjoined to be performed, by the artificers, on Corpus Christi and Candlemas festivals, in ' honour of God, and the blessed Virgin Mary '. The dramatis personæ were represented as follows :

The Fleshers, furnishing -	- St Sebastian and his Tormentors.
The Barbers - - -	- St Laurence and his Tormentors.

The Skinners and Furriers - -	St Stephen and his Tormentors.
The Cordwainers - - -	St Martin.
The Tailors - - - -	The Coronation of Our Lady.
The Litsters - - - -	St Nicholas.
The Websters, the Waulkers, and Bonnet Makers - - -	St John.
The Baxters - - - -	St George.
The Wrights, the Masons, the Slaters, and the Coopers - -	The Resurrection.
The Hammermen, to furnish -	The bearmen of the Cross.

THE SACRAMENT.

[Wm. Kennedy, *Annals of Aberdeen, etc.* (1818), pp. 95-6 ; from the *Council Register*, VIII, p. 186 ; XIII, p. 162.]
    See also under **X. Processions.**
    Dancing. See under **V c, V k,** *Bleeze.*

X. Processions. Every town had the festival of its patron saint . . . and there were processions at Candlemas . . . and other times, with the trades marching in order. [*The Book of Buchan* (1910), V, ii, p. 267.]
    In the beginning of the 16th century various plays and pageants were exhibited by the artificers, who walked in procession through the town on Candlemas. [Robert Wilson, *Historical Account, etc., of Aberdeen* (1822), p. 32.]   Ab.
    The litsters (dyers) . . . were ordained to provide . . . their banners and pageants in the processions on the festivals of Corpus Christi and Candlemas, in the same manner as the other craftsmen. . . . [*Council Register*, XVI, p. 291 ; in Wm. Kennedy, *Annals of Aberdeen, etc.* (1818), pp. 94-7.]
    In 1523 John Pitt, tailor, who had refused to join the Candlemas procession . . . was sentenced by the Town Council to appear on the following Sunday in St Nicholas Church, ' bareheaded and barefooted ' and there to publicly acknowledge his offence. In performing his act of penance, he was to wear on his breast a pair of shears, and, in the time of high mass, to carry a wax-candle as an offering to St Nicholas and thereafter on his knees, humbly to beseech the officiating priest to remit his fault. [*Burgh Records of Aberdeen*, quoted in Chas. Rogers, *Social Life in Scot.* (1884), II, p. 163.]
    Processions of school children. The bairnies of the Old Town Grammar School came to the gate with candles lighted in

their hands, crying, rejoicing, blythe enough. They came up
to the cross and round about goes diverse times, climbs to the
head thereof and sets on a burning torch thereupon. [Gavin
Turreff, *Antiq. Gleanings* (1859), p. 50.] Ab.

The custom, formerly connected with this game (football),
of the schools marching in procession through the town (at
Candlemas) with a gilded ball on the top of a pole has long
been abandoned. [E. J. Guthrie, *Old Scot. Customs* (1885),
p. 93.] Kelso, Rxb.

XI. Outdoor Games, Races, Mock Combats. *Ball game.* The
game of ' ball ' is played only on one particular day of the year
in the month of February, the young men of one district being
pitched against those of another. Similar games are also held
annually about the same season in some of the neighbouring
parishes. [*N.S.A.* III, i, p. 246.] Ancrum, Rxb.

Rules of the Ba'-playing. In olden times nearly every district
had its annual *ba'-playing.* . . . The following were the rules.
. . . It was not allowable to touch the ball with the hand
after it had been cast upon the ground. An opponent might
be tripped when near the ball, and more especially when
about to hit it with his foot, but a competitor could not be
laid hold of or otherwise interfered with when at a distance
from the ball ; the party who out of three rounds hailed the
ball twice was proclaimed victor. [E. J. Guthrie, *Old Scot.
Customs* (1885), p. 26.]

Handball was more popular in the southern districts. [*Ibid.*,
p. 27.]

For several accounts of ball-playing at Shrove-tide or
Candlemas see Vol. I, Movable Festivals, pp. 15-27.

Cock Fighting. D. McTaggart remembers when it was
a common practice to have steel spurs put on fighting cocks
before the fight. He has also known of snuff being put under
their wings with the view that when the cock would fly against
his opponent, the snuff would blind the other one. Of course
Candlemas was the great time for regular cock-fighting . . .
such as took an interest in the practice took great pains to
have their cocks properly trained and prepared. [Mlan MS.]
Islay, Ar.

Cock fighting . . . was a regular annual treat to the people
on Candlemas Day, . . . Two or three hundred of these
bipeds were often placed in pugnacious array at that period,
and under particular auspices. The schoolmasters of the town
requested all their male scholars to produce cocks on that

occasion ; so that, in one school, thirty or forty couple of these feathered combatants would have been mustered to destroy each other ; while the schoolmaster presided in the arena as Master of the Ceremonies. This disgraceful practice has long ceased. [R. Wilson, *Hist. of Hawick* [2] (1841), pp. 177 f.]   Rxb.

See also Vol. I, Movable Festivals, Fastern's E'en.

XII. Religious Observance. A chappel in the Parish of Konesbie the northernmost Parish of all this country opposite Orkney, which is yet more frequented than any of the former, which some wildly superstitious frequent on some day about Candlemas, going about it on their bare knees, and thence going to a water, they cast some of it in handfuls over their heads, and from the water to an Alehouse, where they use to fill themselves drunk ; and when going to these or at them they can scarce even though threatened be prevailed to speak. [John Brand, *A brief description of Orkney, Zetland, Pightland Firth and Caithness* (1701), p. 233.]   Cths.

See also February 4th, offerings to St. Modan.

XIII. Business Transactions. *Candle Dues paid from the Treasury.* In 1474 the Lord High Treasurer paid two crowns to James III and his queen (Margaret of Denmark) ' to offer on Candlemas Day ' at the Altar. Throughout the succeeding reign there are many such entries, the amount often varying from one to three French crowns—that is, from fourteen to forty-two shillings. Occasionally the payment is described as ' the king's offering in his candle ', which seems to imply that the money was inserted in or attached to the candle, then placed on the altar of the Virgin Mary. For with her this day became especially associated. The royal accounts of Scotland not only speak of these offerings as made on Candlemas Day, but quite as often the date is described as ' the Purification ', or ' the Purification of Our Lady '. [D. MacRitchie, *Scottish Review*, Feb. 1st, 1906.]

Rents paid in candles. The tenants of monastic establishments frequently held their lands on the condition of furnishing a quantity of wax to make the candles to be used in the celebration of this festival (Candlemas). [R. T. Hampson, *Med. Aevi. Kal.* (1841), p. 155.]

. . . There will be found mention made in the *Trans. of the Buchan Field Club* . . . that in Catholic times a burden laid upon certain holdings in our district was so many pounds of

candles, or of tallow for making them, to be delivered by
Candlemas. [J. Spence, *Trans. Buchan Field Club* (1896, 8),
iv, p. 223.]   Ab.

Wax as alms. Charter by Henry Bald, Goldsmith, to the
Monastery at Scone. Two booths given to God and the
churches of the Holy Trinity and of St Michael of Scone and
to the abbot and canons, which must render to the Monks of
Cupar yearly one half stone of wax, at the Purification of the
Blessed Mary, in name of alms. [*O.S.A.* vol. 18, pp. 505 f.]
                                                           Scone, Pth.

Rents paid. The rents are paid twice in the year, at Candlemas, or some time in February when the price of the manu-
facture of stockings in winter is mostly collected, and in
September. . . . [*O.S.A.* X, p. 243.]   Ab.

Fines for loupin' the laird's dykes. At Galashiels the tenants
of the barony had to pay a penny fine at the bailie's court
every time they 'loupit' the laird's dykes. At Candlemas,
when the tenantry dined at the tavern with the laird, the pence
were regularly paid with the rents, and went towards the
defraying of the reckoning. [E. J. Guthrie, *Old Scot. Customs*
(1885), p. 214.]   Rxb.

As Candlemas was an important Quarter Day there were
many business transactions at this date.

XIV. Prohibitions. The Church (soon after the Reformation) prohibited plays from being acted upon any subject in
the canonical scriptures, or any play to be performed on
Sunday. [*Council Register*, vol. I, p. 500.]   Aberdeen.

After the period of the Reformation, these ancient pastimes
(plays and pageants) were repressed by acts of the legislature ;
although '*plays, fasts, histories, and antiques*', composed of
profane subjects, and performed by several of the young
citizens, were substituted in their place. These, however,
were condemned by the clergy, but supported, on the other
hand, by the king, who, by his mandate, compelled the clergy
to discontinue their censures against theatrical representations.
[Robt. Wilson, *An Historical Account, etc., of Aberdeen* (1822),
p. 32.]   Aberdeen.

3rd

III. Saint. St Blaise, patron saint of the island of Pladda,
on the south coast of Arran. He had an altar in the nave of
Glasgow Cathedral, and another in the choir of St Giles,
Edinburgh, and a special office in the Aberdeen Breviary.

His legend is given from the *Legenda Aurea* in the *Legends of the Saints in the Scottish Dialect of the 14th Century*. *Scottish Text Society* (1896). Armenian ; bishop of Sebaste in Cappadocia, he suffered martyrdom under Diocletian. He was patron of the wool-combers of Aberdeen, who held a procession through the city on his day with his representative seated on a white horse, a book in one hand and a loaded comb in the other. There was an ' Aisle of St Blaise ' in the cathedral of Dunblane with an altar dedicated to St Blaise and the Holy Blood. Here his cross was carried through the borough at the annual Corpus Christi procession. [*Anc^t. Church Dedications, N.*]

In England he shared the honours of these processions with Jason of the Golden Fleece. His relics were brought to Canterbury Cathedral where was one of his chapels. A special feature of church ceremonies on his day is the cluster of candles placed about his statue or by his picture. This observance was commanded by him to the woman whose pig he had rescued from a wolf when she brought offerings to him in prison : the blazing lights became associated with blazing fires at this time. It has been suggested that fires on February 3rd, his day, were transferred back to February 2nd, his eve. Cf. February 2nd, **V** c. *Candlemas Bleeze*. Chambers, *Bk. of Days*, I, describes the taking out of a thorn in the flesh or a bone in the throat in his name.

The resemblance of his name to the German *blasen*, to blow, led to a belief in his control of storms ; Scandinavian sailors would not refer to his feast and old calendars mark his day with a hunting horn. In parts of France a local pronunciation of his name gave rise to a connection with *blé*, wheat, which explains the invocation of his aid in agricultural rites. Sir D. Lindsay, *Testament & Complaynt of the Papyngo*, I, p. 701, refers to ' Sanct Blase ' as a cautioner for faithful performance of a promise. There were two ancient military orders of St Blaise. [Ed.]

See also *Folk-Lore*, XLV, pp. 77 f. and p. 163 ; *Calendar Customs*, England, II, pp. 130-136.

4th

III. Saint. Modan, M'Aodhan, ' my Aedan ', has several attributions ; see *Celt. Pl.-Names*, p. 289 ; and cf. St Modan of November 14th. The *Bk. of Saints* places him in the seventh century.

At Candlemas. E.S.E. from the Church (of Canisbay) at two miles distance is the town of Freswick upon a bay of the

East or German Sea. The house stands on the S.W. side of
the bay. . . . On the north side of the house a brook . . . runs
into the sea, over which is a bridge of one arch over against
the gate. At the further end whereof is a lately erected chappel
with a vault for burying, in the place where one old Popish
Chappel stood, that in very late times was much resorted to
by . . . people, who by offerings and devotions made to the
saint (Modan) expected recovery of their health. [*Geograph.
Collections*, I, p. 153. The Caithness Section was written about
1726.]   Cths.

7th

III. Saint. James Gammack, LL.D. [*Sc. N. & Q.*, 2nd
series, VIII, April 1907], gives this date for St Ronan, but
Celt. Pl.-Names finds no data to determine his day and there
were several of the name. *d. 737.* Abbot of Kingarth, Bute.
The old parish church, Teampull Ronaig, in Iona may have
commemorated him, also a church at Eoropie in Lewis, An
islet west of Shetland is called St Ronan's Isle. [*Celt. Pl.-
Names.*]

His chapel on the island of Rona, near Lewis, has a celebrated altar. There is a chapel here (on Rona) dedicated to
St Ronan, fenced with a stone wall round it, and they take
care to keep it neat and clean, and sweep it every day. There
is an altar in it, on which there lies a big plank of wood about
ten feet in length ; every foot has a hole in it, and in every
hole a stone, to which the natives ascribe several virtues ; one
of them is singular, as they say, for promoting speedy delivery
to a woman in travail. . . . The inhabitants . . . say that the
cuckoo is never seen or heard here, but after the death of the
Earl of Seaforth or the minister. [M. Martin, *A Descript. of the
Western Isles of Scot.*[2] (1716), Pinkerton, III, p. 581.]

9th

III. Saint. Apollonia, 3rd century. A martyr of Alex-
andria, whose teeth were broken with pincers. Invoked
against toothache. [*Bk. of Saints.*] This saint had some vogue
in Scotland since she is twice mentioned by David Lindsay.

ll. 269 ff.   Thare superstitious pylgramageis
                To mony divers Imageis;

                .   .   .   .   .

                For thare teith to Sanct Apolleine.

ll. 2295, 6. Sanct Apolline on Altare standis,
    With all her teithe in tyll hir handis.
[Sir D. Lindsay, against domestic Idolatry ; *The Monarchy*
(1550), ed. D. Laing, 1879.]

13th

V. Observance. **c.** On Old Candlemas (the 13th of
February), children were wont to carry home-made candles
to the school. A general illumination was produced, and the
remainder of the candles was presented to the schoolmaster.
[Ch. Rogers, *Familiar Illustr^{ns}. of Scot. Character* (1865), p. 166.]

14th

I. Name. St Valentine's Day. Cf. February 29th.

III. Saints. There are several early saints of this name but
none whose legend associates him with the customs of the day.
Valentinus, the Gnostic, 2nd century A.D., is one uncanonised
saint whose followers, the Valentinians, practised rites capable
of interpretation as the origin of these popular customs.

V. Observance. **d.** *Rites of divination.* In February (the
young people) draw Valentines and from them collect their
future fortune in the nuptial state. [T. Pennant, *A Tour in
Scot.*[4] (1769), ed. 1776.]   Bf.
    A Valentine for the year only was also drawn by lot, hence
the name passed to that of a guardian saint. [See Sir Walter
Scott, *The Fair Maid of Perth*, chapters IV and V.]
    At one time it was the custom on St Valentine's Day to draw
names in couples, the pair thus drawn being Valentines for
the rest of the year. This was apt to be an expensive business
for the gentleman, who was expected to present a really handsome gift to his Valentine, whether she pleased his fancy or
not. [A. A. M. D. in *The Scotsman*, Feb. 14th, 1936.]
    On the evening of Valentine Day companies of the young
unmarried men and women met, and drew ' valentines '. This
was done in the following way : The names of all the young
men and women in the neighbourhood were written on slips
of paper. The slips of paper were carefully folded up. The
slips bearing the names of the young men were put into one
bag, and those bearing the names of the young women were
put into another. The young men drew from the bag containing the names of the females, and the young women drew
from the other. The young man or young woman whom each

drew was the ' valentine '. Of course there was much merriment, and sometimes there was a little disappointment if the
wished-for ' valentine ' was not drawn. The slip of paper,
bearing the name was carefully preserved by each, and put
below the pillow to evoke dreams. [Greg., p. 166.] N.E. Scot.

Sixty years ago . . . I remember keeping Valentine day as
it was then kept generally in Morayshire. Printed Valentines
had not then come into vogue among us. A number of the
young people of the town or village assembled in some particular house for the purpose of drawing their Valentines.
Fate had to settle the matter. A sheet of paper was cut up
into slips sufficient in number for the boys or young men who
were to put their fortune to the test. Upon these slips the
names of girls were written. When ready the slips were placed
in a hat and well shaken together. Then the drawing took
place. Slips for the girls were prepared in the same way. . . .
Every one had in like manner (to proceed to the Valentine's
home to announce the event) to establish his claim to his
Valentine. . . . On the presentation of the slip of paper,
every one drawn as a Valentine had to make some small
present to the wooer, such as an apple, etc. As it was with the
boy drawers so it was with the girls. This was the real
original way of observing Valentine day and was undoubtedly
a survival from pagan times. . . . The early church did not
break the custom, but attached to it the name of Valentine
the Martyr, thus giving it a Christian character. Our earliest
English poets make frequent reference to Valentine's day.
But this ancient festival is . . . dead. [J. Spence, *Trans. of
the Buchan Field Club*, IV, p. 225.] Morayshire.

St Valentine's Eve has an observance of its own in the South
of Scotland. The young people assemble and write the names
of their acquaintances on slips of paper, placing those of the
lads and lasses in separate bags apart. The maidens draw
from the former, the young men from the latter, three times in
succession, returning the names after the first and second times
of drawing. If one person takes out the same name three times
consecutively, it is without fail that of the future husband or
wife. Thus, in Burns's song of Tam Glen the maiden sings :

> Yestreen at the Valentine dealing,
>   My heart to my mou gi'ed a sten [leap],
> For thrice I drew ane without failing,
>   An' thrice it was written, Tam Glen.

[Henderson, *F.-L. of the Northern Counties* (1879), p. 94.] S. Scot.

Valentine's e'en and Hallowe'en . . . used to be anniver-
saries observed in every house by the assemblage of young
people, and abundance of mirth. . . . They are hardly known
to the rising generation. [Th. Somerville, D.D., *My Own Life
and Times*, 1741-1814, p. 344.]   Jedburgh, Rxb.

Under *Valentines* the *New English Dictionary* cites an Act of the
Scottish Parliament ' ordaining the commissioneris of shyris to
draw lottis and valentines ʒeirlie at ilk parliament for thair
places '.

The following quotation illustrates the seriousness of this
custom :

When King Charles I was at Edinburgh in 1641, it was
proposed to him that the Lord Chancellor should be chosen
as they do valentines, and the king consented. . . . The
following extract from a letter from Sir Patrick Wemyss to the
Earl of Ormonde, given by Carte in his collection of letters,
1739 [?1639] : ' They are this day about the nomination of
the Lord Chancellor ; but what time that will take up, God
knows. But first it was moved amongst them that every man
should give his voice, after the question was stated, in a piece
of paper, and put them, like *Valentines*, in the clerk's hat ; and
so to be numbered. This His Majesty yielded to in the forenoon ; but in the afternoon came to the House and told them
he had forgot himself, and entreated them to let that alone.
But their hearts are hardened, and till that be granted they
will hearken to no other business.' This plan of electing
a Lord Chancellor, like a valentine, by converting the
clerk's hat into a ballot box, was not carried out ; for in a
subsequent letter, dated the ——— October, 1641, Sir Patrick
says, ' Upon Friday last my Lord London (*sic*] was chosen
chancellor in great state, being nominated by the king, and
approved of by the Parliament.' [*Long Ago : a Journal of
Popular Antiquities*, ed. by Alex. Andrews, Vol. i (1873), pp.
304-5.]

V k. *Gifts.* The learned Moresin tells us that . . . presents
were made *reciprocally* (between men and women) on this day
in Scotland. [Brand (1849), I, p. 57.]

V o. *Observances of birds.* Most birds were believed to pair
on Valentine day.   N.E. Scot.

For *Larks* see *Candlemas*, **V o.**
Cf. *British Calendar Customs*, England, II, Valentine's Day.

18th

III. Saint. Colman. The name is a diminutive of *colum*, a dove, and was adopted by a large number of saints. *Celt. Pl.-Names* quotes the Martyrology of Aberdeen for a Colman of this date, 7th century, as patron of Tarbert, Ross-shire, where he had a chapel. As bishop of Lindisfarne he upheld the Celtic Church in the dispute with Rome over the date of Easter ; he retired from Northumbria when his cause was lost.

24th

I. Name. St Matthias's Day.

II. Saying. If it freeze on St Matthias's Day it will freeze for months together. [D. Grewar, *Sc. N. & Q.*, 3rd series, II (1924), p. 24.]

III. Saint. St Matthias, who was chosen by lot to take the place of the traitor, Judas.

29th

II. Saying. ' Leap year was never a gude sheep year.' On account of the greater length of February. [*Pop. Rhymes*,[1] (1826), p. 291.]

> Now when the Year doth leap,
> Beware of shroves and sheep.

[From an old almanac.]

It is unlucky for beasts and bodies and a heap o' witchcraft is about in Leap-Year. [*County F.-L.* VII (1912), p. 158.] Ffe.

For obligation to accept a proposal of marriage from a lady on this day see *F.-L.* XXX (1919), pp. 64 f. This day and Valentine Day seem to have been connected in some places.

The day is unlucky because it had been cursed by Job. Told . . . by a clerical member of the Club who is at present in office in Wakefield. . . . ' When I was a boy . . . I was much puzzled with there being twenty-nine days in February Leap Year. . . . I knew an old cottar woman . . . and made an opportunity of calling at her cottage and putting the . . . question to her. " Well," said she, " I don't know, but whenever I don't know a thing I go to the funtin [fountain] heed, to the Bible I mean." . . . She took a folio Bible from its shelf and . . . it opened at a certain passage in the book of Job. . . . " And Job cursed the day on which he was born." " Now," she says, " I understand how it is. Job . . . must have been born on the 29th of

February, and God listened to his servant as far as He could. He could not score the day out altogether, but He scored out three out of every four. That was a gain for Job, and so you . . . see how Leap Year came to be different from the rest." '
[J. Spence, *Buchan Field Club, Trans.*, 1896-8, p. 229.]

St Fergus, Ab.
This belief is quoted also from Kintyre. [Mlan MS.]   Ar.

Last Week in February.   X. Procession. *Kate Kennedy's Day.*

The following celebration is observed annually by students of St Andrews attending the United College of St Salvator and St Leonard, during the fourth year.   Kate Kennedy's Day is yearly fixed by the observers for the last week in February or the beginning of March.   The students meet at an appointed place at noon, when they attire themselves in masquerade attire.   They then form a procession.   The leading performer, Kate Kennedy, is dressed in female garb and mounted on horseback.   Kate has a bodyguard, attended by a mounted escort.   A drummer leads the way discoursing martial music. Each member of the procession represents some historical character, such as the Pope, the Stuart kings, Roman citizens, Greek Philosophers, etc.   The cavalcade first proceeds to the college quadrangle, where Kate receives a congratulatory address.   They then visit the private houses of the different professors, who are cheered or hooted according to the esti- mation in which they are held.   The day's proceedings terminate in a banquet. . . .   The origin of this celebration is involved in some doubt.   It seems to combine the memory of St Catherine with a public recognition of the good services of the pious Js. Kennedy, Bishop of the See, who built St Salvator's College in 1456.   A bell was placed in the College steeple by Bishop Kennedy, who dedicated it to St Catherine. This was recast the third time in 1686 when a procession attended its suspension. [E. F. Guthrie, *Old Scot. Customs* (1885), pp. 218 ff.]

The principals and professors in 1878 forbade the cele- bration of ' Kate ', on pain of rustication.   [Westwood, *Guide to St Andrews* (1887).   Quoted in *County F.-L.* VII, pp. 156 f.]

The Dismal Days quoted for February are the 8th, 10th, 17th.

MARCH

MONTH

I. Names. *Màrt* is the modern Gaelic name for March, but this name had other meanings and is sometimes used in the sense of a specified time suitable for agricultural work ; in this sense there were three Màrts. The change of style added to the misunderstanding, and proverbs illustrate the uncertainty of the true meaning. *Màrt* is also Tuesday. See *Seasons*, for Gaelic seasonal names.

II. Rhymes, Sayings. March many weathers.

A night in March is swifter than two in harvest. [*Wcrft. & Sec. Sight*, p. 256.] Hghlds.

A peck o' March dust is worth a king's ransom.

A peck o' March dust is worth its waicht in goud.
[Greg., p. 150.] N.E. Scot.

The well-known verse advising seed-sowing in March is an instance of Màrt as Tuesday ; the third Tuesday of the month must by no means pass without the seed being sown. [Ed.]

> *Leig seachad a'chiad Mhàrt,*
> *'San darna Mhàrt mà's f heudar e,*
> *Ach olc air mhath gan d'thig an t-sìd,*
> *Cuir do shìol 'san f hior Mhàrt.*

> Let past the first March (i.e. Tuesday)
> And second March if need be,
> But be the weather good or bad,
> Sow thy seed in the true March.

[*Wcrft. & Sec. Sight*, p. 255.] Hghlds.

†Snow showers in March are locally called St Causlan's (for Causnan, Constantine) Flaw. The saint's fair was held in this month. [*N. & Q.*, 1st series (1850), p. 188 ; *O.S.A.* I, p. 422.] Angus.
See his day, March 11th.

March sud come in like an adder's head, an gang oot like a peacock's tail.

March sud come in like a boar's head, an gang oot like a peacock's tail.

March sud come in like a lion an gang oot like a lam'. [Greg., p. 150.] N.E. Scot.

A Januar haddock,
A Februar bannock,
And a March pint o' ale.

[*Pop. Rhymes,*[3] p. 169.]

Marry in March when born in June
Then you're sure to win the crown.

[J. E. Cr.]   Deskford, N.E. Scot.

A blustering March through nine Bull-hides will blow,
For this our old Good-dames would have us know.

[' Prognostication,' by G. F., *Philol. and Philom.*, 1685.]

March wind wakens the alder and blooms the thorn.

Who in this world of ours their eyes
In March first opened, would be wise,
In days of peril firm and brave,
Should wear a jacinth to the grave.

March teach, April try,
May will prove if you live or die.

[J. E. Cr.]   Bf.

Though you cannot send a pebble against the north wind
you must sow. [*Wcrft. & Sec. Sight*, p. 256.]   Hghlds.

It is said of an early March, ' there will be no gowk oats this
year.' Gowk oats are oats sown after the 1st of April. [*F.-L.
Record*, II, p. 58.]   Bwk.

When close misty weather comes in the month of March,
the mist is called *ceòban losgainn*, frog's mist. [Mlan MS.] Ar.

During the month of March the saying is, that however
long the wind blows from the south-east the north-west pays
it back. [W. Gregor, *F.-L.* II (1891), p. 479.] Pittulie, Ab.

The month of March seems to have been thought the best
month for hatching chickens, from the saying—

' March cocks is aye crawin'.'

[Greg., p. 142.]   See also V. below.   N.E. Scot.

Am fear nach cuir 's a Mhàirt,
Cha bhuan e 's an Fhogair.

The man who does not sow in March
Will pass Autumn without reaping.

[T. D. MacDonald, *Gaelic Proverbs* (1926), p. 103.]

Am fear a thig a mach 's a Mhàrt
Theid e stigh 's a Ghiblein.

The grass that springs in March
Will shrink away in April.

[T. D. MacDonald, *Gaelic Proverbs* (1926), p. 103.]

March whisker (blusterer) was never a good fisher.

A windy March betokens a bad fish year.   p. 334

A peck of March dust and a shower in May,
Makes the corn green and the fields gay.   p. 43

[James Kelly, M.A., *A Collection of Scottish Proverbs* (1721).]

A dry and cold March never begs its bread.

A March without water
Dowers the hind's daughter.

Bleach as well as summer's sun
March dust and March win'.   (wind)

March water and May sun,
Make clean claes and maidens dun.

March rain spoils more than clothes.

[D. Grewar, *Sc. N. & Q.*, 3rd series, II, p. 38.]

Said by a Mermaid on the margin of the Firth of Clyde
as the funeral of a young woman passed along the high-road:

If they wad drink nettles in March
And eat muggons in May,
Sae mony braw maidens
Wadna gang to the clay.

Muggons, mugwort or southernwood.   [*Pop. Rhymes,*[3]
p. 113.]   Lnk.

March dust and May sun
Makes Corn white and Maidens dun.

March water is worth May soap.

(Water in . . . March is supposed to be of a more cleansing
quality than in any other month.)   [*Ibid.*, p. 146.]

The Mearns, Pth.

Saying for the end of March.   As the month of April draws
near the plover cries out,

Shauve yer bere ;   [barley]
O harrow well, O harrow well,
I will gather for my Sal.

[J. E. Cr.]   Deskford, N.E. Scot.

III. Omens.   Children born in March are not very lucky.
[But see March 11th and 19th.]   [J. E. Cr.]   El.

From weather.

> Thunder in March presages an unlucky year.
> When it thunders in March it brings sorrow.

[*Ibid.*]   Bf.

> March damp and warm
> Does the farmer much harm.

> In March much snow
> To plants and trees much woe.

> As many mists in March you see,
> So many frosts in May will be.

> A wet March makes a sad August.

[D. Grewar, *Sc. N. & Q.*, 3rd series, II (1924), p. 38.]

IV. Observances. *Marbles.* Marbles are played by children in March, but not in February. [J. E. Cr.]   Bf.

Hatching cocks in March. The crow of a cock hatched in March has more effect against evil spirits than one hatched in autumn.

Cf. A goblin came to the door one night and failed to get admittance. He said : ' If it were the red cock of autumn that were in the house he would open the door for me. It isn't that that is in it, but the black cock of the spring March.' [A. Goodrich-Freer, *Outer Isles* (1902), pp. 233 and 240.]   Hdes.

Formerly when the time was reckoned by cock crowing, it was always a March bird that people kept for the purpose, as it was thought that a March bird was more trustworthy. [Mlan MS.]   Islay, Ar.

Wreath made and preserved. In the increase of the March moon, the Highlanders cut withes of the wood-bind that clings about the oak. These they twist into a wreath or circle and carefully preserve it till the next March. And when children are troubled with hectick fevers or when anyone is consumptive, they make them pass through this circle thrice by passing it over their heads. . . . The like they do to cattle in some distempers. This I have often seen. [Rev. L. Shaw, *Hist. of Province of Moray* (1775), p. 232.]   Morayshire.

DAYS

1st

III. Saint. Saint Marnock (*Mo Ernoc*, my Ernoc), was commemorated in east Scotland on this day, known also as Mernanus, Marnanus. The parish of Marnoch, Banff, bears his name. 'Sanct Marnoyss' portable shrine was used for the taking of oaths in perambulation of certain lands belonging to the church of Aberchirder, at which time also his head gave special sanctity. He had a well on these lands. [*Celt. Pl.-Names.*]

An interesting account of the church of Foulis Easter, Perthshire, celebrated for its rare panel paintings, speaks of St Marnan to whom the church was dedicated ; he was a worker of miracles and adored ' like a god on earth '. His ' glorious head ' was washed every Sunday of the year and the water drunk by the sick to their great advantage.—From Aberdeen Breviary. [A. B. Dalgetty, *Hist. of the Church of Foulis Easter* (1933), p. 19.]

V. Observances. b. *Lucky.* By putting on a new dress on the first day of March, one was likely to have luck for the rest of the year. [Mlan MS.]   Ffe.

V o. *Animals, birds, etc.* On the first of March the crows begin to scratch. [*Ibid.*]   *Ibid.*

On this day crows were believed to begin their nests. [Napier, p. 114.]   W. Hghlds.

X. XI. Procession with bell-ringing and mock combat.

†*Whuppity Scoorie.* The following appeared under the heading ' An Ancient Custom at Lanark ' in the *Scotsman* for March 2nd, 1909 : ' The ancient honoured custom known as *Whuppity Scoorie* was celebrated by the youth of Lanark last night, and was witnessed by a crowd of several hundred people. The origin of the custom is unknown, but is generally supposed to herald in the entrance of spring. From the months of October to February the town bell in the steeple is not tolled at six o'clock in the evening, but during the other months it rings at that hour daily. On the first day of March, when the bell is rung for the first time after its five months silence, the boys of the town congregate at the Cross with a bonnet to which a piece of string is attached, and so soon as the first peal of the bell rings out, the parish church is walked round three times, and thereafter a dash is made to meet the boys of New Lanark. On their meeting there is a stand-up fight, the weapons used being the stringed bonnets. This procedure was followed last night, and about seven of the boys returned and paraded the principal streets singing their victorious refrain.' [D. Rorie, in *Folk-Lore*, Vol. XXI. p. 92.]   Lnk.

The custom was observed in 1939. See *Scotsman*, March 2nd.

4th

III. Saints. 'Adrian and others,' 9th century, whose burial place in the Isle of May, Firth of Forth, was visited by many pilgrims in the Middle Ages. Legend says these saints drove out demons and wild beasts before they took up their life of devotion in the island where they were martyred by Danes. Pilgrims' Haven recalls their mission, and the burgh seal of Pittenweem, Fife, represents St Adrian setting forth on his voyage from Hungary, with *Deo Duce* as motto. [The legend is much disputed.] [See *Anc*^{t}. *Ch. Ded. N.*, p. 490.]

6th

III. Saint. Baldred or Balthere ; known as St Baldred of the Bass, the Bass Rock near N. Berwick. He is said to have used a rock as a boat when crossing to the mainland, and a rock near by is called Baudron's Boat. His legend states that his corpse was triplicated in order that each of three churches might possess his body. The river Tyne has a St Baldred's Whirl. [*Ibid.*, pp. 19 f.]   Hdn.

8th

III. Saint. Duthac, Dubhthaich of Tain, an important religious centre, known in Gaelic as *Baile Dhubhthaich*, Duthac's town, where the burgh arms bear his figure. His legend tells how he carried burning coals with impunity in the front of his tunic when sent to bring them for his master's forge. In later years, one of his disciples being robbed of meat and a ring by a kite, the saint called the bird before him and bade it restore the ring, allowing it to keep the meat for itself, At a distribution of the flesh of an ox to the needy at Dornoch the canon set aside a portion for Duthac. He set out in stormy darkness to take the flesh to the saint and was guided over dangerous paths by a light shining from the spit. [Allan Butler, *Lives of the Saints*, ed. 1931.]

Tain was a famous place of pilgrimage ; James IV was a frequent visitor at the shrine of St Duthac and invoked the aid of his favourite saint for the last time in 1513, a few weeks before his death at Flodden. By James IV also a silver-gilt reliquary was commanded to be made for his patron in 1507, 1508. There were chapels of St Duthac at Kirkwall, Orkney, and at Caithness. For rites at Caithness cf. *Christmas*, **V** i.

At his altar in the Dominican monastery at Ayr creditors and debtors met for repayment of loans. At Dundee his chaplain was supported by the Craft of Skinners and Glovers ; in Edinburgh his ' licht ' in a chapel of St Giles was maintained by a grant from the Lord High Treasurer. He had an altar at Arbroath, Angus, and one in the church of St Nicholas at Aberdeen, also churches in other Scottish towns. A mussel-bed near Tain was known as St Duthac's Scalp. [*Anc*[t]. *Ch. Ded. N.*, and *Celt. Pl.-Names.*]

In the 14th century Earls of Ross went to battle in the shirt of St Duthac which hung in one of the churches within his sanctuary at Tain. [*P.S.A. Scot.* XII (1877), p. 135, Note.]

10th

II. Sayings. On the feast of St. Kessock every eel is pregnant. [*Wcrft. & Sec. Sight*, p. 259.] Hghlds.

III. Saint. Kessog, Cassog, Cassoc, or Mackessog ; 6th century. This saint is associated chiefly with Luss on Loch Lomond, and was patron saint of the Lennox, the country around the Loch. *Celt. Pl.-Names* gives his name as a compound beginning with *Cess*, a spear, and he was at one time depicted in military costume with arrows and a bent bow. Local legend derives the name of Luss from a sweet-smelling *lus* or herb which grew on his grave and spread over the church. Kessog had a holy bell and a fair. The privilege of sanctuary was granted by Robert Bruce to the precincts of the church of Luss and placed under the charge of the Earls of Lennox. The saint has several dedications in Scotland where his name was a battle-cry before St Andrew was the patron saint.

V. Observance. e. *Customs of farm, etc.* It is a practice in this parish with many of never beginning to plough till the 10th day of March. However inviting the season may be prior to this period, it matters nothing ; they adhere to the custom of their fathers. [*O.S.A.* XVII, p. 210.] Cf. Feb. 2, **V e.**

Cardross, Dbn.

11th

III. Saint. Constantine, 6th century. He is said to have been king in Cornwall and resigned from the kingship on his conversion to Christianity. He became a monk and an abbot. After some years in Ireland he settled in Scotland and is commemorated in Kintyre, where he suffered martyrdom. The church of Govan on the Clyde is dedicated to him, also the church of St Constantine at Colmonel, Ayr. In Forfar, now Angus, he was known locally as St Causnan (cf. above, March, month, II. *Causnan's showers*). [*Celt. Pl.-Names* and *Anc^t. Ch. Ded.*]

The well of St Cowstan in Lewis was believed never to boil meat though its water stood over a fire for a whole day. [Martin.]

In the graveyard of a church commemorating him, Kil-chouslan, Kintyre, stood a round stone . . . with a large hole in its centre. According to tradition, if a man and woman eloped and were able to join hands through this hole before being overtaken by their kinsfolk they were free from pursuit. [*F. Lore of Sc. Lochs, etc.*, p. 54.]

The joining of lovers' hands through a hole in a small pillar near St Couslan's church was held as an interim tie of great . . . sanctity. Any one breaking this pledge met with a fatal accident. [E. F. Guthrie, *Old Scot. Customs* (1885), p. 167.]

In Campbeltown two churches were dedicated to SS. Cowie and Couslan. While Couslan upheld the honour of lovers' vows, Cowie instituted a custom whereby those unhappy in marriage should be allowed an opportunity of making a fresh choice. [*Ibid.*]

VI. *Belief in luck.* Children born on March 11th are believed to be lucky. [J. E. Cr.]   El.

17th

I. Name. St Patrick's Day ; *Féill Pàdruig*. A date very near the spring equinox ; O.S. March 28th, 29th.

II. Sayings, Rhymes. There is a rhyme said about the time of St Patrick's feast-day which is sometimes quoted as a charm against serpents :

> Patrick's feast-day—half of spring,
> Ivar's daughter will come out of the hole.
> I will not ' be at ' (hurt) Ivar's daughter,
> No more will she ' be at ' me.

However, as there are no serpents in the islands, an explanation suggested by Father Allan strikes one as far more probable. As is well known, the common nettle always tends to spring up around the places occupied, or which have been occupied, by man, and however carefully extirpated it is one of the most common of the many weeds which grow in the crevices of the houses and byres both indoors and out, and the appearance of its first tender leaves is hailed as one of the first signs of spring. What the phrase ' Ivar's daughter ' may mean it is interesting to inquire, but the hint that she does no harm if let alone might well point to the conduct of the common nettle. (Cf. Feb. 1st, **II.**) [A. Goodrich-Freer, *F.-L.* XIII (1902), p. 39.] Hdes.

' The calf-killer of Patrick's feast ' is the name given to the cold east wind which prevails so often in the early spring. [*Ibid.*] *Ibid.*

There is not an herb in the ground, but the length of a mouse's ear of it is out on St Patrick's Day. [*Wcrft. & Sec. Sight*, p. 260.] Hghlds.

After this day the limpet is better than the whelk and is said in consequence to treat it with great indignity. [*Ibid.*] *Ibid.*

The Deadening of St Patrick's Day, *Marbhadh na Féill Pàruig*, means the quiet calm waters that sometimes occur at this season. [*Ibid.*] *Ibid.*

There are particularly high tides on St Patrick's Day . . . according to the saying, . . . And the mad tides of St Patrick's Day. [*Ibid.*] *Ibid.*

On St Patrick's Day each cow-fold will have a female calf and each pool a salmon. [A. R. Forbes, *Gael. Names of Beasts, etc.*]

St Patrick's day in spring, three sights may be seen—i.e. ploughing, sowing, and harrowing ; some versions mention seven sights. [Edward Dwelly, *Gaelic Dictionary*.]

III. Saint. St Patrick of Ireland, bp., *d.* about 461. Most of his many dedications in Scotland are in the south-west. At Portpatrick, Wigtownshire, a rock bore the mark of a foot said to have been that of St Patrick when he stepped across from Ireland at one stride. He has a spring in Kirkpatrick-Durham, Kirkcudbright, and a well near the Clyde at Dalziel. A chapel dedicated to him at Strageith, by the Earn, Perthshire, was much venerated. The *N.S.A.* states, 1837, that on his day neither the clap of the mill was heard nor the plough seen to move in the furrow. *Féill-Padrick*, his fair, was held in the Atholl district, Perthshire. He was popular in the Hebrides. Among Gaels the wheatear is known as *fear na Féill-Padruig*, as it was believed to make its appearance at that date. [*Anc*t. *Ch. Ded. in Scot. N.*]

As ' the herdsman Patrick ' he was one of the saints invoked during milking in Gaelic-speaking Scotland. [*Car. Gad.* I, p. 259.]

Herding incantations call on St Patrick and St Patrick's milkmaid to attend the cattle to the pastures. [*Trans. of the Gael. Soc. of Inverness*, XVIII (1891, 2).] Hghlds.

In art St Patrick is represented with a crozier, a harp, or with the serpents he is said to have driven from Ireland. (Cf. February 2nd.)

IV. Omens. a. *Weather*. A certain sign of the day is held in the Hebrides to be a south wind in the morning and a north wind at night. The saint comes from Ireland to see his parishioners in Barra and other places on the west of Scotland and has a favourable wind coming and returning. [*Wcrft. & Sec. Sight*, p. 259.] Hdes.

V. Observances. a. *Work forbidden*. †At Muthill is . . . St Patrick's memory held in such veneration (that farmers and millers left off work on his day). [E. J. Guthrie, *Old Scottish Customs* (1885), p. 118.] Muthill, Pth.

V i. *Visiting wells, etc.* In this Loghgreveren there is one high mountaine on the north syde thereof. And on the mid parte of the mountaine there is a chappell called Craikquerre-lane. And in this high craig where the Chappell stands, there is verie manie fresh springs and fountaine waters. And sundrie and divers multitudes of men and woemen from all Countries doe convein and gather togidder to this Chappell in the springtyme one day before St Patrickmess day and drinking everie one of them of this spring and fresh water alleadges that it shall recover them to their healthes againe, of the sicknes or desease which they have before their comeing to that place and uses the same yearlie, once a time in the year certaine of them doth come for pilgrimadge, and certaine others in respect of their sickness bygone, of which they have recovered their health and certaine of them for their sickness present. And as they are persuaded to be restored to their health by the help and assistance of that holie saint, and the drinking of the waters. This holie place hes sundrie spring founts and wells of fresh water for divers . . . kynds of deseases. . . . There is one fountaine springing out of the sand of the sea, of fresh water, not ane myll distant from the sanctuarie or holie Chappell in a toune called Ardnacloch which when anie in these pairts are sick, if the sick dieth, a dead worme is found in the bottome of the water or fountaine and if the sick shall recover a quick worme is found in it. [*Geograph. Coll.* II, p. 154.] Appin, Ar.

G. Henderson quotes the rite for St Patrick's day ; the

sick would collect the day before in order to use the water at dawn on the next day. [Ed.]
Cf. Section, Wells, Vol. I.

18th

III. Saint. The Archangel Gabriel of the Annunciation ; ' Bearer of Good Tidings.'

> For gude novellis, as I heir tell,
> Sum takis thare gait to Gabriell.

[Sir D. Lindsay, *The Monarchy*, ll. 2377-8.]

19th

III. Saint. Joseph, spouse of the Virgin Mary. ' The churches and altars dedicated to him in all parts of the world are literally numberless.' [*Bk. of Saints.*]
In Scotland he was invoked for sheep.

IV. Omens. *Weather.* If it is clear on St Joseph's day it will be a fertile year. [D. Grewar, *Sc. N. & Q.*, 3rd series, II (1924), p. 38.]

IV. d. *Birth on this day of good augury.* Cf. March 11th.
Children born on March 19th are very lucky. Birth on this day ensured that a man would not be shot in battle. A glamour came over the enemy, who thought he was shooting at him but aimed in another direction. [J. E. Cr.]

A Hghld. Superstition.

20th

III. Saint. St Cuthbert. The saint's earliest home is believed to have been on the river Tine, near the monastery of Tiningham, by Dunbar. The famous vision by which he saw the soul of Bishop Aidan carried to heaven by angels and thus learned of his death, came to him while watching sheep on the hills by the river Lauder near the Tweed. This vision made him decide to enter a monastery, and he was received at Old Melrose by the prior, Boisil, who recognised in him ' a servant of God '. When the abbot, Eata, went to Ripon, Cuthbert was one of his company, but in 661 the king of Northumbria expelled the Melrose monks, having resolved to establish the ' use of Rome ' in his kingdom. The monks returned to Melrose, an offshoot of Lindisfarne, where Cuthbert succeeded Boisil as prior. It was at this time he visited country districts, preaching to the people, from whom arose the legends related below. The Synod of Whitby in 664 made good the claim to observance of its rites by the Roman Church, and Cuthbert was converted to its rule. The abbot now invited him to his Abbey of Lindisfarne to assist in establishing the Roman use there where St Colman had early introduced from Iona the rule of the Celtic Church. In 676 Cuthbert left the Abbey to live as a solitary, first in a cave on the mainland, then to an island of the Farne group, where he lived in his cell for nine years. When offered the see of Hexham he refused to leave the island till a visit from the king persuaded him to accept the high office ; Eata, Abbot of Lindisfarne, however, gave up to him the Abbey of his earlier life in exchange for that of Hexham. After two years he retired again to his cell, the scene of his death on March 20th, 687. He was buried at Lindisfarne, where he was held in great honour ; many miracles were reported from his shrine.

In 698 when the monks opened his coffin, wishing to place his remains above the floor of the church, they found them uncorrupted and retained the chasuble for use as a relic. During the Danish invasion of 793 his body was unmolested, but at a later invasion, in 875, the bishop feared desecration and fled, taking the saint's body with him to Cumberland. Its wanderings continued for seven years, and with it travelled the famous Lindisfarne Gospel which bears to this day the marks of its fall into the sea. An attempt to land the remains of the saint in Ireland was unsuccessful, storms turned back the boat, which took refuge on the shores of Galloway ; from here the body went again to Northumbria. It lay at Chester for a hundred years, was moved to Ripon and at the last to Durham. There are legendary accounts of wanderings to other places and of miracles there. In 1105 the body was said to have been found still uncorrupted, and with it the head of King Oswald, king of Northumbria, killed in 642. In art Cuthbert is represented bearing the head of Oswald in his hands ; in Henry VII's chapel, Westminster, he bears it, crowned, in his left hand. [See *Dict. of Christ. Biog. and Lit.*]

When the tomb was opened in 1899 the frontal bone was again found and replaced. [J. C. Wall, *Shrines of Brit. Saints*, pp. 206 f.]

Celt. Pl.-Names quotes a Latin life which tells of the saint's voyage with his mother and others in a stone currach, and their landing in the Rinns, Galloway. Bede makes use of another legend according to which Cuthbert set out with two friends on a missionary voyage. After landing they were held up for three days by a violent storm ; feeling their strength fail them, Cuthbert prayed for help, whereupon three large cutlets from a dolphin were found on the shore, the wind fell, and they were able to return home. He is said to have visited the Tay from Melrose, where he set up a cross near Aberfeldy, and called forth a spring of water which filled his ' Bath ', a hollow in the rocks, visited by many pilgrims. At Farne Island he made pets of the eider ducks. The Burgh Arms of Kirkcudbright, which bears his name, represent him seated in the stern of a boat with St Oswald's head on his knee. He has several dedications in Scotland both east and west, but is not commemorated in the Highlands, where his support of the Roman church set a limit to his popularity. His monastery at Melrose was replaced by a chapel to St Cuthbert on *Tom Naomh*, ' Holy Knowe,' a place visited by many pilgrims.

His church under the Castle rock in Edinburgh is believed to be of a very old foundation. There are many legends of his migrations ; according to one his body lay for a while at Kirkcudbright after landing at Galloway. He was one of three titular saints at the priory of Coldingham, on which Robert Bruce bestowed the right to take five harts yearly from the royal forest of Selkirk, in commemoration of the translation of his body from a church in Durham to the Cathedral in 999. His shrine at Durham was the most splendid in England after that of Becket ; it was destroyed in 1539. Durham Cathedral owed its sanctuary rights to the saint's relics ; fugitives were admitted at any hour of the day or night and were maintained at the Cathedral's expense. His banner was highly prized ; it was carried by Edward I on his invasions of Scotland, was with the English forces at Neville's Cross, 1346, and at Flodden in 1513.

Bede wrote of ' the brightness of his angelic face '. [*Anc*^t. *Ch. Ded.*, *N.*]

One of the most interesting of legends is that which tells of Cuthbert's appearance in a vision to King Alfred ; it was quoted by Fox and much discussed in the fierce disputations of his time.

In the meantime, while King Alfred, accompanied with a few, was thus in the desert wood (Etheling in Somersetshire, where he was hiding from the Danes) . . . according to certain stories a poor beggar there came and asked alms of the king :

and the night following he appeared to the king in his sleep, saying his name was Cuthbert, promising (as sent from God unto him for his good charity) great victories against the Danes. [*Acts and Monuments of John Fox* [4] (ed. 1877), II, p. 23, quoting Wm. of Malmesbury ; Rog. Hoveden, etc.]

> Saint Cuthbert sits, and toils to frame
> The sea-born beads that bear his name :
> Such tales had Whitby's fishers told,
> And said they might his shape behold,
> And hear his anvil sound. . . .

Note.—Since his death (Cuthbert) has acquired the reputation of forging those *Entrochi* which are found among the rocks of Holy Island, and pass . . . by the name of St Cuthbert's Beads. While at this task, he is supposed to sit during the night upon a certain rock, and use another as his anvil. [Sir W. Scott, *Marmion*, II, xvi.]

V. Observances. e. *On Farms, etc. Sowing on St Cuthbert's day.* †The farmers, whatever the state of the weather, obstinately adhered to the immemorial practice of beginning to . . . sow on the 20th of March. [*O.S.A.* XX, p. 474.]

Dowally, Pth.

XII. Religious Observance, sacrifice. *Sacrifice of a bull.* On the Festival of St Cuthbert a bull was offered in sacrifice at his church in Kirkcudbright. The account of this is in the *Libellus de admirandis Beati Cuthberti Virtutibus*, written in the 12th century by Reginald of Durham, a monk sometimes known also as of Coldingham.

A bull of ferocious strength was dragged to the church as an offering to the saint. Clerics (scollofthes) attached to the church set about taking the bull out to be baited for the amusement of the people and led him into the graveyard. Protests were made by those in charge against proceedings of such levity in the Saint's sanctuary and on his very holy day, to which one of the clerics replied that there was no Cuthbert present, neither could he manifest his power there for all his little stone-built church. The baiting began and the bull, though closely pressed by the crowd, singled out the mocker to be tossed on his horns. [*Surtees Society*, vol. I (1835), p. 179.]

Kcbt.

This incident has been read as a sign of changing opinion in Galloway as to animal sacrifice on a saint's festival. Sacrifice of animals to avert pest or other sickness continued for many centuries in this part of Scotland but has no connection with the calendar.

For sacrifice of a bull on the festival of a saint cf. August 27, Saint Maol Rubha.

XIII. Business Transactions. *Dues paid in wax.* †For many years the lords of Bemersyde, Tweedside, were bound by deed to pay yearly to the abbot and convent of Old Melrose half a stone of wax or thirty pennies, on the day of St Cuthbert, for the chapel of St Cuthbert, under penalty of paying thirty pennies to the lamp of the chapel for every month after the date mentioned during which any cessation shall have occurred of the payment of the wax or the thirty pennies at the covenanted time. The date of the deed is supposed to have been between 1260 and 1270, and one of the witnesses was Thomas the Rhymer of Ercildoune. [See John Russel's *Haigs of Bemersyde* (1881), pp. 68 f.]   Borders.

25th

I. Name. Lady Day, Our Lady Day. Feast of the Annunciation. *Féill Moire an t-sanais*, the Feast of Mary of the Greeting. *La na caillich* (Lady Day).

II. Rhymes, Sayings. One of the feasts most regarded, especially in earlier times, is that of the Annunciation, as to which there is a saying :

> Mary's feast—day of Patrick's feast,
> The noblest day that will come,
> The noblest that has gone.

It is a week later than St Patrick's day. [A. Goodrich-Freer, *F.-L.* XIII (1902), p. 40.]   Hdes.

III. Saint. The Virgin Mary. Her cult in Scotland does not differ from the cult as observed throughout Europe. She has many churches, chapels and altars and is joint titular with many saints. Like Bride, she was invoked during milking in the Highlands. There is a reference to her character as patron saint of poultry in Dunbar's *Ballad of Kynd Kittock*,

ll. 22-6.   And thair zeiris sevin
  Scho levit ane gud lyfe,
  And was our Leddies henwyfe,

  .   .   .   .   .   .
  Ay quhill scho was in Hevin.

[*Poems by Wm. Dunbar* (c. 1490), Sc. Texts Soc^ty., ed. 1907, p. 24.]

She was famous as patroness of fountains and wells. The wearing of her nut was practised in the Highlands. These nuts are of various colours, but the one most prized has the cross indented on its sides. The writer had in his possession one of these nuts from the Hebrides mounted with a silver cross. It had been duly blessed by a cleric and was believed to be possessed of great virtues. It used to be worn about the neck . . . and every one who thus carried it was believed to be under the special protection of the Virgin Mary. She guarded him from evil courses, led him on the right path, and saved him from various calamities, such, for instance, as sudden death—*Bàs obann*. It was specially useful in the case of women in travail, and the belief in its efficacy is not yet a matter of the past.—These virtues were told by an Uist crofter. [W. Mackenzie, *Trans. of the Gael. Soc. of Inverness*, XVIII (1891-2).]
Hghlds.

The Shrine at Loretto. The chapel of Our Lady at Loretto stood at the eastern gate of Musselburgh. . . . Expectant mothers sent handsome presents of money accompanying their child-bed linen, which latter was consecrated for a good fee, to promote their safe delivery and recovery. . . . It was esteemed the most noted shrine in Scotland. King James V performed a pilgrimage from Stirling to it before he sailed for France to woo and win his future queen. . . . The materials of the ruined . . . chapel . . . were employed in the erection of the present town gaol. For this piece of sacrilege, it is said, the inhabitants of Musselburgh were annually excommunicated at Rome till the end of the last century. [E. J. Guthrie, *Old Scot. Customs* (1885), pp. 111 f.]

This was one of the most famous of Our Lady shrines. It was named after the Santa Casa at Loretto in Italy, believed to have been the home of the Virgin in Nazareth miraculously transplanted in 1295, and claimed to possess part of the stone on which the angel Gabriel stood at the Annunciation. It was known also as Allariet or Lariet chapel. The frequent pilgrimages to Loretto were noted by Sir D. Lindsay :

I have seen pass ane mervellous multytude
. . . .
For tyll adore ane image in Loreit.

[*Ane Dialog betwix Experience and ane Courteour*, ll. 2661 and 2664.]

The Cathedral of Iona, known as *Eglis Mór*, ' the Great Church ', was dedicated to the Virgin. As patroness of the

Knights Templars, introduced to Scotland by David I, her name was connected with many chapels.

26th

I. Name. Called in the Western Isles ' the old woman's day '. On this day the *Cailleach* was believed to try to beat down the growing grass, and when unable to do so threw away her birch wand. [Mlan MS.] Ledaig, Ar.
For the legend in full see *Seasons*.

30th

III. Saint. Regulus or Rule, 4th century. His personality remains a mystery. The legend runs that when the Emperor Constantius desired to remove the relics (of St Andrew the Apostle) from Achaia to Constantinople, St Regulus (the custodian) was warned by an angel to retain portions of them and afterwards take them to the western regions of the world, there to found a church in the apostle's honour. He succeeded in landing with the relics at Muckros or Kilrymont in Fife, now known as St Andrews. St Rule's Chapel stands near the cathedral, and its tower is one of the oldest edifices in Scotland. Scott, *Marmion*, I, xxix, speaks of his cave. His date is variously given as of the fourth or eighth century.

29th, 30th, 31st.
The Three Last Days of March

I. Name. The Borrowing Days. These days being generally stormy, our forefathers have endeavoured to account for this circumstance by pretending that March *borrowed* them from April that he might extend his power so much longer. [Jamieson.] They are also called the three Hog days, ' hog ' being a young sheep.

They are perhaps the days called in Tiree *tri latha na boin ruaidhe*, three days of the Red Cow. (*Wcrft. & Sec. Sight*, p. 255.] Hghlds.
This name is that used in Ireland where the cow takes the place of the hogs. [Ed.]

II. Rhymes, Sayings.

> March said to Aperill
> I saw three hoggs on yonder hill,
> An' if you'll lend me dayis three
> I'll find a way to gar them dee.

> The first o' them was wind an' weet
> The neist o' them was snaw an' sleet,
> The third o' them was sic a freeze
> It friz the birds' nebs till the trees ;
> An' when the three days were past an' gane,
> The silly poor hoggies cam' hirplin' hame.

[Jas. Ferguson, ' Old Sc. Sayings, etc.,' in *Chambers's Journal*, Feb. 1916, p. 107.]

Another version :

> March borrowed from April
> Three days, and they were ill ;
> The first it was snaw an' sleet,
> The second it was caul' an' weet,
> The third it was sic a freeze
> The birds' nibs stack t' the trees.

[Greg., p. 150.]   N.E. Scot.

A fable says that these days were borrowed by March . . . for the purpose of destroying some young sheep, but the attempt proved a failure.

There efter i entrit in ane grene forest, to contempil the tendir ӡong frutes of grene treis, because the borial blastis of the *thre borowing dais of Marche* hed chaissit the fragrant flureise of evyrie frut tree far athourt the feildis. [*The Complaynt of Scot.*, Chap. VI (1548), Er. Eng. Text Soc^ty. (1872), pp. 37 f.]

V. Observances. a. *Things unlucky or forbidden. Borrowing or lending.* The superstitious would neither borrow nor lend at this period, for the Israelites borrowed extensively from the Egyptians with no intention of repaying the loan. [D. Grewar, *Sc. N. & Q.*, 3rd series, II (1924), p. 39.]

Lest witchcraft may be worked with the loan. [Jamieson.]

There is a Highland explanation also connecting them (these days) with the departure from Egypt. They were days borrowed by the Israelites for the killing of the Paschal lamb. ' Some went on this side of the hillock, some on that.' [*Wcrft. & Sec. Sight*, p. 254.]   Hghlds.

The dismal days for March, from an old almanac, are the 15th, 16th, 19th.

APRIL

MONTH

I. Name. April ; *an Giblean ; Céitein na h-òinsich*, the May of the silly one. The month preceding Beltane (O.S.) was called *Céitein na h-òinsich* . . . the word *òinseach* denoting both a silly woman and a cuckoo. The habits of the bird, . . . have earned for it the reputation of being silly . . . and premature glimpses of fine weather are supposed to mislead it as to the advent of May. [*Wcrft. & Sec. Sight*, p. 272.]   Hghlds.

This period is often taken as being April 19th to May 12th, after the change of style. For cuckoo lore of this season see *Seasons, Spring*. *Cailleach*, old woman or hag, is a term sometimes used in the north as the first week of April.

For the lore of the *Cailleach* and her rhyme see *Seasons*.

For a fuller version of the *Cailleach's* verse see *The Celt. Rev.*, V, pp. 65-7. Cf. March 26th.

II. Rhymes, Sayings. Of an April day . . . it was said, ' It's an April day, it's sheetin' an' glintin'.' [Greg., p. 150.]
                                                                    N.E. Scot.

In Scotland the advent of the cuckoo calls forth the old season's spite, and the consequence is ' a gowk storm '. Hence the proverb :

> In the month of Averel
> The gowk comes over the hill
> In a shower of rain.

[*F.-L. Record*, II (1879) ; Jas. Hardy, *Pop. Hist. of the Cuckoo*.]

Aiberhill (April) wi's braid yax (axe) an' copper bill hacks the feet. [J. E. Cr.]   St Combs, Ab.

> An April flood
> Carries away the frog and his brood.

> April rains for men, May for beasts.

> April and May are the keys of the year.

> Plant your 'taters when you will.
> They won't come up before April.

[D. Grewar, *Sc. N. & Q.*, 3rd series, II (1924), p. 54.]

III. Omens. *Weather.*

A dry April not the farmer's will,
April wet is what he would get.

April cold and wet fills barn and barrel.

A cold April
The barn will fill.

When April blows his horn,
It is good for hay and corn.

'Twixt April and May if there be rain,
It's worth more than oxen and wain.

If the first three days of April be foggy,
Rain in June will make the lanes boggy.

A wet April, a dry June.

[D. Grewar, *Sc. N. & Q.*, 3rd series, II (1924), p. 54.]

Cuckoo oats and woodcock hay
Make a farmer run away.

That is, if oats cannot be sown till the cuckoo is heard
(April), and the autumn is so wet that the aftermath of hay
cannot be got in till woodcock shooting (mid-November), the
farmer must be a great sufferer.

A frosty winter and a dusty March, a rain about April,
Another about the Lammas time when the corn begins to
fill,
Is weel worth a pleuch o' gowd, and a' her pins theretill.

This ' plough of gold ' rhyme is believed to have been composed
by George Buchanan, a native of Stirlingshire, when asked
what would buy a plough of gold. [J. E. Cr.]   Ab.

When April weeps, then May will chirp and sing ;
For April showers make May flowers to spring.

[' Prognostication,' by G. F., *Philol. and Philom.* (1685).]
Omen from successful fishing. If one did not catch fish in
April he would be unsuccessful as a fisher (fresh water) during
the year. [J. E. Cr.]   Corgarff, Ab.

Cf.   An April fish
            A dainty dish.
                    [*Ibid.*]

X. Boundary Riding, Wappenshaws.
See Vol. I.

The chief days for Wappynshaws in Banff were in April, usually on the 23rd. The Marches were also most commonly visited during this month in Banff. [N. Sp. Club, *Annals of Banff*, I.]

Bf.

Latter Half of April

I. Name. *Bailc na Bealltain.* The fourteen days preceding May-day were known as *Bailc na Bealltain*, the balk or ridge of *Bealltain*. The sea is then as it were awakening, and is more obedient to the winds. *Bailc* means a ridge, also swelling, strength. The weather threatens frequently without breaking. [*Wcrft. & Sec. Sight*, p. 267.]

Hghlds. and W. Is.

DAYS

1st

I. Names. All Fool's Day. *Là na Cubhaig*, Cuckoo Day ; *Là na Gogaireachd*, day of fooling ; *Là nan car*, day of tricks.

V. Observances. a. *Unlucky or forbidden.* People should not begin any particular work on April 1st. [Mlan MS.]

Kintyre, Ar.

V n. *Pranks and tricks. Sending on a gowk's (cuckoo's) errand.* What compound is to simple addition, so is Scots to English April fooling. In the northern part of the island they are not content to make a neighbour believe some single piece of absurdity. There, the object being, we shall say, to befool simple Andrew Thomson, Wag No. 1 sends him away with a letter to a friend two miles off, professedly asking for some useful information, or requesting a loan of some article, but in reality containing only the words :

> This is the first day of April,
> Hunt the gowk another mile.

Wag No. 2, catching up the idea of his correspondent, tells Andrew with a grave face that it is not in his power, etc. ; but if he will go with another note to such a person, he will get what is wanted. Off Andrew trudges with this second note to Wag No. 3, who treats him in the same manner ; and so on he goes, till some one of the series, taking pity on him, hints the trick that has been practised upon him. A successful affair of this kind will keep rustic society in merriment for a week, during which honest Andrew . . . hardly can show his face. The Scots employ the word gowk (which is properly a cuckoo) to express a fool in general, but more especially an April fool, and among them the practice above described is called *hunting the gowk*. [Chambers, *Bk. of Days*, I, pp. 435 f.]

The old custom of sending one on gowk's messages is still kept up in force. [Mlan MS.]   Barra, W. Isles.

Young people, attracted by the singular cry of the cuckoo, being anxious to see it, are often very assiduous to obtain this gratification. But as this bird changes its place so secretly and suddenly ; when they think they are just within reach of it, they hear its cry at a considerable distance. Thus they run from place to place, still finding themselves as far removed from their object as ever. Hence the phrase, *Hunt the gowk*, may have come to be used for any fruitless attempt ; and particularly for those vain errands in which persons are sent on the first day of April.

Nor is it unlikely, that the custom of sending one on what is called ' *a gowk's errand* ', on the first day of April, has had its origin, in connexion with what is mentioned above, from the circumstance of the bird's making its appearance in our country about the beginning of this month. It is said, indeed, that it is generally about the middle of April that it is first observed. But if we reduce this to the old style, it will fall within a few days of the beginning of the month ; and it is well known that it is silent for some short time after its arrival ; its note, which is that of the male, being a call of love. [Jamieson.]

†An evil charm rests on the ' April Fool ', but it can be got rid of if the person sent on the fool's errand can manage to turn the table against the one that had made a fool of him during that day. [Mlan MS.]   Kintyre, Ar.

VI. **Beliefs in Evil Spirits, etc.** *The Devil's Croft.* In a good many parts of the country there were pieces of land left uncultivated, though there was no natural obstacle to their being so. They were dedicated to the Devil, and went by the name of ' The Devil's Craft ' or ' The Gueedman's Craft '. In Corgarff there were two such spots. They had a rampart of stones round them to prevent any man or beast from going over them. They had also to be some distance from water. (Told to my informant by an old man of 83 years of age, who died about 21 years ago (1894).) They were sprinkled yearly with milk on the first of April (O.S.). (My informant was not exactly certain of the day and hour.) This oblation was to keep the evil one out of ' the hoose, the milk-hoose, the byre an' the barn '. If the guidman crossed the forbidden ground, he lost the best tooth in his head ; if the gueedwife did so, she lost a moggan [stocking] ; if a horse, a shoe came off ; and if a cow, a hoof fell off.

One of the places was at Delnadamph (Stag-haugh) on the south side of a hillock called Tornashaltic (Fire-hillock), and the other at Tornahaish (Cheese-hillock). [W. Cramond.]

Corgarff, Ab.

Other names attached to these patches of land were, Clouttie's Craft (Croft), and the Helliman's Rig. [J. E. Cr.]

N.E. Scot.

1st and 2nd

V n. *Pranks.* We learn from the Wilkie MS. that the second of April shares on the Borders the character which the first bears all England over. There are two April-fool days there, or, as they call them, ' gowk days '. Unsuspecting people are then sent on bootless errands, and ridiculed for their pains. [Henderson, *F.-L. of the Northern Counties* (1879), p. 92.]

Borders

1st, 2nd, 3rd

I. Name. *Three borrowed days.* Old people . . . used to have a saying that April borrowed three days from March. Hence this fable :

A duck brought out twelve ducklings in March, and on the 11th of April, the end of March, O.S., the duck was very proud of her brood, and thinking all danger was now past she said—' Here am I with my twelve nice ducklings.' But before three days had passed all the ducklings except two were dead owing to the severe weather that had set in. [Mlan MS.]

Durness, Sld.

Days of the six black hogs. Long ago an old woman had six beautiful white hogs (young sheep), she lost them on the first day of April and they remained away for three days. When they returned their wool was quite blackened with the east wind, and ever since the first three days of April have been called *Laithean na sè oisgean* (*othaisgean*) *dubha*. [*Ibid.*] Islay, Ar.

Week after the Borrowing Days

V. Observances. e. *Farm customs.* m. *Food and drink.*
Bleeding cattle. All the cattle were bled within the week after

the ' borrowing days ', i.e. 13th, 14th, and 15th of April after the change of style, but not on the last ' borrowing day '. Nor was a Sunday allowed to pass before the process of bleeding was gone through. The blood was carefully preserved, mixed with oatmeal, and baked on the ' girdle ', as a kind of unleavened bannock. Three of these bannocks were given to each member of each ' cottar's ' family on the farm. It was no small offence if the bannocks were refused. The remainder of them was used by the household. [J. E. Cr.] Corgarff, Ab.

1st Saturday

I. Name. *Glen Saturday.* †The first Saturday in April or other day indicated by notices from the Castle in the shopwindows, on which the people of Kilmarnock are allowed to gather daffodils in the Castle grounds, Glen of Craufurdland. [*E.D.D.*, p. 640.]   Ayr.

2nd

VII. Natural Phenomenon. †It used to be a common notion that during the sittings of the Aberdeen Synod on the second day of April and October the weather was bad. [J. E. Cr.]   Keith, Ab.

15th

V. Observances. i. *Visiting wells.* The natives (Roman Catholic) observe St Katherine's anniversary ; all of them come to the well (St Katherine's) and having drunk of it they make the *Dessil* round it sunways. This is always performed on the 15th day of April. [Martin, p. 278.]   Eigg, Hdes.

The saint is probably St Catherine of Siena, whose day was April 29th, later April 30th.

25th

I. Name. St Mark's Day.

III. Saint. The apostle Mark.

V d. *Rite of divination.* St Mark's Day is on April 25th. In some parts of the country it was once held that if a person went boldly and sat in the church porch until one o'clock next morning he or she would see the ghosts pass of all the neighbours who were to die within the year. [M. Manson, *John O'Groat's Journal*, Dec. 15, 1911.]

30th

III. Saint. Catherine of Siena. A well-known nunnery in Edinburgh, at a place called the Sciennes, was dedicated to St Catherine, 1517. She had several dedications in Scotland. Cf. 15th above. Edin.

V. Observance. b. *Enjoined and lucky.* Elder leaves gathered on the last day of April cure wounds—and hung on doors and windows [*sic*]. [Lean's *Collectanea* (1903), Vol. II, pt. i, p. 390.]

Dismal days for April are 15th, 21st.

MAY

MONTH

I. Names. May, *Màigh, Cèitean, Samhradh, Miòs bòchuin* (month of swelling). *Cèit,* dimin. of *Cèitean* is used in poetry.

II. Sayings, Rhymes. The first few days in May are commonly looked for to be cold and wet, they go by the name of ' the gab o' May ' or ' the caul' gab o' May ' in the inland parts of the country. [J. E. Cr.]

Of May there are various and contradictory sayings :

> May comes in wi' warm shoors
> An' raises a' the grais ;
> An' a' the floors o' May an' June
> They do incraise.

But there is another side to this picture . . . the first days were supposed to come accompanied by cold and wet, and hence were called the ' Gab o' May '. [Greg., p. 150.]

Fishermen's sayings. During the first half of the month of May the sea assumes a dull colour, so that anything falling into it overboard is much sooner lost to sight than at other times. This ' thickness o' the wattir ' or the ' growth o' the sea ' goes by various names : ' The cleansan o' the sea ' (Peterhead) ; ' the gammicks o' May ' (Pittulie) ; ' the May-sob ' (Pittulie). Fishermen agree in saying that during this season the sea rises much more quickly and under less force of wind than at other seasons. Old Footdee fishermen call this excitability of the sea ' the ready row ' (ready roll), and say that it is caused by the thickness of the water. The fishermen of Pittulie and other villages say that ' the sea is prood (proud) in May '. [Rev. W. Gregor, *F.-L. J.*, III (1885), pp. 306 f.] N.E. Scot.

Haddocks spawn during the last weeks of March and the first of May. For a few weeks they are lank and soft. Many of them are split up, salted, and sun-dried on the rocks along the beach. They are called ' speldans ', ' spellans ', ' camerals ' and ' harrowsters '. For the first six days of May fishermen say they are ' prood ', i.e. less keen in taking the bait, and that they will not catch at all during daylight. They become

keener in seizing the bait after this date and get into better
condition : hence the saying :

> A haddock's never gueede
> Till it gets three dips o' the May fleed.   (flood)

[Rev. W. Gregor.]   N.E. Scot.
This saying quoted also from Lnk. in *Pop. Rhymes.*
Landsmen's Proverbs.

> Be not sure of hay till the end of May.

> Be it weal or woe,
> Beans blow before May doth go.

> A hot May makes a fat churchyard.

> He who sows oats in May
> Gets little that way.

> A swarm of bees in May is worth a load of hay.

> Shear your sheep in May
> And shear them all away.

> Castna a clout till May be out.

or, not so frequent :

> Castna a clout till the May be out.

> Come it early, come it late,
> In May comes the cowquake.

In many years the ' cowquake ' occurred between the 6th
and 21st of May.   Oftener it comes between the 9th and 14th.
And the week commencing after that on the 17th is very often
colder than the week before or after.   [David Grewar, *Sc.
N. & Q.*, 3rd series, II (1924), pp. 69 f.]

> For a warm May
> The parsons pray ;
> For an east wind in May
> 'Tis their duty to pray.   [J. E. Cr.]

> If April hath been kind and wept for thee,
> We wish the fruits of that monethes tears to see.

[' Prognostication,' by G. F., *Philol. and Philom.* (1685).]
Rhyme for eating Muggins in May.   See *March, Month,* **II.**
Bird rhyme. The yellow ammer (*Emberiza citrinella*).   Cham-
bers says that this bird (called devil's bird in the north of

Scotland) is the subject of an unaccountable superstition on the part of the peasantry, who believe that it drinks a drop, some say three drops, of the devil's blood each May morning —some say each Monday morning. Its nest, therefore, receives less mercy than that of almost any other bird. Its somewhat extraordinary appearance, all of one colour, and that an unusual one in birds, is the only imaginable cause of the antipathy with which it is regarded. The boys of our own northern region, who call it the yellow yorling or yellow yite, address it in the following rhyme of reproach :

> Half a paddock, half a toad,
>   Half a yellow yorling :
> Drinks a drap o' the de'il's bluid
>   Every May morning.

Scotch children also hang by the neck all the yellow ammers they can get hold of. They often take the bare ' gorbals ', or unfledged young, of this bird, and suspend them by a thread tied round the neck to one end of a crossbeam, which has a small stone hung from the other. They then suddenly strike down the stone end and drive the poor bird into the air. This operation they call ' spangie-hewit '. [Swainson, *F.-L. of British Birds* (1886), pp. 71, 72.]

Of the yellow-hammer it is said :

> Half a poddock, half a tead,
> Half a drap of deil's bleed,
> In a May morning.

[Greg., p. 140.]   N.E. Scot.

The drop of blood is used to paint its eggs. [*F.-L. J.*, VII, p. 175.]

III. Weather Omens and Lore. Crops in the North of Scotland depend a good deal on the weather in May, and this fact is embodied in several proverbs.

> Him it leuks at's crap in May
> Gangs mournin' for aye.

> May makes the hay.

> A misty May an' a drappy June
> Pits the fairmer in gueede tune.

> A misty May an' a drappy June
> Macks the crap come in soon.

A misty May and a drappy Jeene
Macks an eer hairst, an seen deen.

[Greg., pp. 150, 151.]   N.E. Scot.

A wet May and a winnie   [windy]
Brings a fou' stackyard and a finnie.   [of good quality]

[*Pop. Rhymes,*[3] p. 145.]

Thunner in May
Hunger for aye.

                 Aberdour, Pitsligo ; Ab.

Thunder in May
Macks meat to the kye.

[Rev. W. Gregor.]   Corgarff ; Ab.

A May flood never did good.

[J. E. Cr.]

A May wet was never kind yet.

but

May showers make milk and meal ;
Water in May, bread all the year.

A wet May
Makes a big load of hay.

A dry May brings nothing gay.

A windy May makes a fair year.

A cold May is kindly
And fills the barn finely.

[David Grewar, *Sc. N. & Q.*, 3rd series, II (1924), pp. 69 f.]

A warm May and a weeping June
Bring the hairst richt sune.

[Jas. Ferguson, K.C., in *Chambers's Journal*, Feb. 1916, p. 108.]

A misty May and a dropping June
Brings the bonny land o' Moray abune.

Much of Morayshire is of a sandy nature, and the crops in May and June require a good deal of moisture, or else they become stunted. [Greg., p. 111.]   Morayshire.
A similar rhyme given in *N. & Q.* comes from Fife.

Better is snow in May than to be without rain. [*Wcrft. &
Sec. Sight*, p. 272.]   Hghlds.

> If warm May day be threatening
> And it be dry the third day
> And it be east wind after that,
> There will certainly be fruit on trees.

[*Ibid.*, p. 267.]   Hghlds.
Beliefs in luck and ill luck, partly omens. Unlucky. It is regarded as very unlucky to take a branch of pink or white haw-
thorn into the house in May as it is regarded as an omen of
death. [J. E. Cr.]   N.E. Scot.
   To wed in May is to wed poverty. [*Ibid.*]   *Ibid.*
May is an unlucky month to marry or to be born in :

> O' marriages in May
> Bairns die in decay.

A May bird's aye cheepin', i.e. a child born in May is always
complaining, unhealthy. [D. Rorie.]
   Proverb against marrying in May. The aversion to marrying
in May finds expression in the very ancient and well-known
proverb, ' Marry in May, rue for aye,' and thousands still
avoid marrying in this month who can render no more solid
reason for this aversion than the authority of this old proverb.
In former times there were reasons given, varying, however,
in different localities. That parties so marrying would be
childless, or, if they had children, that the first-born would
be an idiot, or have some physical deformity ; or that the
married couple would not lead a happy life and would soon
tire of each other's society. [Napier, p. 43.]   W. Scot.
   A family was sure to be overwhelmed with calamity and
misfortune had the head of the house chanced to marry in
May. [John Fraser, *Chap-Books of Scot.* (1873), p. 53.]
   To wear a green dress.

> Married in May, and kirked in green,
> Baith bride and bridegroom won't long be seen.

[*Antiquary*, vol. III, p. 111.]
   To wean a child. (In Scotland) it is—or recently was—con-
sidered unlucky to wean a child in May. [A. W. Mair,
Hesiod, Addenda, p. 164.]
   Kittens. Kittens brought forth in May are looked on as

unlucky. They are commonly put to death. [*Ethnog. Survey of the U. Kingdom*, 5th Report (1897), p. 456.]   Dalry, Ayr.

Hens not set. A hen is not set during the month of May. The saying about chickens hatched in May is :

> Come oot in May
> Moorn for aye.

[*Ibid.*, p. 471.]   Portlogan, Galloway.

Omen from blades of corn, by the sunwise turn. Aberdeen, May 22, 1597. Jonet Wischert, spouse of John Leyis ; Indytit for passing to the greyne growing corne in May, xxij yeir sensyne or thairbe, sitting thairwpone tymonis in the morning, befor the sone rysing, and being thair found and demandit quhat scho was doing, thow answerit, I sall tell thow, I have been payling the bledis of the corne ; I find it wil be ane deir yeir ; the bled of the corne growis withersones ; and quhan it growis sonegatis about [clockwise], it wil be ane gude chaip yeir. [*Miscellany of the Spalding Club* (1841), I, p, 96.]

Ab.

IV. Observances. The month of May led in the summer and life out-of-doors after the cold dark northern winter. Observances are mostly festivals, merry-making, visits to wells and shrines for healing, and processions of young people to ' bring in May '. Some rites belong especially to the eve and day of Beltane, but others continue during the month and are true May observances, revels of the early summer. The heavy work of the in-gathering is still ahead and full fruition has not come, it is the awakening and growth of vegetation visible to the eye that claims tribute in the general celebrations of Maytide. But as life quickened evil forces were believed to gather strength for renewed attacks on the well-being, food and activities of man ; sorcery was practised in many forms, and witches were feared. Healing powers, however, were also strong at this season, and visits to healing wells, made at the beginning of every quarter, were more frequent and carried out by greater numbers at the beginning of May, when the magic of the waters was held to have full sway. See Section *Wells*, Vol. I.

The revels at this season were not left without control ; both civil and ecclesiastical authorities organised rites aiming at leading merry-makers along lines of safety, for at such celebrations respect for official law and order was in abeyance. We find, therefore, such figures as Robin Hood and Little John, or Abbots of Unreason, Bon Accord, Narent, etc., appointed in charge. These appointments were made annually and any ' burgess chosen to the office ' who neglected his duty to the public in this matter and had failed to provide an acceptable substitute was punishable by a heavy fine. Guilds and fraternities of trades and crafts were also responsible for public entertainment, especially in connection with pageants and mumming, but their observances were related to the patron saints and were held on commemoration days. [Ed.]

A notable early reference to the king and queen of May in summer sports is that made by the wife of Robert the Bruce. A quotation from a history of Fife runs :

Robert the Bruce's coronation at Scone in 1306 seemed to his queen an ominous ceremony. . . . To her it seemed that her lord could not escape being offered up a victim to the forlorn hope of Scotland's independence. ' Alas! ' she exclaimed, ' we are but king and queen of the May! Such as boys crown with rushes in the summer sports.' [1] [Js. Wilkie, *Hist. of Fife* (1924), p. 115.]

Another version. Aestimo quod rex aestivalis sis ; forsitan hyemalis non eris. [*Floris Historiarum* (R.S.), iii, p. 130.]

Earliest known documentary reference to the May game in Scotland. The earliest definite reference to the May game which I have found is in the minutes of the Faculty of Arts at St. Andrews, 1432. The old practice of the ' magistri ' and ' scolares ' bringing in May or summer . . . in disguise on horseback, bearing the insignia of kings and emperors, is condemned as useless and dangerous :

Nov. 21, 1432. Item prohibemus modum quem annis preteritis habuerunt magistri nostri et scolares importando mayum seu estatem vz in habitibus dissimulatis mutuo procuratis a militibus et dominis in equis in armis in insigneis regalibus symeando reges et presides seu imperatores nec tantum prohibemus tanquam inutilem infructuosum et periculosum sed etiam vel magistris quam scolaribus dampnablem reprobamus et condempnamus statuentes si causa recreacionis velint omnes adire campos ad capiendum ayerem quod vadant . . . in vestibus propriis suo gradui statui et honori condecentibus et simul audiant missam in regressu ad villam omnibus aliis superfluitatibus postpositis et vanitatibus pretermissis. . . . [Anna J. Mill, M.A., *Med. Plays in Scot.* (1927), pp. 19 and 284.]   Ab.

---

[1] This quotation unverified.

Literary references to Maying now in print begin with one of Wm. Dunbar : *The Golden Terge.*

XV

And every one of thir, in grene arrayit,
On harp and lute full mirrely thay playit,
And sang ballatis with michty nottis cleir ;
Ladies to danss full sobirly assayit,
Endlang the lusty rever so they mayit.

[Ed. H. Bellyse Baildon (1907), *The Poems of Wm. Dunbar* (*c.* 1490).]

Later we find a reference to dancing and carolling at May-time in Scotland in Gawain Douglas's translation of the *Aeneid* (1512-13), often quoted :

Sum sang ring sangis, dansis ledys, and roondis
Wyth voces shill, quhill all the daill resoondis ;
Quharso thai walk into thar caraling,
For amorus lays doith all the rochis ryng.
Ane sang, *The schip salis our the salt fame,*
Will bring thir merchandis and my lemman hame.
Sum other singis, *I wil be blyth and lycht,*
Myne hart is lent apon sa gudly wycht.

[Ed. John Small (1874), IV, p. 86.]

May pastimes are described by Alex. Scott, from about 1568 :

And now in May to madynnis fawis   [obtains]
With tymmer wechtis [tambourines] to trip in ringis
And to play vpcoil with the bawis.

In May gois gallandis bring in symmer,
And trymly occupyis thair tymmer,
With Hunts vp, every morning plaid.

In May gois dammosalis and dammis,
In gardyngis grene to play like lammis ;
Sum at the baireis [lists] they brace [embrace] like
  billeis [lovers] ;
Sum rynis at barlabrikis [hide-and-seek] like rammis ; . . .

[Alex. Scott, from the Bannatyne MS. (1568). Printed for the Hunterian Club (1896), II, p. 445.]

Barla-Breikis, Barley-Bracks. A game generally played by young people in a corn-yard. . . . One stack is fixed on as the *dule* or goal, and one person is appointed to catch the rest of the company, who run out from the *dule* ; he does not leave it till they are all out of his sight. Then he sets off to catch them. Any one who is taken cannot run out again with his associates, being . . . a prisoner, but is obliged to assist his captor in pursuing the rest. When all are taken the game is finished, and he who was first taken is bound to act as catcher in the next game. (Well known in England, where the rules of the game were slightly different.) [Jamieson.]

Bringing in May. It is principally from official prohibitions that we learn of the festivals of May. In 1555 the Parliament of Scotland (ch. 40, II, 500, ed. 1844) decreed that any women or others ' about simmer treis singand', who perturb the Queen's Lieges as they pass through the boroughs and ' landwart ' towns . . . were to be put on the cuck-stools of every borough or town. At Perth the same penalty awaited the ungodly pastime practised on Sunday evening in the chief streets, ' especially filthy and wngodly singing about þe Mayis'. [Kirk Session Minute Books, Perth, May 3, 1591. See A. J. Mill, *Med. Plays in Scot.*]   Pth.

Visits to the Spynnie Wood (Elgin) for May celebrations of a suspected merriment continued for many years. In 1626 two women promised not to go to the wood of Spynnie ' or any suspect place ' ; if accused again of this they were to ' stand in the jogis a haill day '. At an earlier date nineteen men and eleven women had been punished for being in this wood from Saturday eve at eleven o'clock till four on Sunday morning. [N. Sp. Club, *Rec^{ds} of Elgin*, II, pp. 170 and 195.]   El.

May 25. In 1638 offenders are sent to ward for being at the Spynnie wood on a Sunday night.

Elgin had another forbidden resort.

†May 9, 1628. The kirk officer is ordained ' to go throw the toun with the bell intymating to ilk person or persones that sall be found in the Chanerie kirkyard dancing or louping or foot-balling, to pay a merk'. [*Elgin Records*, II, p. 204.]   El.

In 1639 and 1641 people are forbidden to resort to the Channery Kirk or ' any superstitious place ' for prayer or ' pretendit devotion '. [*Ibid.*, pp. 235 and 238.]

†A famous fair, known as ' The Sleepy Market ', was held during the month of May at Kennethmont. Its transactions were carried on during the night, being attended probably by merriment unpleasing to the civic authorities. Soon after the middle of the 18th century an attempt was made to hold the fair by day, ' but so strong was the prepossession of the people in favour of the old custom that rather than comply . . . they chose to neglect it altogether '. [*O.S.A.* XIII, p. 17.]   Ab.

A break with old custom brings bad luck. [Ed.]

†At Perth the Dragon-hole at Kinnoul Hill was noted for special May observances ; Rob. Chambers describes it as difficult of access, ' and old tradition had her stories about it '. It was believed to have been the abode of a Caledonian prince ; and the Rev. Ch. Rogers, *Scot. Social and Domestic* (1869), p. 216, tells of a stone connected with it which was held to make the person who held it invisible. William Wallace was traditionally reported to have taken refuge in the cave.

The prohibition runs :

1580. The Assembly of ministers and elders understand that the resort to the Dragon Hole, as well by young men as women, with their piping and drums striking before them through this town, had raised no small slander to this congregation, not without suspicion of filthiness following thereupon. (They) have with the consent of the magistrates . . . statute and ordained that no person . . . resort to the Dragon Hole, as they had done in times bygone, namely in the month of May . . . also that they (who transgressed) shall make their public repentance upon Sabbath-day in presence of the people. [Ed. by Js. Maidment, *The Spottiswood Misc.*, ii, pp. 238 f. (1845).] Pth.

The appointed lords of these pastimes were the Abbots of Unreason or Unrest, Lords of Inobedience, and Priors of Bon Accord, who inherited their powers from festivals of midwinter held about cathedrals, in colleges and schools, and at Courts. By the time that prohibitions of May pastimes were in force we find the Abbots, Priors, and Lords put in the same class as Robin Hood, Little John and Queens of May, all equally under censure as figures in the games of May. While yet uncensured there recognition was widespread. The Lord High Treasurer's accounts and Burgh records quote payments for the expenses of their office and penalties for neglect in performance of the duties attached. They had power to punish grave disorders and to summon and fine those who refused expected appearance in ' ridings ' and processions. [Ed.]

The Lord of Misrule was known by various names in different towns. In Peebles, Abbot of Unrest ; Inverness, Abbot of Unreason ; Arbroath, My lord of Rason ; Aberdeen, Abbot or Prior of Bonaccord, also, rarely, Abbot ' out of ressoun ' ; Edinburgh, and in the Court Records, Abbot of Narent, latinised to Narentia [explained in *Mediaeval Plays in Scot.* as ' of no rent or benefice '] ; also Lord of Inobedience.

Abbots were officially appointed to take the lead in popular frolics. . . . They organised folk-games and ridings of the marches. . . . Traces of some or all of these activities are preserved in the records relating to Aberdeen, Arbroath, Ayr, Dalkeith, Dumfries, Dundee, Dunfermline, Edinburgh, Elgin, Errol, Glasgow, Haddington, Inverness, Kelso, Lanark, Peebles, Perth, St Andrews, Stirling. [I. F. Grant, *Social and Economic Develop^t of Scot. before 1603* (1930), pp. 553-555.]

Local Records from Haddington illustrate the serious nature of the Abbot's duties.

May 8, 1536. Memorandum, John Ryklynton and two others were chosen to ' be abbot off wnresson ' which they all three forsook and were ' content ylk man to pa xls to the kyrk maister & he to maik cownt thairof to the town '.

April 24, 1539. This day it was delivered that G. Rychart-son should pay to the treasurer ' xxs at witsonday nixt heir eftir & oder xxs at Ʒoull nixt thaireftir quhilk xls georg ves awand the town becaufs he vald nocht be abbot of Wnresson '.

April 24, 1539. This day the council delivers that the ' baillies pafs & put the actis to executioun of the abbot chesing as thai will anfser on thair aythis & that Incontinent but delay '. . . . [A. J. Mill, *Med. Plays in Scot.* (1927), pp. 250 f.]

Early in the 16th century Robin Hood and Little John were firmly in the saddle as lords of the May ceremonies and re-joicings. They and their company had been adopted long before by the folk and had been known in folk-plays and dances. Walter Bower, in his continuation of Fordun's *Scotichronicon*, early 15th century, mentions their popularity in plays and songs among the ' *Stolidum Vulgus* ', but in these early refer-ences in Scottish literature they have no seasonal character, and are not specially figures of May. [Ed.]

Andrew of Wyntoun, Canon of the Priory of St Andrews, in his *Orygynale Cronykil of Scot.* (Bk. vii, Ch. x, ll. 3525-8) introduces them as ' waythmen [forest rangers] . . . commendit gud ' [Ed. *S.T.S.*, 1914.]

The *Cronykil* was written before 1424 ; the reference is to an earlier date, but the introduction of these two figures seems to have been for decoration. It may at least be taken as evidence that by 1424 they were familiar to Scotsmen as woodland characters and not out of place in a sober chronicle. [Ed.]

In the *Complaynt of Scot.* (1549) Robin Hood is the hero of a ballad : I sall rehers so mony as my ingyne can put in memorie —thai dancit . . . the northt of Scotland, huntis vp . . . Robene hude, thom of lyn. . . . [Ed. Js. A. Murray, *E.E.T.S.*, extra series, XVII (1872), p. 66.]

By 1568 poets claim him for May.

> In May quhen men yeid everich one
> With Robene Hoid and Littill Johne,
> To bring in bowis and birken bobbynis.
> > [the seed-pod of the birch]

[Alex. Scott, *The Evergreen*, ii, p. 187. Bannatyne MS.]

But following soon after is the lament :

> Now all sic game is fastlingis [quickly] gone,
> But gif it be amangis clovin robbynis.   [*Ibid.*]

The Act of 1555 which forbade the election of ' Robert Hude, Little John, Abbot of Unreason, Queens of May or otherwise ' was therefore not a cause of rejoicing.

In 1561 the Edinburgh bailies and Council decree against ' the auld wikit maner of Robene Hude ', but in 1592 the General Assembly had occasion to denounce the profanation of the Sabbath by making of Robin Hood plays, which had not been forgotten. [*Book of the Universal Kirk*, p. 414.]

The change in policy may have been disturbing, for in 1518 the Lord ' Erle of Aranis ' gave serious reasons to the Linlithgow bailies to ' excuse him fra the office of Litiljohn, to the quhilk he was chosin for this yeir . . . for to mak sportis and joscositeis in the town '.   And there was remitted to him ' the vnlaw gif ony he has incurrit for excepping of the said office '.   Those responsible for his appointment are discharged from ' ony poynding of him tharfor '.   [John Foular's *Protocol Books.*]

May 6, 1555.   The quhilk day, Robert Murro wes creat burges and mad his aith as vse is, and fand his hand and his land to do thai thingis that concernit till his aith . . . and to pay his burges siluer to my lord Robene Hude. [A. J. Mill, quoting Records of the Burgh of Peebles, *Med. Plays in Scot.* (1927), p. 263.]

The May Queen has a history of many centuries.   As we know her in Scottish records she seems to appear in solitary state.   Standing at first in beauty among other maids of the year when associated with Maypole rites, she ranks before the Kings of May or Summer as an emblem of spring.   If confused with Maid Marian in May celebrations elsewhere she has, as far as written evidence goes, no such parallel in Scotland. [Ed.]

'Dancing round the Maypole . . . in May was widely practised and was very popular among the young people.' [Js. Brown, *Hist. of Sanquhar* (1891), p. 371.]

In these dances the Queen would be a leading figure. But the pole lived on after her banishment by law. In June 1625, five men and a piper are noted in the Presbytery Records of Lanark as profaners ' in fetching hame a maypole and dancing about the same wpon pasche sonday '. [A. J. Mill, *Med. Plays in Scot.*, p. 263.]

From the same source we have the references in the Lord High Treasurer's Accounts :

1506 . . . to ane Quene of Maij at the Abbey ʒet.   xiiijs.
. . . to ane Quene of Maij on the gait as the king passit to the Abbot of Halyrudhous garding.   vs.
. . . to the Quene of Maij in Air [Ayr].   vs.

[Med. Plays in Scot., p. 323.]

These summer festivals were inaugurated on the first day of May, when the young men and maidens . . . sallied forth into the woods, returning laden with green boughs or ' May bushes ', which they placed above their doors as a protective against evil influences. At the same time, a young tree cut in the woods and stripped of its branches, was erected as a ' May Pole ' or ' Summer Tree ', and round it the country folk danced and sung according to immemorial usage. [D. MacRitchie, ' Anc[t] Summer Festivals', *Scot. Review*, Aug. 10, 1905.]

The dignity of state, even in the case of ' inverted status ', brought abuses, and the Lords of May set up observances of a sumptuous kind, while they were not always able to restrain excesses or even criminal acts during their reign, Presbyteries and boroughs had more causes than one to pronounce judgment against them. [Ed.]

These ancient games, dances, farces and plays . . . were attended with unnecessary expenses to the lords of Bon-Accord, who vied with each other in their sumptuous banquets . . ., the first Sunday in May and the Tuesday after Pasche being the ordinary days appropriated for these exhibitions ; and, at length, the people having become weary of such recreations and amusements, they appear to have declined. [Wm. Kennedy, *Annals of Aberdeen* (1818), p. 93.]   Ab.

April 30, 1562. Disregarding the Act of Parliament of 1555, it had been intended to elect persons to bear such offices (of Robin Hood and Little John) this approaching May, and under colour of Robin Hood's play to raise sedition and tumult, therefore such ' vnleissum gammis ' are forbidden . . . under uttermost danger and peril. [Scot. Burgh Records Soc^{ty}, *Rec^s of the Burgh of Edinburgh,* 1557-1571, p. 131.]

St. Andrews, Ffe.

Thieves took advantage of masks and disguises to enter houses for robbery.

Jan. 16, 1508. Adam Mure is convicted of Stouthreif [robbery with violence], by way of ' Mummyng ', having his face muffled, under silence of night, of a certain sum of money from Sir Don. Moffet. . . . Hanged. [Pitcairn, *Rec^{ds} of the Court of Justiciary.*]

The folk, however, lamented that ' All merines is worne away ', and a return to gaiety is prayed for.

> All borrowis tounis euerilk man zow prayis
> To mak baine fyris fercis & clerk playis
> And throw zour rewis (streets) carrous dance & ſing.

[S.T.S. (1920) Maitland Quarto MS. v, *Poems by Sir R^d Maitland (c.* 1580), ed. W. A. Craigie.]

Duties of supervision devolved upon citizens without the old names. In 1673 two brothers, Ed. Fountain of Locheil and Capt. Js. Fountain, had their patent formally proclaimed throug^t Scotland as masters of the Revels within the kingdom. They thus possessed a privilege of licensing and authorising balls, masks, plays, and such-like entert^{mts}, for which they exacted fees. [R. Chambers, *Domestic Annals,* II, pp. 400 f.]

Before this, gipsies had taken over the parts of older actors in the summer play.

It is stated by Father Hay, the genealogist of the St Clairs of Roslin, that during the latter half of the 16th century two towers at Roslin Castle were known as ' Robin Hood ' and ' Little John ' because they were annually the temporary residence of a company of gipsies, who acted several plays at Roslin during May and June, the inference being that the chief of these plays was ' Robin Hood '. . . . The revellers were unaware in later times that these observances had once a religious meaning, although no doubt they had an instinctive feeling that it would be unlucky to abandon them. (D. MacRitchie, ' Anc^t Summer Festivals ', *Scot. Review,* Aug. 10, 1905.]

Free from blame, archery became the chief feature of practices connected with the Robin Hood games. ' Chief among the festive amusements were the Robin Hood games, consisting mainly of archery.' [J. M. Mackinlay, *Glasgow Herald*, Aug. 8, 1891.]   Edin.

May Races. In the reign of James IV horse-racing was instituted as a royal pastime. During the reign of Queen Mary district horse-races were instituted. In 1552 an annual horse-race was established at Haddington, the winning prize being a silver bell. The silver bell competed for at the Lanark races probably belongs to this period, it is 4½ in. in length and 4½ in. at its greatest diameter, to it are attached 17 shields inscribed with the names of the winners. The oldest shield bears the date 1628. During the reign of Js. VI horse-races were established in the principal centres. In 1608 Paisley appointed one with a silver bell prize ; Cupar, Fife in 1621, with a large silver cup as prize.

After the Restoration there was a keen renewal of racing. In 1661 it was actively revived.

In Lanark the third Tuesday in May ; at Haddington, 22nd of May, the prize a silver cup. At Dumfries, 1662, a silver bell ordered as a prize to be run for every first Sunday of May by the work-horses of the borough. In Peebles was voted a silver cup for an annual race on May-day. Later it became very degraded and a Racing Society was set up by persons of high rank, the Hunters' Club, 1777. [Chs. Rogers, *Soc. Life in Scot.*, II, pp. 305 ff.]

May Festival. †At Kinglassie Common a green sward indicates what was once styled the Ba'field or Bowling Green, where the farm-servants in the vicinity held an annual festival after earing-time, in ' the merry month of May '. The custom has long since fallen into desuetude. [Wm. Blair, *Rambling Recollections* (1857), p. 47.]   Ffe.

Golf. †The meetings of the St Andrews Golf Club are in May and October when competitions are keen. [Chs. Rogers, *Social Life in Scot.* (1884), II, p. 301.]   Ffe.

Boundary Ridings in May. See *Calendar Customs Scot.*, Vol. I.

Waulking the Cloth. A domestic custom of great interest was the cloth waulking ; when practised in earlier days the cloth was waulked by the women in the open air, but now this occupation is carried on indoors and begins in the month of June instead of May. During the waulking the women sang and recited legends and tales thus kept alive in the popular memory.

Lucky undertakings. The first week in May is very fortunate for any undertaking to men ; the second to women. [Dr Crammond.]   Cullen ; N.E. Scot.

PLATE VI

Waulking the Cloth.
After Pennant, 1772.

Agricultural operations done about Beltane are especially lucky. The period extends over the first sixteen days of May. [A. Goodrich-Freer, *F.-L.* XIII (1902), pp. 40 f.]   Hdes.

Invalids in May sunshine. It was an article of belief in the hygienic code of the old Highlanders that the invalid suffering under no matter what form of internal ailment, upon whom the sun of May once fairly shed its light, was pretty sure of a renewed lease of life, until at least the next autumnal equinox. [Rev. Alex. Stewart, *Nether Lochaber* (1883), p. 226.] Hghlds.

DAYS

Beltane Eve. Beltane eve is the last night of April according to official calendars, but in the mind of the folk it is the beginning of Beltane, the chief festival of May. The day began with its preceding night, especially is that true of Hallowmas and Beltane, the two dividing terms of the primitive year. The ancient habit of thought clings to the modern New Year and will have been detected by many who read this record, but later custom has there made its rule firm, and a line of division runs clear cut between past and present wherever the older instinct, impregnable at other points, consents to yield to the dictates of later forms. [Ed.]

V. Observances. a. *Unlucky or forbidden.* *To give away rennet.* If any came to ask for rennet (for the preparation of Beltane dishes), it should on no account be given to them. It would be used for taking the substance out of the giver's own dairy produce. [*Wcrft. & Sec. Sight*, p. 270.]   Hghlds.

V b. *Lucky or enjoined.* *To hang up rowan branches.* (On May eve) the house was hung with rowan-tree. [*Ibid.*]

The reason why the witches shunned any place secured by the ' ran-tree ' is revealed in the Wilkie MS. ' A witch who is touched with a branch of rowan, by a christened man, will be the victim carried off by the devil when he comes next to claim his tribute.' [J. M. McPherson, *Primitive Beliefs in N.E. Scotland* (1929), p. 221.]   N.E. Scot.

This sacred tree cannot be removed by unholy fingers. [*Remains of Nithsdale Song*, p. 290.]   Dfs.

Rowan-tree, roun-tree or roan-tree ; the mountain ash, *Pyrus Aucuparia.* The northern name is of Scandinavian origin [*N.E.D.*]. A tree believed from ancient times to be efficacious against evil influences. Gael. *luis.*

Juniper. Branches of juniper were hung at May-eve above doors and windows . . . to keep witches away. [Mlan Ms.]

V c. *Fire, ashes, etc.* Two fires were kindled by one another on May-eve, in every village of the nation, as well thro'out all Gaule, as in Britain, Ireland and the adjoining lesser Islands. . . . One of the fires was on the carne (that is, a stone barrow), another on the ground. [John Ioland, *Hist. of the Druids* (1814), p. 117.]

At May-eve . . . and on the eve of the first day of November . . . all the people of the country . . . extinguished their fires. Then every master of the family was religiously obliged to take a portion of the consecrated fire to kindle the fire anew in his home. [*Ibid.*]

See also *Fires*, under May 1, **V c.**

V d. *Rites of divination. A snail's trail.* It was a custom among young women to put a snail under a bowl on a table on the evening before May-day, and it was believed that on the following morning they would find their future husband's name written on the table by the snail's trail. [Mlan Ms.]

Islay, Ar.

Live creatures in a hole. It was common in many parts of the Highlands to dig a hole in the garden or other place about the house, with the view of finding what would be in it next morning. A living creature foretold marriage, a dead creature widowhood, and an empty hole non-marriage. [*Ibid.*]

Hghlds.

It used to be a custom among young people in Islay to go on May eve to a march between two properties or two farms where each dug three little holes which were left open all night. On the following morning they went back to examine the holes and discovered certain important events in their future according to what might be found in the holes. [*Ibid.*]   Islay, Ar.

Yarrow and dreams. Girls pluck a sprig of yarrow on May eve, and having addressed it in the words of the following rhyme, place it under their pillow, that they might dream of their sweetheart ; under the impression that the nature of the sweetheart's appearance will indicate the reality or un-reality of his affection. The rhyme is :

Good morrow, good morrow, sweet yarrow to thee ;
If I see my true love in white, his love to me is ever bright.
If he appears to me in blue, his love to me is ever true.
If he appears to me in black, his love to me will lack.

[Mlan Ms.]   Ar.

V e. *Customs of farm, byre, barn or pasture. Protection against witches. Tar.* Tar was put behind the ears of the cattle and at the root of the tail. [*Wcrft. & Sec. Sight*, p. 270.]   Hghlds.

Tar and rowan. The reciter has often enough seen people in Islay putting tar on the horns and ears of cattle and tiny rowan berries to the cows' tails on *Oidhche Bhealtuinn* [May eve]. This was usually accompanied by the repeating of some good words and was intended to protect the beasts from being blighted by the Evil Eye. [Mlan MS.]   Islay, Ar.

Rowan on the byre. On Beltane-eve a cross made of rowan tied with red thread was placed in each opening of the walls of the byre. [*F.-L. J.*, VII, p. 277.]   Corgarff, Ab.

Urine. The animals were sprinkled with urine to keep them from fighting. [*Wcrft. & Sec. Sight*, p. 270.]   Hghlds.

V m. *Food. Beltane bannocks.* I append statements relating to Beltane cakes collected, . . . with the names of my informants.

Bannocks were baked the evening before Beltane, the first day of May (O.S.), and were called Beltane bannocks. They were made of oatmeal in the usual way, but they were washed over or ' watered ' with a thin batter composed of whipped egg, milk or cream, and a little oatmeal. Before being laid on the ' brannithr ' (Keith), ' branner ' (other districts), i.e. gridiron, the upper side was rubbed over with this batter. When the underside was sufficiently baked or ' fired ', the bannock was turned, and the underside was now rubbed over with the batter. The bannock was then allowed to hang over the fire on the gridiron till fully baked.—Janet Davidson (aged 81), Kingussie.

The same custom was followed in Daviot, Strathnairn, but with this difference, that the bannocks were baked any time during the day before. It was accounted unlucky if anyone's bannock broke in the baking.—Mrs Robertson (aged 72), born in Daviot, now at Lynnchat, Alvie.

In Dyke the bannock was baked very thick, and the upper side was smeared or ' watered ' with a batter made of whisked eggs, milk, and oatmeal. A peat on fire through and through, quite without smoke and clear, was held over the upper side till the ' watering ' was dry. The bannock was then turned, and the side that had been under next the fire and was baked was now washed over with the batter, and the bannock was allowed to hang over the fire till it was fully baked. One was prepared for each of the family.—Mrs Munro, Dyke.

In Corgarff, the bannock was about four inches in diameter

and washed over with whisked egg. One was made for each member of the family, and marked so that it might be known for whom it was intended.—J. Farquharson, Corgarff, Ab. [Collected by Rev. W. Gregor, *F.-L.* VI (1895), pp. 3 ff.]

Rites observed in connection with these bannocks on the following morning are described under *Beltane,* **V** d.

V i. *Visits to stones, altars, etc.* In a cave near Portpatrick an altar once stood, and people resorted there on May eve and washed the bodies of diseased children with water and afterwards tied a farthing or some such offering to the altar. [*Dumfries & Galloway N. & Q.,* I, p. 6.]   Galloway.

V j. *Bloodshed and sacrifice.* Mr Maciver remembers of hearing in his native island of Lewis, when he was young, of the old practice that existed there long before, of sacrificing a sheep on May eve. It was said to have been done with the view of securing luck throughout the year. According to Mr Macphail, who is also a native of Lewis, this old sacrifice was called *Tamnadh* (?) [*Damnadh,* ' doom ' (?)]. [Mlan Ms.]
Lewis, Hdes.

VI. Beliefs in Witchcraft, Fairies, and Occult Powers. The chief festivals of witches were on Beltane Eve and Hallowe'en, when new members of the community were introduced, and various rites and practices of magical forms were prescribed. These ' Sabbaths ' or assemblies seem to have been conducted on similar lines over most of Europe. When under examination country people stated that they had seen witches ride to such meetings on horses, sticks, or the wind. A characteristic feature of these organisations in Scotland was perhaps the prominent part played by the woman as leader. A queen ruled the court of Elfin and was mentioned in confessions at Aberdeen and other places, but the Devil or Beelzebub, known under various names, was the supreme lord. There is a copious literature on this subject.

Penalties for witchcraft, sorcery, and the practice of magic, black and white, were imposed by both civic and religious authorities for centuries, and most of the customs quoted as observed at Beltane, Hallowe'en, St John's Eve and New Year had as their aim the counteracting of these dreaded powers. They were, for the most part, called into action without reference to the ' Sabbaths ' or special recognition of Beelzebub, but companies of witches and sorcerers were supposed to act in organised communities and to consult together how best to strengthen their influence. [Ed.]

On the night preceding May Day . . . witches were awake, and went about as hares to take their produce . . . from the cows. [*Wcrft. & Sec. Sight*, p. 270.] Hghlds.

Fairy gaiety. Beltane eve was the night on which fairies were supposed to make their social calls. They were seen dancing on this night. [Mlan MS.] Islay, Ar.

The date given here is May 12, due to the change of style. [Ed.]

The nights before Beltane were the period of fairy festivities and raids on human beings. [J. G. Campbell, *Superstitions of the Highl^ds & Isl^ds of Scot.* (1900), p. 18.] Hghlds. and W. Is.

Kirk's essay on *Fairies, Elves and Fauns* relates what was known of fairies two centuries ago, and all the stories gathered since . . . may be regarded as a mere amplification . . . of what was well known and universally believed at the time of the Reformation. [Rev. J. Macdonald, *Trans. Gael. Soc. of Inverness*, XXI (1896-7), p. 270.]

Belief in movement of a stone. Stone washes itself in the stream. †In the north of the Stewartry, there is a green howe dipping down to the joining of two hill streams, on the face of the hill stands a great white stone and it was a matter of belief that every May eve this stone came down to wash itself at the meeting of the waters, and then returned to the hillside to stand guard over the sleeping valleys for another year. [John Glover, *Dumfries and Galloway N. & Q.*, I, p. 66.]

The Stewartry.

X. *Beltane Watch.* April 25, 1571. †The said inqueist ordanis the half of the toone to walk nychtlie quhill Beltane ewin, and the haill toun to walk on Beltane ewin, Beltane at ewin, and the morne efter Beltane day quhill thai se quhat stay may cum in the cuntre for resisting of thevis. [Sc. Burgh Records Society (1872), *Records of the Burgh of Peebles*, p. 326.] Ps.

1st

I. Names. *May Day. Beltane, Yellow or Golden Beltane.* Gael. *La buidhe Bealltuinn.* The old derivation of the name from words interpreted ' the fire of Baal ' is no longer accepted. The first element, *beall*, is cognate with O.E. bael and English bale, as in bale-fire [*Scot. Nat. Dict.*, 1934]. The second element is taken as from Gael. *teine*, fire. ' Beltane is the first day of May ' [*Car. Gad.* I, p. 182]. The name is given also to Rood day, May 3, St Helen's day ; this use is ' frequent in documents of the 16th century'. See *Dict. of the Older Scot. Tongue*, ed. W. A. Craigie (1932), where the relevant quotations are given.

Later evidence shows the observance of Beltane rites on both May 1 and May 3 in different places. *The Burgh Records of Peebles* (1621), p. 85, notes the three fairs of the town, ' the first thereof beginning yearly upon the third day of May, called Beltane day'. May 2 is found also with the name of Beltane, and even Whitsunday and Johnsmass, June 24, are so called. [Ed.]

Where the Church was powerful . . . Rood day would be the important festival and Beltane would gradually become incorporated with it, the names Beltane and Rood day becoming synonymous. . . . Where the Church was weaker the festival would be kept according to older custom on the first day of May. [Napier, Appendix, p. 164.]

From another account we must infer that the 1st of May was called Whitsuntide in some northern parts, not that the date of Beltane was later than that explainable by the change of style, i.e. May 12, later 13. [Ed.]

Là Bealltuinn (May-day, Whitsuntide). . . . The first of May was held as a great Druidical festival. . . . Fires were kindled, etc. . . . [Rev. Alex. Macgregor, *Highland Superstitions, etc.*, p. 43 (1901). First appeared in Vol. II of the *Celtic Magazine*.]

But there was a distinct dating of Beltane on May 3, Rood Day, even where the older date was known to be May 1. ' That there were two days known as Beltane at the beginning of the last (i.e. 18th) century is evident from a book of Scotch proverbs (1721) published by Js. Kelly, in which occurs the following :

' " You have skill of man and beast. Ye was born between the beltans."

' In all probability the discrepancy originated through the Church substituting a Christian festival for a heathen one.' [Napier, Appendix, p. 163.]

Cf. A. D. Cumming :

The festival of Beltane was celebrated in former times on the first of May, both in the Highlands and Lowlands of Scotland. [*Old Times*, p. 159.]

On the first of March
The craws begin to search ; (or scratch, *cf*. March 1, **V** o.)
On the first o' April
They are sitting still ;

By the first o' May
They're a 'flown away ;
Croupin' greedy back again,
Wi' October's wind and rain.

[*Pop. Rhymes,*[3] p. 165.]

II. Sayings and Rhymes. New year's day to-day, Beltane to-morrow ; meaning—that whatever day New year's day fell upon, Beltane fell on the day following. [*Wcrft. & Sec. Sight*, p. 270.]

' For ever ' is longer than till Beltane. [D. Macintosh, *Gaelic Proverbs* (1785), p. 38.]

Referring to assurance that the longest winter must have an end. [Ed.]

I'll bring your Yule belt to the Beltane bore. [*Denham Tracts* (1875), II, p. 90.]

The belt is worn tighter at Beltane than at Yule. [Ed.]

Herds wha count their hogs afore Beltane hae often to count twice. [And. Cheviot, *Proverbs* (1896), p. 165.]

The saying, ' the mournful linnet of Beltane ' refers to the cold weather often prevalent at this time. [*Wcrft. & Sec. Sight*, p. 270.] Hghlds.

Snow at this time was known as ' Snow about the mouth of May-day '. [*Ibid.*]

IV. Omens. *From the day on which Beltane fell.* The only exception to the luck of Thursday [St Columba's day] was when Beltane fell on that day. [*Car. Gad.*, I, p. 163.]

It was thought that certain boy infants would die if Beltane fell on a Thursday, . . . according to the saying, ' Many a woman will be without an infant son, when Beltane falls on Thursday '. [*Wcrft. & Sec. Sight*, p. 297.]

Woe to the mother of a wizard's son, when Beltane falls on a Thursday. [D. Macintosh, *Gael. Proverbs*, p. 146.]

IV d. *Omen from the hair of the foot.* In the West of Scot., on hearing the cuckoo for the first time (on May 1), pull off your shoes and stockings, and if you find a hair on the sole of the *left* foot, it will be the exact colour of the hair of your future spouse. If no hair is found, then another year of single life must be endured. [*F.-L. R.*, II, p. 89.] West Scot.

IV e. *Omens from birds.* Cf. **V o.** below, the Cuckoo.

IV f. *Omen from a plant.* Highlanders regard Beltane as the first day of summer. Forecasts for the season are made from it. If a birch shows a leaf the size of the lug of a mouse, it presages a prosperous year. [J. E. Cr.]   Hghlds.

V. Observances. The customs under this heading should be read with those given under May 2 and May 3, to which dates some Beltane rites have passed.

V a. *Unlucky or forbidden. To give out eatables or drink.* People here in Mull believe it very unlucky to give milk or any eatables out of the house on May-day. [Mlan Ms.]
                                                            Isle of Mull, Ar.

To give out fire or water. No one would give fire or water out of a bowl on May Day—to do so was unlucky. [J. Glover, *Dumfries & Galloway N. & Q.*, I, p. 66.]   S.W. Scot.

To use fire or water. If possible fire and water were not to be used. [*Ibid.*]

To give out kindling. No fire on this, or any other first day of a quarter of the year, was given out of the house. It gave the borrower the power of taking the milk from the lender's cows. [*Wcrft. & Sec. Sight*, p. 271.]   Hghlds. and W. Isles.

If on the 1st of May a person begged fire of a neighbour and got it, the remnant cinders were drowned by the latter. [Mlan MS.]   W. Isles.

I remember myself when matches were not common . . . and people would be going to their neighbours for a kindling when their fires would go out. And I remember that people would not be willing to give a kindling to anyone about the time of Bealtuin, for the notion was pretty common that if one gave away a kindling out of his house at that time he would be in danger of giving his good luck away with it. [*Ibid.*]   Arran, Ayr.

To allow a woman to cross a certain stream before a man. †The natives in the village of Barvas retain an ancient custom of sending a man very early to cross Barvas river every first day of May, to prevent any females crossing it first ; for that, they say, would hinder the salmon from coming into the river all the year round. They pretend to have learned this from a foreign sailor who was shipwrecked on that coast a long time ago. [Martin, p. 7.]   Lewis, Hdes.

V b. *Lucky or enjoined. Washing the face with May dew.* Other things forbidden are noted under **V c.**, *Rites of fire*, etc.

From an Aberdeen almanac of 1692 :

> O Lustie May, fair, mistie and gay,
> Makes Trees, Herbs, Bloom on every bray.
> In this moneth gather more dew of Grace,
> Then of May-dew to wash your Face.

It was not so very long ago that Edinburgh citizens thronged
in hundreds to the summit of Arthur's Seat on May-morning
for the purpose of washing their faces in May dew, in accordance with the old belief that they would thereby render
themselves beautiful for at least a year to come. Latterly no
doubt the custom was kept up in a spirit of jest . . . but as
certainly the efficacy of May dew was seriously believed in in
earlier times. [D. MacRitchie, *Scot. Review*, Aug. 10, 1905.]
                                                                 Edin.

In Perth they climbed Kinnoul Hill for the same purpose,
with a lingering belief in the old saying—that those who wash
their faces in May dew will be beautiful all the year. [Hen-
derson, *F.-L. of the Northern Counties* (1879), p. 85.]   Pth.

Washing the face with dew gathered on the morning of
the first day of May kept it from being tanned by the sun and
becoming freckled. [Greg., p. 151.]   N.E. Scot.

The custom is reported also from Fife, Galloway, Kirkcudbright, Roxburgh, and Ross-shire.

From Hone, *Every-Day Book*, we have an early account.

To the Editor of the Every-Day Book.

EDINBURGH, *April 20, 1826.*

My Dear Sir,—Allow me, without preface, to acquaint you
with a custom of *gathering the May-dew* here on the first of
May.

About four o'clock in the morning there is an unusual stir ;
a great opening of area gates, and ringing of bells, and a
' gathering ' of folk of all clans, arrayed in all the colours of
the rainbow ; and a hurrying of gay throngs of both sexes
through the King's-park to Arthur's-seat.

In the course of half an hour the entire hill is a moving
mass of all sorts and sizes. At the summit may be seen a
company of bakers, and other craftsmen, dressed in kilts,
dancing round a Maypole. On the more level part ' next
door ', is usually an itinerant vender of whiskey, or mountain
(not May) dew, your approach to whom is always indicated
by a number of ' bodies ' carelessly lying across your path,
not dead, but drunk. . . .

These proceedings commence with the daybreak. . . . About
six o'clock, the appearance of the gentry, toiling and *pechin*
up the ascent, becomes the signal for serving men and women
to march to the right-about ; for they well know that they

must have the house clean, and every thing in order earlier than usual on May morning.

About eight o'clock the ' fun ' is all over. . . .

I am, &c.,

P. P., Jun.

[Hone, *Every-Day Book*, ii, p. 609.]

Sometimes the dew is believed to have magical powers. Dew collected on the first day of May is supposed to confer witch power on the gatherer, and give protection against an evil eye. [Napier, Appendix, p. 170.]   W. Scot.

Wishing with the dew. On the first day of May girls went to wash their faces in the dew and *wish* before sunrise—while doing this they name some lad and wish in their own mind that he may become their sweetheart, and they get their wish.   Rs.

Marginal Note.—Ask the grass to give them their wish and they will get it. [Mlan MS.]

Ivy-sprigs with dew. In Ross-shire the lasses pluck sprigs of ivy, with the May-dew on them, that have not been touched by steel. [Rich. Folkard, *Plant Lore* (1884), p. 30.]   Rs.

Decking the house and the horse with flowers and green. In my remembrance, the first of May, in the country west of Glasgow, was honoured by decking the house with tree branches and flowers. Horses were also similarly decked. [Napier, Appendix, p. 167.]   Lnk.

See May, Month, for bringing in a Maypole.

Decking a statue with flowers. It was formerly a custom with the boys (of Heriot's Hospital, Edinburgh) to dress Heriot's statue with flowers on the first of May, and to renew them on this anniversary festival when they received their new clothes. [*Gentleman's Magazine*, 1745, p. 686.]   Edin.

Watching the sunrise from a hill-top. In my grandfather's youth it was the custom for the young men and maidens of Lawers to climb to the summit of Ben Lawers on that day (Beltane) to see the sun rise, and it was a race between the young men which of them would first reach and drink out of a spring called ' the Lady of Lawers's well '. [J. Mac-Diarmid, *Trans. Gael. Socty. of Inverness*, xxv (1901-03), p. 131.]
Pth.

Sunrise watching noted also from Arthur's Seat, Edinburgh, and from hills of Fife.

Luck by a snail. If you catch a snail by the horns on the first of May and throw it over your shoulders you will be lucky throughout the year. [Dr Crammond.]   Cullen, Bf.

PLATE VII

May-Day Dancers at Arthur's Seat, Edinburgh.
From Hone, 1826.

V c. *Rites of fire, torches, ashes.* The fire rites of May and of the summer solstice at St John's Eve were the most remarkable and the most carefully observed of seasonal customs. Incinerated earth and layers of charcoal have been noted on hill-tops and were described by older students of folk custom as the marks of Beltane fires. They are not quoted here, as it is impossible to distinguish remains of Beltane fires from those of beacons, which were common on hill-tops. The same difficulty is found in dealing with place-names formed from words meaning fire or burning. [Ed.]

The Beltane bonfire. The advent of summer was at one time signalised in a striking manner by the ' Beltane Fires ' which blazed all over the British Isles in May and June. The antiquity of this custom is indicated by the fact that these bonfires were kindled by the primitive method of ' forced ', or ' need ' fire (Gaelic *tein'-èigin*), i.e. from combustion produced by the violent friction of two pieces of wood. Any more modern method was denounced as profane. . . . Although Beltane synchronises with May Day, the summer solstice has always been the favourite season for the great annual fire-festival on the Continent of Europe. [David MacRitchie, ' Anc[t] Summer Festivals ', in the *Scottish Rev.*, Aug. 10, 1905.]

The ancient Irish Glossary of Cormac states :

Belltaine Mayday, i.e. bil-tene, i.e. lucky fire, i.e. two fires which Druids used to make with great incantations. And they used to bring the cattle [as a safeguard] against the diseases of each year to those fires. [In margin.] They used to drive the cattle between them. [Cormac's *Glossary*, p. 18, ed. Whitley Stokes (1868).]

Most authorities hold with Cormac that there were two fires between which cattle and even children were passed. Criminals were made to stand between the two fires, and hence the proverb in regard to a person in extreme danger— as the Rev. D. Macqueen gives it, ' He is betwixt two Beltein fires'. [Alex. MacBain, *Celt. Mythol. and Religion* (1917), p. 167.]

Pennant speaks of things passing between two Beltane fires. [*Tour in Scot., etc.*[2] (1772), Pt. I, p. 435.]

On May Day all the fires of the district were extinguished and *tein'-èigin*, need-fire, was produced on the knoll. This fire is divided in two and people and cattle rushed through for purification, and safe-guarding against mischance and murrain during the year. . . . The ordeal of passing through the fires gave rise to a proverb which I heard used by an old man in Lewis in 1873 : ' A Mhoire! Sonnie, it were worse for me to do that for thee than to pass between the two great fires of Beall.' [*Car. Gad.*, I, pp. 182 f.] Hghlds. & Is.

The making of the fire. All the fires in the parish were extinguished, and then eighty-one married men, being thought the necessary number for effecting this design, took two great planks of wood and nine of them were employed by turns, who by their repeated efforts rubbed one of the planks against the other until the heat thereof produced fire, and from this forced fire each family is supplied with new fire. . . . [Martin p. 113.] W. Isles.

A native of Caithness said that a countryman told him that he had himself taken part on one occasion in raising fire by this means. Eighty-one men were engaged on it, divided into nine shifts, nine on each shift, and they had to work the sticks against each other as fast and with as much pressure as possible. [Mlan MS.] Cths.

Upon any small island in a river or lake, a circular booth of stone or turf is erected, on which a couple, or rafter of birch-tree, is placed and the roof covered over. In the centre is set a perpendicular post fixed by a wooden pin to the couple, the lower end being placed in an oblong groove on the floor ; and another pole is placed horizontally, between the upright post and the leg of the couple, into both which, the ends, being tapered, are inserted. The horizontal timber is called the auger, being provided with four short arms, or spokes, by which it can be turned round. As many men as can be collected are then set to work, having first divested themselves of all kinds of metal, and two at a time continue to turn the pole by means of the levers, while others keep driving the wedges under the upright post so as to press it against the auger, which by the friction soon becomes ignited From this the Need-fire is instantly procured, and all other fires being immediately quenched, those that are rekindled both in dwelling-houses and offices are accounted sacred. . . . [Js. Logan, *The Scottish Gael* (1831), II, pp. 68 f.]

In Mull, 1767, a hill-top was selected, within sight of which all fires were put out, and then the pure fire was produced by turning a wheel over nine spindles of wood until the friction caused combustion. Mull.

Need-fire workers should carry no *iron*, by the earliest accounts. . . . Though latterly restricted to act as a charm against plague [and murrain], the need-fire shows clear traces of a higher religious purpose. It was lighted at the great festivals of the solar and lunar year, and from them all the fires of the neighbourhood, previously extinguished, were relighted. Priests presided, and men and cattle passed through them.

The ' Druidic ' incantations and the ' tinegin ' were not used within the last century . . . for lighting *the Beltane fire* ; their use seems latterly to have been restricted to raising the need-fire during cattle plagues. [Alex. MacBain, *Celt. Mythol. and Religion* (1917), pp. 159-167.]

The Beltane feast seems to have been performed on hills or eminences. The sacrifices were offered *in the open air*, frequently upon the tops of hills. But since the decline of superstition it has been celebrated by the people of each hamlet on some hill or rising ground around which their cattle were pasturing.

The night before, all the fires in the country were carefully extinguished, and next morning the materials for exciting this sacred fire were prepared. The most primitive method seems to be that used in the islands of Skye, Mull and Tiree. A well-seasoned plank of oak was procured, in the midst of which a hole was bored. A wimble of the same timber was then applied, the end of which they fitted to the hole. But in some parts of the mainland the machinery was different. They used a frame of green wood, of a square form, in the centre of which was an axletree. In some places three times three persons, in others three times nine, were required for turning round by turns the axletree or wimble. If any of them had been guilty of murder, adultery, theft, or other atrocious crime, it was imagined that the fire would not kindle, or that it would be devoid of its usual virtue. So soon as any sparks were emitted by means of the violent friction, they applied a species of agaric which grows on old birch-trees and is very combustible. This fire had the appearance of being immediately derived from heaven and manifold were the virtues ascribed to it (against witchcraft and malignant diseases both in human species and cattle ; it changed the nature of strongest poisons).

After kindling the bonfire with the *tein-eigin* the company prepared their victuals. As soon as they had finished their meal (they sang and danced for a while round the fire). Towards the close of the entertainment the person who officiated as master of the feast produced a large cake baked with eggs and scalloped round the edge, called *am bonnach beal-teine*. It was divided into a number of pieces and distributed in great form to the company. There was one particular piece which whoever got was called *Cailleach beal-teine*, the Beltein Carline, a term of great reproach. Upon his being known, part of the company laid hold of him and made a show of putting him in the fire, but the majority interposing he was rescued. In some places they laid him flat on the ground, making as if they would quarter him. Afterwards he was pelted with eggshells and retained the odious appellation during the whole year. And while the feast was fresh in people's memory they affected to speak of the *Cailleach beal-teine* as dead.

(The festival was longest observed in the interior Highlands ; towards the W. coast the traces are faintest.) . . . [Alex. Allardyce, from MSS. notes of *c.* 1760, *Scot. and Scotsmen in the 18th cent.* (1888), II, pp. 429 ff.]

Mull, Ar. ; Skye & Tiree, Iness.

Dancing round the flames.

> But o'er his hills, in festal day,
> How blazed Lord Ronald's beltane-tree,
> While youths and maids the light strathspey
> So nimbly dance with Highland glee.

The fires lighted by the Highlanders on the first of May are termed *The Beltane-tree*.[1] [Sir Walter Scott, *Glenfinlas*, Verse IV, note, p. 686. Ed. J. Logie Robertson (1894).]

At Bel-tein on the 1st of May the herds of several farms gather dry wood, put fire to it, and dance three times southways about the pile. [T. Pennant, *Tour in Scot.*[4] (1769), Appendix II, p. 309.]

El.

Rowan carried round the fire. In the counties of Ross and Sutherland young men formerly walked round the Beal fires carrying branches of the mountain ash garnished with sprigs of heath. [Ch. Rogers, *Social Life in Scot.*, I, p. 13.]

Rs. & Sld.

Torches lighted. Into fires so raised (need-fires), young men dipped torches, which they bore hastily to their respective villages, and thence to the nearest eminence. [*Ibid.*]

(At Beltein) the Highlanders passed through the fire and they thought it a religious duty to walk round their fields and flocks with burning matter in their right hands, a practice once universal throughout the country. [James Logan, *The*

---

[1] The term ' Beltane-tree ' arose from a confusion of the first syllable *bel-* with Gael. *bile*, a tree. [Ed.]

Scottish Gael, 1831, vol. II, p. 337. Ed. by Rev. A. Stewart, 1876.]

Leaping through the flames. In the Western Isles it was long customary to pass children and cattle through the smouldering embers. In some cases fathers took their children in their arms, and leapt thrice through the flames. [*Ibid.*]

At the Beltane festival . . . in the northern counties, children kindle great fires and, as part of a ceremonial, rush wildly through the flames. [Ch. Rogers, *Social Life in Scot.*, I, p. 13.]

Hghlds.

Leaping by lot. Upon the first day of May, which is called *Baltan* or *Bàl-tein*-day, all the boys in a township or hamlet meet in the moors. They cut a table in the green sod, of a round figure, by casting a trench in the ground of such circumference as to hold the whole company. They kindle a fire, and dress a repast of eggs and milk of the consistence of a custard. They knead a cake of oatmeal, which is toasted at the embers against a stone. After the custard is eaten up, they divide the cake into so many portions, as similar as possible to one another in size and shape, as there are persons in the company. They daub one of these portions all over with charcoal until it be perfectly black. They put all the bits of the cake into a bonnet. Every one, blindfold, draws out a portion. He who holds the bonnet is entitled to the last bit. Whoever draws the black bit is the devoted person who is to be sacrificed to *Baal*, whose favour they mean to implore, in rendering the year productive of the sustenance of man and beast. There is little doubt of these inhuman sacrifices having been once offered in this country as well as in the East, although they now omit the act of sacrificing, and only compel the *devoted* person to leap three times through the flames ; with which the ceremonies of this festival are closed. . . . [*O.S.A.*, XI, p. 620.]

Callander, Pth.

Its later form . . . was somewhat as follows : the day was set apart as a holiday ; a hole was dug in a hill and a fire lit therein. Lots were cast and he on whom the lot fell had to jump clear over the fire seven times, while the young folks capered round in a circle ; then they all sat down to cook eggs and eat them. [John Horne, *Caithness* (1905), p. 112.]

Cths.

According to a few accounts the fire was kindled with a flint. [Alex. MacBain, *Celt. Mythol. & Relig.* (1917), p. 167.]

Fire not given out till tithes had been paid. The custom practised (at Beltane) by the druids in the isles of extinguishing all the fires in the parish until the tithes were paid, upon payment of them the fires were kindled in each family, never till then. [Martin, p. 105.]   Hdes.

It was not safe for them to kindle a fire in their houses any more, until they boght it from beil's druids. . . . The first day of summer was called the beil-fires day. [Letter from J. Dewar in J. F. Campbell's *Pop. Tales of the W. Highl*[ds], New Ed. (1895), I, Introd. liii.]

In Rannoch and the uplands of Lochaber the *Tein' eigin* was produced within living memory. My father, who died at the age of eighty-two, remembered taking part as a boy in the production of *Tein' eigin*. . . . It was then the custom for each family in the district to receive a brand from the sacred fire to kindle the domestic hearth. But those who were in arrears of rent, had failed to pay their just debts, had been guilty of theft or meanness, or were known to have committed certain offences against good morals, were deprived of the privilege, and this was regarded much as expulsion from one's club would be viewed by us. [Rev. Js. Macdonald, *Trans. Gael. Soc*[tv] *of Inverness*, XIX, 1893-4, p. 273.]

Iness & Pth.

The fire gives virtue to water and cakes. Water boiled at Beltane fires is believed to acquire medicinal virtue. Cakes toasted at these fires are held to be spiritually sustaining. [Ch. Rogers, *Social Life in Scot.*, I, p. 13.]

Sometimes a large bannock of oat or barley was rolled through the Beltane bonfire. [Rev. W. Gregor.]   Keith, Bf.

An old man near Galashiels remembers hearing his father speak of the Beltane fires on a cairn visible on a hill from the road between Galashiels and Langshaw. The cairn was pointed out to me (the editor) by Mr Ion C. B. Jamieson of Langshaw. . . . The rite of leaping through the flames was observed on the cairn at Beltane each spring. (September 1934.) [*F.-L.*, Dec. 1934, p. 344.]

Beltane fires in this part of the country have long been extinguished. [Hugh Miller, *Scenes, etc., of N. of Scot.* (1850), p. 62.]   Rs.

The custom out of favour. I have myself conversed with old men who, when boys, were present at, and took part in, these observances ; and they told me that in their grandfather's time it was the men who practised these rites, but as they were generally accompanied with much drinking and riot, the clergy set their faces against the customs, and subjected the parties observing them to Church discipline, so that in

course of time the practices became merely the frolic of boys.
[Napier, Appendix, p. 169.]

Late dates of the fires. A woman in Arran said that her father
and the other men of the townland made the neid-fire on the
knoll on the Yellow Day of Beltane. They fed the fire from
great bundles of sacred faggots brought to the knoll on
Beltane Eve. . . . The last neid-fire in Arran was in 1820.

The last Neid-fire made in N. Uist was in 1829. It was
brought from Sail Dharaich, Sollas, after they had extinguished
their own fire, and produced from an oak log by rapid boring
with an auger by the exertions of nine nines of first-begotten
sons.

The last fire in Helmsdale was *c.* 1818, in Reay *c.* 1830.
[*Car. Gad.*, II, pp. 340 f.]   W. Is. & Hghlds.

The Beltane fire was kindled in Ayrshire till about 1790.
[Rev. Alex. Macgregor, *Highl^d Superstitions, etc.* (1901), p. 43.]

V d. *Rites of divination or augury.* (Other rites under **V c.**)
At Beltane, as at Hallowe'en, when the invisible world was
believed to show its powers to man, secrets could be learned
and the future foretold by rites of divination. [Ed.]

Drawing of cakes from a hat by lot to select the one to jump
through the Beltane flames is described in the preceding
section, **V c.**

Divination for marriage was practised chiefly at Hallowe'en ;
a few rites were used at Beltane.

By a snail. Take a snail on the morning of May Day and
shut it up in any kind of dish. Omens are drawn from the
figures made by the slime. The diviners tried to detect the
form of letters in the slime marks. [*Ethnog. Survey of the U.
Kingdom*, 5th Report (1897), p. 478.] Kirkmaiden, Galloway.

Cf. the similar rite on May eve.

By the yarrow. On the 1st of May, ' atween the sin an' the
sky,' the girls went to the fields where Milfoil (*Achillea millefolium*) Yarrow or ' hunirt-leaft girss ' [hundred-leaved grass]
grew, shut their eyes and pulled what came first to hand,
repeating the words :

> Oh! it's a bonnie May mornin',
> I cam t' pu' the Yarrow,
> I hope before I go
> To see my marrow.

They then opened their eyes and looked in all directions
as far as the eye could reach, and if a man was seen, the girl

was to get a ' marrow '.—Told by Mrs Sutherland, who has done this. [Rev. W. Gregor.]   Aberdour, Ab. ; N.E. Scot.

Young girls on the first night of May, O.S. (May 12) adopted the following mode of finding out who was to be their lover. Without speaking a word they went out ' atween the sin and sky ' and gathered the flower Yarrow (*Achillea millefolium*), repeating the words :

> Good morrow, good morrow
> To thee, brave Yarrow,
> And thrice good morrow to thee.
> I pray you tell me [to-night] or to-morrow
> Who is my true lover to be.

They carried it home, put it below their pillow, went to bed without speaking a word. Neither did they speak till morning. During the night they dreamed and saw their lover. [*Ibid.*]   *Ibid.*

From rolling bannocks. After 4 o'clock in the afternoon all the members of the household went to the top of a rising ground or slope, and rolled the bannocks [baked on May eve as described] to the bottom. Omens of good or bad fortune, or of death, were drawn from the way in which they rolled. If one fell before it reached the bottom, some evil was to happen to its owner. If one broke, its owner was to die before next Beltane. Each rolled the bannock three times. [Rev. W. Gregor, *Kilns, Mills, etc.* (1894), p. 32.]   Corgarff, Ab.

At Dyke, Nn., the bannocks were eaten, each by its owner. [*Ibid.*]

The bannocks are all arranged in a line, and on their edges let down the hill, etc. When this has been done (the children) assemble round a rousing fire of collected heath and brush-wood and the bannocks are soon demolished. [W. Grant Stewart, *Pop. Superstit*[s], p. 181.]   Hghlds.

Eggs with the bannocks. In the neighbourhood of Kingussie . . . bannocks and hard-boiled eggs continue to be rolled down the hills on the first of May. Till quite lately these bannocks were used for purposes of divination. [*F.-Lore of Scot. Lochs, etc.*, p. 298.]   Iness.

Egg-rolling, probably with divination. In Strathnairn . . . on the 1st of May, which they called Beltane Day. The children used to roll eggs, coloured blue, yellow, etc., down the hill. [*F.-L. J.*, VII (1889), p. 265.]   Iness.

The rolling of coloured eggs is believed by some to be an Easter rite, extended by children to Beltane. [Ed.]

Bannocks used to dream on. (After rolling the bannocks) the young folk ate part of them, left each a ' bittie ' on the hill to the ' cuack ', i.e. the cuckoo, and carried a piece home. This piece was put under the pillow in the name of the sweetheart to find out if dreams would reveal the future as to marriage. [Rev. W. Gregor, *Kilns, Mills, etc.* (1894), p. 31.]

Kingussie, Iness.

Divination from stones round the fire. When the (Beltane) bonfire burned low, and the devotees were departing, a ring of stones was placed round the ashes, one stone for each person present. If any should be removed or amissing in the morning, it was a sign of an early death to the individual represented. [*Old Times*, p. 160.]

W. Isles.

V e. *Farm customs, Barn, Byre, Pasture.* (*Farm customs with fire, see* **V c.**) *Herds' tribute to unseen powers and animals.* On the first of May the herds of every village hold their Beltein, a rural sacrifice. They cut a square trench on the ground, leaving the turf in the middle ; on that they make a fire of wood, on which they dress a large caudle of eggs, butter, oatmeal, and milk ; and bring, besides the ingredients of the caudle, plenty of beer and whisky, for each of the company must contribute something. The rites begin with spilling some of the caudle on the ground, by way of libation ; on that every one takes a cake of oatmeal, upon which are raised nine square knobs, each dedicated to some particular being, the supposed preserver of their flocks and herds, or to some particular animal, the real destroyer of them ; each person then turns his face to the fire, breaks off a knob, and flinging it over his shoulder, says, ' This I give to thee, preserve thou my horses ; this to thee, preserve thou my sheep ' ; and so on. After that they use the same ceremony to the noxious animals. ' This I give to thee, O fox ! spare thou my lambs ; this to thee, O hooded-crow ! and this to thee, O eagle ! '

When the ceremony is over they dine on the caudle, and, after the feast is finished, what is left is hid by two persons deputed for that purpose ; but on the next Sunday they re-assemble, and finish the reliques of the first entertainment. [Pennant, *Tour in Scotland* (1790), vol. i, p. 112.]

In Kincardineshire the latter part of the formula was somewhat different : ' This to you, O mists and storms— spare our pastures and our corn ; this to you, O eagle—spare our lambs and our kids ; this to you, O fox and falcon—spare our poultry.' [*Old Times*, p. 161.]

Herds' Festival. On the first of May, O.S., a Festival called Beltan is annually held here. It is chiefly celebrated by the Cow-herds, who assemble by scores in the fields, to dress a dinner for themselves of boiled milk and eggs. These dishes they eat with a sort of cake baked for the occasion, and having small lumps in the form of nipples raised all over the surface. [*O.S.A.*, V, p. 84.]   Logierait, Pth.

Herds' meal of eggs and milk by a fire on a hill-top. Reported also from Ayr. [*Scot. N. & Q.*, Oct. 1894.]

The shepherds in Perthshire still hold a festival on the 1st of May, but the practices at it are now much modified. [Napier, Appendix, p. 170.]   Pth.

Cf. the festival with casting cakes in divination under section **V** c.

Cows milked through a hole in a cake. A cake was made at Beltane on May Day. This cake had a large hole in the middle, through which each of the cows in the field was milked. In Tiree it was of triangular form. [G. Henderson, *Survivals in Beliefs among the Celts* (1911), p. 260.]   Hghlds.

Rowan on the farm. On . . . Beltane the people of Strathspey make a hoop of rowan tree through which all the sheep and lambs are forced to pass evening and morning. [John Ramsay, *Scotland and Scotsmen in the 18th Century*, II, p. 454. Ed. by Alex. Allardyce (1888).]

To keep the witches at a distance there were various methods and all of approved value. On bonfire night (1st May, O.S.) small pieces of rowan-tree and woodbine were placed over the byre doors inside the house. Sometimes it was a single rod of rowan, covered with notches. There is the well-known rhyme :

> The rawn-tree in the widd-bin
> Haud the witches on cum in.

[Greg., p. 188.]   N.E. Scot.

One (cross of rowan tied with red thread) is also placed in the midden, at all times a favourite place of rendezvous with the black sisterhood. [*Pop. Superstitions* (1822), pp. 259 f.]
                                                      Hghlds.

Herds' meal, bonfire, with staves of wood kept from Maundy Thursday. Upon *Maundy Thursday*, the several herds cut staves of Service Wood about three feet long, and put two cross sticks into clefts in one end of the staff. These staves they laid up till the first of May. On that day several herds met together ; every one had two eggs, and a bannock or thick cake of oat meal crusted over with the yolks of eggs.

They raised a pile of dry wood or sticks on a hillock, and striking fire with a flint they kindled the pile. Then they made the *Deas-Soil* [sunwise turn] thrice round the fire ; after which they roasted their eggs, and ate them with a part of the bread. The rest of the bread they brought home, to be eaten by the family ; and having adorned the heads of their staves with wild herbs, they fixed them on the tops, or above the doors of their several cotes ; and this they fancied would preserve the cattle from diseases till next May. [Rev. Lachlan Shaw, *Hist. of . . . Moray* (1775), p. 241.]

Red threads. The farmers . . . hope to preserve the milk of their cows and their wives from miscarriage by tying red threads about them ; they bleed the supposed witch to preserve themselves from her charms. [Pennant, *Tour* (1769), p. 156.]

Bf.

Another and even more effectual method was to tie to each animal's tail by a scarlet thread a small cross made of the wood of the rowan-tree ; hence the rhymes :

> Rawn-tree in red-threed
> Pits the witches t' their speed.

and

> Rawn-tree in red threed
> Gars the witches tyne their speed.

[Greg., p. 188.]

N.E. Scot.

Fire in the byre doorway. Sixty years ago my informant has seen fire put down in the byre doorway on Beltane, and the cows were made to pass over it. [*Ethnog. Survey of the U. Kingdom*, 5th Report (1897), p. 468.] Dalry, Galloway.

Cattle driven sunwise round the fire. Every fire was put out and a large one lit on the top of the hill, and the cattle driven round it sunwards (*dessil*), to keep off murrain all the year. [A. Goodrich Freer, *F.-L.* (1902), XIII, p. 41.] Outer Hdes.

Cattle driven through the fire. When the sacred fire was kindled, the people rushed home and brought their herds and drove them through and round the fire of purification. [*Car. Gad.*, II, p. 340.] Hghlds.

Rowan crosses get virtue from fire. At Easter a cross of rowan dipped in pottage had been placed over the doors of the stable, byre, and sheep-cot. On Beltane these were removed, carried to the sacred fire to receive fresh virtue, and borne back to their former positions. [*Old Times*, p. 162.] Hghlds.

Use of tar. People who believed in their (witches') existence were . . . earnest to counteract their machinations. Tar was

put behind the ears of the cattle and at the root of the tail.
[*Wcrft. & Sec. Sight*, p. 270.]   W. Hghlds.

Salt as a charm.   See above, Section *Quarters, Summer*.

Charmed water in use when cows without milk.   A wooden cog
filled with water out of a running brook with a piece of silver
at the bottom and the four paws of a living cat dipped in the
cog ; this was sprinkled on the calf before daybreak next morning, or before the sun would rise, when the milk would come
back to the cow.   [Mlan MS.]   Ar.

Power of crystal balls.   They (the people of Scotland) have
the *Ombriae pellucidae* (which are crystal balls, or hemispheres,
or depressed ovals) in great esteem for curing of cattle ; and
some on May Day put them into a tub of water, and besprinkle
all their cattle with that water, to prevent their being elf-
struck, bewitch'd, etc.   [James Britten, from a letter, 1699,
from Mr Ed. Lhwyd, late Keeper of the Ashmolean Museum
in Oxford, to a friend.   *Folk-Lore Record*, IV (1881), p. 168.]

Charm with a hair rope.   Sometimes a superstitious ceremony
was performed by *giseagach* [superstitious] women who were
not content with their own milk supply.   Early on Beltane
morning one or two persons . . . would draw a hair rope along
the dewy grass, saying : ' *Bainne an té so shios, bainne an té so
shuas, 'nam ghogan mhor fhéin.*' (Milk of this one above, milk of
this one below, into my own big pail.)   If the neighbours had
only one cow each, *bo* or *boin* could be substituted for *té*. . . .
That work was called gathering dew. . . .   It was recently
told me by one who has frequently seen such ropes that they
were made of the long hair which grew on the tails of the
Highland cattle, and were generally used as cart ropes.   [Js.
MacDiarmid, *Trans. Gael. Soc*ᵗʸ *of Inverness*, XXV (1901-03),
pp. 131 f.]   Breadalbane, Pth.

This charm was seen performed south of the Tay about
1897.   [*Ibid.*, XXVI (1904-07), p. 46.]

The migration to the summer sheiling.[1]   On the first of May the
crofter people migrate from their winter homestead to the
summer sheiling.   All the families of the townland bring their
flocks of horses, cattle, sheep and goats together in one spot,
and then drive them in a *triall* or procession up the hills to the
bothies.   They carry with them bedding, meal and dairy
utensils, spades, sticks, ropes, etc.   Having seen to their flocks
and the repairing of their huts, the people resort to their
sheiling feast.   This consists principally of a male spotless

[1] This custom now observed only in migration to the I. of Lewis in the
month of June.

PLATE VIII

Towing Cattle to the Isle of Lewis for the Summer Pasture ;
the last of the Sheiling.

From a photo taken by Miss F. Nicholls, June 1938.

lamb killed that day. Formerly it was sacrificed, now it is eaten. Friends and neighbours share this feast and all wish each other luck and prosperity with increase of their flocks. . . . [*Car. Gad.*, I, pp. 190 f.]   Hghlds.

In the *triall* the sheep lead, the cattle follow according to their ages ; then come the goats and finally the horses, with creels slung across their backs laden with domestic gear of various kinds. The men carry spades, etc., . . . while the women carry bedding, meal and dairy utensils. About their waists the women wear a cord of wool, or a belt of leather, called *crios-feile*, kilt girdle, underneath which their skirts are drawn up and fastened, to enable them to walk the moor with . . . ease. All who meet them on the way bless the *triall* and invoke upon it a good day. . . . (After the food is made ready) the people bring forward their stock, each man his own, and count them into the fold. The herdsman . . . and one or two more . . . count the flocks as they enter. (After the feast the blessing of Abraham, Isaac and Jacob is invoked.) Protestantism prevails in Lewis, Harris, and N. Uist, and the people confine their invocations to the Trinity : Roman Catholicism prevails in Benbecula, S. Uist, and in Barra, and . . . the people of these islands invoke, besides the Trinity, St Michael of the three-cornered shield and flaming sword, patron of their horses ; St Columba of the holy deeds, guardian of their cattle ; Bride of the clustering hair, the foster-mother of Christ ; and the golden-haired Virgin, mother of the White Lamb. (Bride is called also, ' shepherdess of the flocks '.) [*Ibid.*, pp. 191 f.]

The Hymn of the *triall* is given in full in *Carmina Gadelica*.

When (Beltane) arrived, it was necessary, whatever the state of the weather, though people sank ankle deep in snow, to get the cattle away to the summer pasture. [*Wcrft. & Sec. Sight*, p. 270.]   Hghlds. & W. Is.

All the cattle were put to pasture on the same day—Beltane. Each herd on setting out with the animals got a bannock, called the Beltane Bannock. [Rev. W. Gregor, *Kilns, Mills, etc.* (1894), p. 32.]   N.E. Scot.

The cattle were driven to the sheiling on May 1 with a switch of rowan. [*The Antiquary*, XLII (1906), p. 372.]

Next morning (after Beltane eve) the crosses (made of rowan and tied with red thread), were tied to the tails of the animals when they were driven to the grazing grounds on the hills, and each ' hird ' received a rowan wand to drive them. My informant told me that on one occasion when the

' hirds ' were driving home their cattle they were obliged to leave a weakly one behind them. After housing the animals the ' hird ' to whose care the animal was committed set out to bring it home. An old woman called him back, gave him a rowan club with a cross cut on the end of it, and told him everything would now go well. [The rowan switch or club was sacred and thrown away after use.] [*F.-L. Jour.*, VII (1889), p. 277.] Corgarff, Ab.

The shieling life continued until the crops were ripening, and it afforded a prolonged picnic under rough conditions. . . . [Rev. Canon MacCulloch, *The Misty Isle of Skye*.]

' *Sheelins* ' on Jura. Land on a bank covered with sheelins —the habitations of some peasants who attend the herds of milch cows. These formed a grotesque group. Some were oblong, many conic, and so low that entrance is forbidden, without creeping through the little opening, which has no other door than a faggot of birch twigs, placed there occasionally ; they are constructed of the branches of trees, covered with sods ; the furniture a bed of heath placed on a bank of sod, two blankets and a rug ; some dairy vessels, and above certain pendant shelves made of basket-work to hold the cheese, the product of the summer. [Th. Pennant, *A Tour in Scot. & Journey to the Hebrides* [2] (1776), part I, pp. 246 f.] Is. of Jura, Ar.

V f. *Household customs. Churning and cheese making.* By having a churning feast and a cheese made before sunrise the fairies were kept away from the farm for the rest of the year. [*Wcrft. & Sec. Sight*, p. 270.] Hghlds.

Certain cakes eaten in the house. In Glenorchy and Lorne a large cake is made (at Beltane) which they consume in the house. In Mull it has a hole in the middle through which each of the cows . . . is milked in turn. [Cf. *Farm customs*, **V e.**] In Tiree it is of triangular form. . . . There are no vestiges of this custom in Skye or the Long Island, the inhabitants of which have substituted the . . . St Michael's cake (at Michaelmas). [Alex. Allardyce, *Scot. & Scotsmen in the 18th Cent.* (1888), p. 451.] Ar.

Cheese custom. When the breeding ewes were ' clippit ' or shorn, they were milked. From the milk was made a cheese, and this cheese was kept till the first day of May. On the morning of that day an oatmeal bannock was baked for each member of the household. An egg was whipped and spread over it, first on one side, and then on the other, in the act of being ' fired ' or baked. When it was laid on the gridiron the sign of the cross was made over it, as also when it was turned. About nine o'clock a.m. the goodman cut the cheese with the kitchen knife, after making the sign of the cross over it. A slice of cheese was laid on a piece of each bannock for each one of the household. Each piece of each bannock and each slice of cheese had to be eaten by each member of the family before sunset. The remainder of the 'kebback' or cheese was kept till Lammas . . . when the whole had to be eaten before sunset, even although the dogs had to get part of it. [Rev. W. Gregor, in *F.-L.*, VI (1895), p. 5.]

H. Macintosh, Corgarff, Ab.

There was also a cheese made, generally on the 1st of May, which was kept to the next Beltane as a sort of charm against the bewitching of milk-produce. [A. Goodrich-Freer, in *F.-L.*, XIII (1902), p. 41.] Outer Hdes.

Consecrated cake. The custom of . . . baking a consecrated cake, etc., on the first of May is not quite worn out. [*O.S.A.*, XV, p. 517, note.] Kirkmichael, Pth.

V h. *Water customs.* See *Water boiled over the Beltane fire*, **V c.**; and *Water poured over a crystal ball*, **V e.**

V i. *Visiting a church.* May 10, 1599. †On this day the minister of Stobo and John Fawsyde and the Minister of Innerleithen, William Sanderson, along with the Bailies of Peebles and certain other gentlemen who had been appointed to lie in wait and apprehend any who should come in pilgrimage to the Cross Kirk of Peebles as had been the custom for hundreds of years before the Reformation, now reported to the Presbytery that they had apprehended certain men and women from Hawick, Selkirk, Minto and other places. [Dr Gunn, *The Book of Stobo Church.*] Ps.

V k. *Gift of food left on a hill-top.* In the parish of Watten, Caithness, the late Rev. A. Gunn remembered, some seventy years ago, each family in the district sending one of its members on May-Day morning, before sunrise, to deposit a bannock of bread and some cheese on the top of a hill called Heathercrow. When the sun rose the cowherds were at liberty to take and eat the offering. . . . Of those who performed such actions none could tell their meaning. It was unlucky to omit it—that was all. [*Trans. Gaelic Soc. of Inverness*, XIX (1893-94), p. 273.] Cths.

Gifts of bannocks to children with eggs. On the first day of May the children received each an egg and a cake ; with these they proceeded to the hill. They gathered materials, formed a bonfire, and roasted their eggs in the ashes. [Rev. W. Gregor, *Kilns, Mills, etc.* (1894), p. 31.]   N.E. Scot.

V m. *Customs of food and drink. Beltane bannocks.* The (Beltane) cake was commonly baked between 9 and 10 o'clock in the morning. It was kneaded entirely in the hand and not on the hearth ; it was placed in front of a peat fire with a stone to support it, and baked in that position, After being so baked it was put into the child's hand and not put on any table or dish. It must never be put from the hand, except to be baked in front of the fire. If laid on anything it was nothing more than an ordinary bannock. It was called ' tcharnigan ' (spelt phonetically), because it was made entirely in and by the hand (*déarnagh*, hand), and the word means ' hand-cake '. It has also been interpreted ' the little defence or guard '. [Rev. W. Gregor, *Kilns, Mills, etc.* (1894), p. 31.]   Achterneed, Rs.

Curds and cream. It is still customary in the W. Highlands to have curds and cream on the first day of May ; towns-people largely take advantage of it by making journeys to the farms and homes within reach, where the time-honoured feast is in readiness for them by previous arrangement. This custom seems to be of very great antiquity. . . . In olden times the feast seems to have been partaken [of] by the family encircling a fire in the open air, and besides milk there were sometimes eggs and oatmeal cakes used ; the whole bearing the air of a religious service. The element of worship has long disappeared. [Mlan Ms.]   W. Hghlds.

Good food. (At Beltane) people had a feast in their houses with better food than ordinary. [*Wcrft. & Sec. Sight*, p. 271.]   Hghlds.

Gratulations to the Moneth of May.

> Butter, new cheise, and beir in May,
> Connan, cokkelis, curds and quhey. . . .

[Poems of Alex. Scott, in J. Sibbald, *Chron. of Scot. Poetry* (1802), III, p. 162.]

V o. *Birds, etc. The Cuckoo.*[1] The folklore of the cuckoo may be quoted as seasonal since its first appearance is dated for Beltane.

May-day is spoken of as the Yellow (or golden) Beltane, and is hailed with joy. It is said that on this day ' The

---

[1] The cuckoo takes the place of the nightingale in the Hebrides.

cuckoo comes from her winter home ', later, it will be observed, than the ' April ', when ' come he will ', of more genial climates. However, the cuckoo is a bird of very short and of merely occasional passage in the treeless Hebrides, and indeed in some islands is practically unknown. [A. Goodrich-Freer, in *F.-L.* (1902), XIII, p. 40.]   Hdes.

' Gug-gug ' said the cuckoo, on the yellow day of Beltane. [*Car. Gad.*, II, p. 324.]   Hghlds. & Is.

The arrival of the cuckoo was looked for, and boys shouted, ' Cuckoo! cried the "gowk" on yellow Beltane day '. [*Wcrft. & Sec. Sight*, p. 271.]   Hghlds.

Rooks' nests. And quhair it be taintit [attainted] that thay (rukis) big, and the birdis be flowin, and the nest be fundin in the treis at Beltane, the treis sal be ffoirfattit to the king. [Acts, James I, 1424, c. 21. Edit. 1566. See Jamieson (1879), under Beltane.]

VI. Witchcraft, Beliefs in Fairies, etc. After the great meeting of May eve witches were active.

May dew. Witches gathered May dew that they might work their incantations with it (on May 1). [*Ethnog. Survey of the U. Kingdom*, 5th Report, p. 456.] Kirkmaiden, Galloway.

Witches were believed to make butter from May dew (on May 1). [*Ibid.*]   *Ibid.*

An old man named David Bell used to tell that going home early one May-day morning he saw three sisters that had the reputation of being witches, drawing pieces of flannel along the grass to collect the dew. When the flannel was soaked the moisture was wrung out. This took place about seventy years ago at a place called Thornybog. [*Ethnog. Survey of the U. Kingdom*, 5th Report, p. 456.]

Watching against sorcery. It is a common belief among Celts, that if one does not watch his cattle on the morning of *La Bealtuinn* (Beltane), some evil-disposed person may take the produce away, and add it to their own ; and it is believed that should one succeed in doing this, he will retain the milk thus taken away for the whole month of May, and those from whom it has been taken will have none for that time. [Mlan Ms.]   Islay, Ar.

Witches ride and dance. Even at present witches are supposed, as of old, to ride on broomsticks through the air. In this country the 12th of May is one of their festivals. On the morning of that day, they are frequently seen dancing on the surface of the water of Avon, brushing the dews of the lawn,

and milking cows in their fold. [12th for 1st May, O.S.]
[*O.S.A.*, XII, p. 465.]   Kirkmichael, Bf.

Fairy Rades. The not yet wholly exploded belief in fairies,
fays, and elves, still closely connects itself with . . . Fairy
Rades. . . . This grand annual festival occurred on the first
day of May. [*Denham Tracts* (ed. 1895), vol. ii, pp. 110-15.]

Fairy Rades. The designation given to the expedition made
by the Fairies to the place in which they are to hold their great
annual banquet on the first of May. [Jamieson.]   N. Scot.

Mermaids seen in May. †Near the place where the Dee
payeth its tribute to the German Ocean, if curious observers
of wonderful things in nature will be pleased thither to resort
on the 1st, 13th, and 29th of May, and in divers other times
in the insueing summer . . . they will undoubtedly see a pretty
company of mermaids, creatures of admirable beauty, and
likewise hear their charming, sweet, melodious voices. Cf.
Harvest time to the 7th and 14th of October. From an Aberdeen Almanac for 1488. [James Napier, *Folk-Lore Record*, II,
1879, p. 106.]   Ab.

IX. **Dancing.** See under **V** c. *Rites of fire, etc.*

X. **Boundary Riding and Wapenshaws.** See Vol. I.

XI. **May-day Sports.** *Competing for a ' Siller Gun '.* †In
August 1617 James VI made a state visit to Dumfries ; he
presented to the magistrates a small silver gun, mounted on a
wheeled carriage, that it might be competed for as a prize at
the annual wapinschaws. . . . But May-day sports had
generally taken their place. Along with these sports the
possession of the silver gun was, at Dumfries, the subject of
an animated competition. . . . Proceedings commenced with
a procession of the traders, . . . while the ' Siller Gun ' gleamed
in the sunshine. [Ch. Rogers, *Social Life in Scot.* (1884), II,
pp. 294 f.]   Dfs.

Other sports. In May-day sports ' Tossing the kebar ' was
a favourite pastime, as were ' casting the bar ', and ' throwing
the hammer '. ' Climbing the greasy pole ' never failed to
excite hearty laughter. [*Ibid.*]

The Peebles Festival at Beltane was for many years celebrated for its races, sports and festivity. It was attended by
all the inhabitants of the South of Scotland arrayed in their
gayest dress. The date changed to suit Sunday observance,
or for other local causes, but was always as near Beltane as
possible. After 1766 it ceased to be kept. [Ed.]

This carnival to hail spring was a landmark of time for the lowland Scot. . . . The origin of our saying, 'Peebles for pleasure,' comes from this spring gathering. [E. B. Simpson, *F.-Lore in Lowland Scot.*, p. 6.]

Peebles to the Play.

> At Beltane, quhen ilk bodie bownis
> > To Peblis to the Play,
> To heir the singin' and the soundis,
> > The solace, suth to say.
> Be firth and forrest furth they found,
> > Thay graythit tham full gay ;
> God wait that wald they do that stound,
> > For it was their feist day,
> > > Thay said
> > Of Peblis to the Play.

[J. Sibbald, *Chron. of Scot. Poetry* (1802), I, p. 129.]

Beltane horse-race. Cf. *May races*, May, Month, **V.**

The prize. May 4, 1648. Compeirit personallie ane noble and potent lord George lord Ramsay, who haveing with ane gray stoned young hors win the silver bell of Peblis, by running thryce about the stowpes of Whythauch, hes receavit the said bell, haveing appendit therto thrie little belles and eight pendicles, all weyand ane pund tuo ounces and ellevine drope weicht of silver (finds caution that the same will be returned on 4th May next year 'with his lordship's addi- tione therto'). [*Records of the Burgh of Peebles*, p. 382. The Scottish Burgh Records Society, Edinburgh (1872).]

At March 24, 1684, and again at March 5, 1688, an order is made by the Council that the prize shall not be run for unless there were three horses to run for it. [*Ibid*, p. 121.]

But at May 3, 1688, at the desire of Lord William Douglas, 'who is thair neighbour, and uther company conveened' that the prize might be run for by two horses. [*Ibid.*, p. 122.]

There are orders for the purchase of the silver cup and the saddle as prizes for the race, in 1633, and later. The towns arms to be on the cup. [*Ibid.*, pp. 55, 56, 59, 63, 69, 86, etc.]

The end of the festival. . . . After passing through various hands, the Whitehaugh Muir (where the sports took place) had for some time formed part of the estate of Haystown, and as such the town had paid yearly to the tenent the sum of ten merks Scots, for its use at Beltane. The land coming into the management of Dr James Hay, he began to enclose and im- prove it in a manner which rendered it unfit for the customary

festivities. At first, the town gave little heed to these operations, but at length taking the matter up, the council feigned
to crave the opinion of a lawyer on the subject. On the 17th
February, 1766, a memorial is copied into the records, repre-
senting that the town from time immemorial has used the
Whitehaugh Muir for its Beltane and other races, 'which
have drawn large numbers of persons from all parts of the
Kingdom' and it is important to know 'what measures the
town should take to recover its right and privilege to the said
courses and muir'. This memorial does not appear to have
been sent to any lawyer, and there is no more about it. Having
twenty-seven years earlier dispossessed itself of King's Muir,
the town was now left without a sufficiently large space of
ground whereon to hold the great annual gathering. An
ancient festival, commemorated by two royal poets, and from
which alone the town derived any celebrity, was therefore
suffered to die out. 'Peebles to the Play' was extinct. [Wm.
Chambers, *History of Peeblesshire* (1864), p. 264.]

Holiday amusement. Frolic of Robin Hood and Little John. By
far the most popular of public amusements was the annual
frolic of Robin and Little John on the first of May. In this
performance all who chose could take a part, and the result
was generally horse-play of the coarsest kind. [*Ab. Journal
N. & Q.* (1906-16), IV, p. 190.]

XIII. Business Transactions. Beltane was a quarter day.

2nd

I. Name. *Eve of Rood Day.* Sometimes included in the
term Beltane.

V. Observances. b. *Rites lucky or enjoined. Rowan and woodbine placed over the byre door, and house and stable doors.* [Greg.,
p. 167.]

Related also by Pennant, 1769.

At Cullen the farmers preserved their cattle against witchcraft by placing boughs of the mountain ash and honeysuckle
within the cowhouses on the second of May. [E. F. Guthrie,
Old Scot. Customs (1885), pp. 108 f.]   Bf.

They cut a piece of this tree (roun tree), peel it, tie a red
thread round it and put it on the lintel of the byre. . . . Then,
it is supposed, their cattle are proof against skaith. This
charm is especially observed in Angus on the evening preceding Rood-day. [Jamieson.]

On the 2nd of May—the eve of the Rood-day—it was customary to make small crosses of twigs of the rowan-tree, and to place them over every aperture leading into the house, as a protection against evil spirits and malevolent influences. [Rev. John B. Pratt, *Buchan* [3] (1870), p. 24.]

In Strathdon pieces of ' rawn tree ' were put into every byre on the ' reed day '—rood day [eve?], May 2, O.S., by the goodman after sunset ; this had to be done in secret. Pieces of it were placed over the stable door to prevent the witches from entering to take out the horses for their midnight rides. [*F.-L. J.*, VII (1889), p. 277.] Ab.

Rowan branches tied round cattle with scarlet threads. [Jamieson, under *Rown-Tree*.]

V c. *Fire, ashes, etc. Bone-fires to burn witches.* In some districts fires were kindled on the 2nd of May, O.S. They were called *bone-fires*, . . . and were kindled by every farmer and cottar. Old thatch, or straw, or furze, or broom was piled up in a heap and set on fire a little after sunset. Some of those present kept constantly tossing up the blazing mass, and others seized portions of it on pitch-forks or poles, and ran hither and thither, holding them as high as they were able, while the younger portion, that assisted, danced round the fire or ran through the smoke, shouting, ' Fire! blaze an' burn the witches ; fire! fire! burn the witches '. In some districts a large round cake of oat or barley-meal was rolled through the ashes. When the material was burned up, the ashes were scattered far and wide, and all continued till quite dark to run through them still crying ' Fire! burn the witches '. [Greg., p. 167.] N.E. Scot.

VI. Witches, Fairies, etc. *Fairies dance.* The fairies came out of their dwellings on Reed Even and had their first dance. They had their last dance on the 31st October, when they retired to their dwellings. These dwellings were green knolls scattered all over the country. There was always a well near these green hillocks. No one would have drawn water from the well and drunk it after the first day of May after sunset. Whoever did so was caught by the fairies and carried off to their dwelling and kept there for a year at least [Rev. W. Gregor.] N.E. Scot.

XIII. Municipal Business. *Collection of the burgh mails.* May 12, 1656. The roll of the burro maill to be regulate and collected in tyme comeing yearlie, the morne after Baltane day, be the town thesaurer, who is to be comtable to the toun thairfore. [*Records of the Burgh of Peebles*, Scottish Burgh Records Soc. (1910), p. 35.]

For this piece (land), Crunzeane and his successors were to pay 'yerelie to the Baillies, Counsale, and communite, two shillings of annuel rent on the morne efter Beltane day, the time of the collecting and gaddering of the Burro males'. [MS. Reg., 1543-67, f. 129.]

XIV. Prohibition. July 5, 1599. The brethren each reported diligence in regard to the ordinance of the Presbytery as to those persons who made Banefires to the effect that such persons were now being tried before their Kirk Sessions. . . . This refers to the survival of kindling of fires at Beltane. . . . [Dr Gunn, *The Book of Stobo Church.*] Ps.

3rd

I. Names. *Rood Day. Invention of the Holy Cross. St Helen's Day in Spring.* The feast of the Invention of the Holy Cross commemorated a belief that the Cross had been discovered by St Helena at Jerusalem in 326. The other Holy Rood day is on September 14. In Aberdeenshire Roodsmas of May was the chief festival of the Cross, in Clydesdale this was in September.

In Caithness 'Roodsmas in Barlan' was the spring observance ; barlan being the time of the barley or bere sowing. Roodsmas in harvest was the festival of September.

It is known in many parts as Beltane. See May 1, and cf. R. Motherby, *Pocket Dict. of Scot. Idiom* : 'Beltine, Beltane, the third of May.' Also Herd, *Scot. Songs*, Glossary (1776), II, p. 244.

Highlanders call the day 'the dismal day' and hold it as unlucky. [Pennant, p. 111.]

The day of the week on which it falls is called 'the Avoiding Day of the Year'. [*Wcrft. & Sec. Sight*, p. 274.]

Explanation of the name Avoiding Day. This is the third day of summer, and its name is almost the only part of the beliefs concerning it that now survives. The writer searched far and wide for an explanation of the name, and only once heard one that was satisfactory. It was on this day that the fallen angels were expelled from Paradise, and on it people should avoid doing any kind of evil. If caught in the act, they will be similarly expelled from the regions of forgiveness, and be visited with 'judgement without mercy'. [*Ibid.*, p. 273.]

II. Saints. St Helen's festival was kept on August 18, but her connection with Rood Day gave rise to the name of 'St Helen's Day in Spring'.

St Fumac [who is not recorded elsewhere]. Botriphinie, six miles from Keith, had as patron St Fumac, whose wooden image was washed yearly with much formality by an old woman (quho keeps it) at his fair on 3rd of May in his own well here. The image was swept away by a flood at the beginning of the 19th century and stranded at Banff, where it was committed to the flames by the parish minister as a monument of superstition. [Sp. Club, *Illus. of Antiq. of the Shires of Banff & Ab.*, II, p. 253, note.]   Bf.

V. Observances. a. *Things unlucky or forbidden. To go on a journey.* If the 'Avoiding Day of the Year' falls on a Friday it is unlucky to go on a journey. [*Wcrft. & Sec. Sight*, p. 273.]
                                                        Hghlds.

To allow kindled coal to be carried out of the house. People would not allow a (burning) coal to be carried out of their house to that of a neighbour on . . . Rood Day, lest it should be employed for the purpose of witchcraft. [*Ethnog. Survey of the U. Kingdom*, 4th Report (1896), p. 41.]

By extension of ill luck. To begin anything important. A Highlander never begins anything of consequence on the day of the week on which the 3rd of May falls, which he styles *La seachanta na bliadhna*, the dismal day. [Pennant, p. 111.]
                                                        Hghlds.

To marry. None get married on that day of the week upon which this day fell. [E. F. Guthrie, *Old Scot. Customs*, p. 63.]
                                                        Pth.

To dig peat or count the stock. The day of the week on which the 3rd of May . . . falls is esteemed unlucky for many things —especially for digging peat or taking an account of the sheep or cattle on a farm. [R. T. Hampson, *Med. Aevi Kal.* (1841), p. 387.]

The bad luck of this day reported also from N.E. Scot. [Rev. W. Gregor.]

V b. *Things lucky or enjoined. To milk a cow's milk on to the ground.* Both witches and fairies are believed to be at work, particularly in carrying off the milk. . . . Many, accordingly, milk a little out of each dug of a cow on the ground. It is believed that this will make the cows *luck* or prosper during the whole summer, but that the reverse will be the case if this ceremony be neglected. [Jamieson, under *Rude-day*.]

To gather dew for healing. Some who have tender children, particularly on Rude-day, spread out a cloth to catch the dew, and wet them in. [*Ibid.*]

See also **V h**, *Water*.

V e. *Water custom. Creaming the well.* A woman who was born towards the end of last century and died about the middle of this, had a croft that now forms part of the farm of Atherb, parish of . . . She had the custom of taking grass and water into the house before sunrise on the morning of the Reed Day. She placed the water—' the cream o' the well '—into the bole or small niche on the right side of the hearth, and the ' flower o' the grass ' into the one on the left side. Both were allowed to stand there till after Sunday. This was done to secure food and water during the season. [Rev. W. Gregor.] N.E. Scot.

In May 1723, the minister informed the Session that Margaret Robertson in Byres of Balmerino had complained to him, that James Paton in Culter ' had scandalised her in her good name by saying that she went to Nine Wells on the Road-day morning [i.e. Rood Day, the Invention of the Cross, 3rd May], to take away her neighbour's milk ', or, as the charge was afterwards expressed, ' to get the cream of the water, and to take away her neighbour's butter '. The parties having been cited, Paton declared that what he had said was, that he ' heard of a woman in Byres that went to Nine Wells on the Road-day morning to gett the cream of them, that she might gett other people's butter, but named no woman '. Witnesses were summoned and examined on oath, but their evidence was not decisive, and the conclusion of the case is not recorded. [Rev. J. Campbell, *Balmerino and its Abbey* (1899), p. 462 ; *C.F.-L.*, VII, p. 16.] Ffe.

V e and **V i.** *Visiting a stone.* A woman, on the morning of that day, had to take a ' three-luggit cap ' ' atween the sin an' the sky ' and draw water. Fasting and without shoes and stockings she carried it to the highest part of the pasture and poured it on the highest stane there. Clachcutts (short stone), about three and a half miles above the Brig of Luig in Corgarff, was such a stone. My informant's grandmother did this in her youth and had her bare feet cut by the heather. This would be over a hundred years ago. [Rev. W. Gregor.]

Corgarff, Ab.

VI. Beliefs in Witchcraft, Fairies, etc. *Trailing the tether.*
On Rood-day, the fairies are supposed to *trail* or *drag the
tether* over the clover in order to take away the milk. Hence,
if one had an uncommon quantity of milk from one's cows,
it is usually said ' You have been drawing the tether '.
[Jamieson.]

One of the early days of May

V i. *Running round stone circles or mounds.* At Stirling, on
one of the early days of May, boys of ten and twelve years
divest themselves of clothing, and in a state of nudity run
round certain natural or artificial circles. Formerly the
rounded summit of Dumyat, an eminence in the Ochil range,
was a favourite scene of this . . . pastime, but for many years
it has been performed at the King's Knot in Stirling, an
octagonal mound in the royal gardens. [Ch. Rogers, *Social
Life in Scot.*, III, p. 240.]   Stg.

X. Procession. †Only fifty years ago the spring festival
received municipal honours in Edinburgh, where, on the
first Sunday after Beltane, the magistrates used to walk down
the Canongate in procession, decorated with flowers and
carrying large nosegays. [C. F. Gordon Cumming, *In the
Hebrides* (1883), p. 233.]   Edin.

First Sunday

XII. Festival. *The Popinjay.* The Festival of the Popinjay
is still (1870), I believe, practised at Maybole in Ayrshire.
' They had then a custome every year to solemnise the
first Sunday of May with danceing about a Maypole, fyreing
of pieces, and all manner of revelling then in use. (A youth
of the family of Somervilles) goes to Hamiltoune and there
bestowes all the money that for a long time before he had
gotten from his friends . . . upon ribbones of diverse coloures,
a new hat and gloves. But in nothing he bestowed his money
more liberallie than upon gunpowder, a great quantitie
wherof he buyes for his owne use, and to supplie the wantes
of his comrades ; thus furnished, . . . he returnes to Delserf
by seven a clock . . . puttes on his cloathes and new hatt,
flying with ribbones of all culloures ; and . . . with his little
phizie (fusee) upon his shoulder, he marches to the church
yaird, where the May-pole was set up, and the solemnitie of
that day was to be kept.' [Quoted by Scott from his own

edition of a MS. history of the Somerville family, published 1815.]

The Popinjay, an ancient game formerly practised with archery, but at this period (1679) with firearms. This was the figure of a bird, decked with party-coloured feathers, so as to resemble a popinjay or parrot. It was suspended to a pole, and served for a mark at which the competitors discharged their fusees and carabines in rotation, at the distance of sixty or seventy paces. He whose ball brought down the mark, held the proud title of Captain of the Popinjay for the remainder of the day, and was usually escorted in triumph to the most reputable change-house in the neighbourhood, where the evening was closed with conviviality, conducted under his auspices, and, if he was able to sustain it, at his expense. [Sir Walter Scott, *Old Mortality*, ed. 1870, p. 31, and note above from p. 424.]   Ayr.

First Monday

XI. Birch-boughs and Foot-races. †In Dumfries a curious custom was observed on the first Monday of May when the ' Muck-men ' as they were called, or day labourers, and servants of the heritors, paraded through the streets of the burgh with ribands and sashes, swords and dirks. They then marched out to Dalscairth wood, where each provided himself with a branch of birch, and went thence to the race-ground, which was as it is supposed at the Stoop. Here there were running contests, and the successful competitors carried off the town's silver ' muck-bell '. [*Dfs. & Galloway N. & Q.*, I, p. 48.]   Dfs.

First Wednesday

XIII. Proclamation. *Change of Beltane fair-day.* March 3, 1656. The magistrattes and counsellores, taking in consideration that the prophanatioun of the Sabbath is occasioned by keeping of faires upon Satterday and Moonday, and that the fair day commonlie called Beltane day, falles this year upon the Satterday, for preventing whereof it is resolved and hereby enacted that the said fair called Beltane fair-day shal be kept and holdin within this burgh this year upon the first Weddensday of Maii, and so furth yearly in all tyme comeing. [*Records of the Burgh of Peebles*, 1652-1714, Scottish Burgh Records Society (1910), p. 34.]

8th

II. Sayings. It would appear that some peculiar sanctity was ascribed to the 8th of May, from the old Scottish Proverb, ' You have skill of man and beast, you were born between the Beltans '; i.e. the first and eighth of May. . . .

9th

III. Saint. The feast of St Nicholas (see December 6), associated with many celebrations, was in some towns, especially at St Andrews, transferred from December to May 9, the day of the saint's translation to Bari, in S. Italy ; an event which furthered the popularity of his cult. As patron of the Grammatici his day was observed with great festivity, for which the later date seemed more suitable. The change took place in 1414, when fresh rules were made. [Ed.]

The collecting of money from house to house as the boy-bishop passed with the saint from the castle to the monastery was forbidden, and there was to be no bringing in of May in guise. . . . Cock-fighting at this festival was allowed for two or three days, and not for two or three weeks as formerly. [J. Robb, *Scot. Hist. Review*, IX, pp. 355 f. Quoting Acta, 1400-1450.] Ffe.

14th

†In some districts of Perthshire the day of the week on which May 14 happened was regarded as unlucky during the remainder of the year. [Ch. Rogers, *Familiar Illust^{ns} of Scottish Character* (1865), p. 166.] Pth.

16th

III. Saint. *Brénaind Mocu Atli*, the Brandon famous as the ' Voyager '. In the east he was the patron of Boyndie in Banffshire, where his feast was kept on May 16, and his fair in Brannan Howe on May 26, O.S. ' The Brannan Stanes ' are in this parish. He appears to have been the special patron of Bute, for the Butemen were of old called the ' Brandans '. [*Celt. Pl.-Names.*] Bf.

The stones of St Brandon, the patron saint of Banff, stood on a field about a mile to the west of Banff. Tradition has it that a battle between the Scots and the Danes was fought on this field. Near the same place is the Brandon How (. . . Brangin How), where long ago St Brandon's Fair was held ; this fair is now held in Banff, Rain, called ' the Brangin sob ', is looked for at this time. [Greg., p. 114.]   Bf.

15th

I. Name. *Whitsun term day.* Whitsun was one of the fixed term days of Scotland. The 15th was Whitsun as a term day irrespective of the Church date for Whitsunday, fifty days after Easter, later the 25th by change of style.

22nd

This day was marked by ' sports ' of a singularly barbarous nature.

XI. Sports. *Cat hunt.* †At Haddington, in connection with the races [run on the 22nd of May], the burgh carters persecuted a sport so utterly inhuman as wholly to demoralise all who might engage in it. By a local witness it is thus described : ' A cat was confined in a dryware cask containing soot, and hung at the end of a beam fixed to the top of the cross. Each rider was armed with a wooden mall, and rode at full speed under the barrel, and gave it a blow with his mall, which operation was continued until the barrel was staved. The poor frightened cat on its release was pursued by the assembled crowd, and was very often trampled to death. The magistrates felt it their duty to put a stop to this barbarous custom ; but the carters, as long as their " play " existed, continued to ride their " Bassies " for three times in a circle opposite the cross.' [1] [Ch. Rogers, *Social Life in Scot.*, II, pp. 310, 311.]   Hdn.

The carters' race. ... From a beam, a living goose was hung up by the feet, and all who could procure horses had an opportunity, as they trotted through between the upright posts, of showing their dexterity, by catching hold of the goose's head, and giving it a pull. This diversion was continued to the no small gratification of the company, till one, more fortunate than his neighbours, had the happiness of pulling the head from the body. The goose being now no longer able to afford any more sport, was taken down, and a cat, inclosed in a barrel, hung up in its room. Every horseman being provided with a mall, struck the end of the

[1] Martine's *Reminiscences of Haddington*, p. 100.

barrel as he rode through below it ; by frequent repetition
of this, the head of the barrel was at length stove in, when the
cat, mad with the cruel usage, darted out all covered with
soot ; and from a principle of self-preservation was dispatched
as quickly as possible, by the happy swains who had collected
to witness the diversions of the day. [*F.-L.* XVIII, p. 337.]
Lowlands.

25th

I. Name. *Flitting Day.* The 25th of May, as the Whitsunday term (old style), is a great day in Scotland, being that
on which, for the most part, people change their residences.
The Scotch generally lease their houses by the year, and are
thus at every twelve-month's end able to shift their abode. . . .
Every Candlemas a Scotch family gets an opportunity of
considering whether it will, in the language of the country,
sit or flit. [*Bk. of Days*, I, p. 679.]

The Marches or boundaries of certain parts of Peebles
Common were ' sett ' on this day, 1665 ; ' according as foure
or fyve indifferent honest men, vpon their oathes . . . shall
depone and declaire.' [*Records of the Burgh of Peebles*, May 24,
1665, p. 64.]　　　　　　　　　　　　　　　　　　　　　Ps.
March Ridings. See Vol. I.

29th

V. Observance. c. *Bonfires.* The 29th of May, when bonfires
were lighted by order of the magistracy, and at which they
attended ' under the penalty of 40ˢ, to see the solemnities kept '.
But whether this was in honour of the king or a relic of the old
. . . observance of Whitsuntide—the Beal-tine . . . of Celtic
times—the records give no intimation. [J. Paterson, *Hist. of the
Regality of Musselburgh* (1887), p. 135.]　　Musselburgh, Edin.

XIV. Prohibition of extravagant spending. Dec. 22, 1683.
The counsell discharges the magistrates in all tyme comeing
to spend anything out of the tounes purse . . . upon the 29th
May [1] bot eight pounds and a four gallad barrell of aill ; . . .
and discharges any more publict dinners. [*Records of the Burgh
of Peebles*, Scot. Burgh Recᵈˢ Soc. (1910), p. 111.]　　Ps.
Dismal days for May are the 7th, 17th, 20th.

[1] King's birthday.

PRINTED IN GREAT BRITAIN
BY ROBERT MACLEHOSE AND CO. LTD.
THE UNIVERSITY PRESS, GLASGOW